N A T I V E
FLORIDA
P L A N T S

Robert G. Haehle is a horticultural consultant and gardening writer. He has a B.S. degree in environmental design from the University of Massachusetts and an M.S. degree in horticulture from the University of Delaware's Longwood Program. Former county agent for Broward County, Florida, he is the radio host of "Garden Line." In Maryland, he served as educational horticulturist and director of Brookside Gardens in Wheaton and as county agent for Howard County. Mr. Haehle has written numerous columns and articles for *The Sun-Sentinel, South Florida Home & Garden, Florida Nurseryman,* and others.

Joan Brookwell received her B.Lit. degree in journalism from Rutgers University. For more than 25 years, she worked at the *Sun-Sentinel* in Fort Lauderdale as a reporter, feature writer, assistant city editor and, for ten years, as home and garden editor. Currently, she is a freelance writer and photographer living in Fort Lauderdale.

Low-Maintenance Landscaping and Gardening

NATIVE
FLORIDA
PLANTS

Robert G. Haehle • Joan Brookwell

Gulf Publishing Company
Houston, Texas

NATIVE
FLORIDA
PLANTS

Gulf Publishing Company
Book Division
P. O. Box 2608 ☐ Houston Texas 77252-2608

10   9   8   7   6   5   4   3

Library of Congress Cataloging-in-Publication Data

Haehle, Robert G.
   Native Florida Plants : low maintenance
landscaping and gardening / Robert G. Haehle and
Joan Brookwell.
        p.   cm.
      Includes bibliographical references and index.
   ISBN 0-88415-425-4 (alk. paper)
      1. Native plant gardening—Florida. 2. Native
plants for cultivation—Florida. 3. Landscape
plants—Florida. 4. Low maintenance gardening—
Florida. 5. Landscape gardening.
   I. Brookwell, Joan. II. Title.
   SB439.24.F6H34   1999
   635.9′51759—dc21   98-44073
                                                                    CIP

Photographs by Joan Brookwell.
Cover design by Senta Eva Rivera.

Printed in Hong Kong.

Printed on Acid-Free Paper (∞).

Contents

ACKNOWLEDGMENTS

We've come across few people who are more helpful, generous, and enthusiastic than the men and women who grow or otherwise work with plants. Invariably, nursery operators, park managers, horticulturists, educators, and other individuals have gone out of their way to lend us a hand in our search for plants and information about them.

Here's an example: A nursery operator answered all our questions, apologized that she didn't have the specific shrub we wanted, then sent us to her competitor down the road, and even called ahead to make sure he would be there. Ever run across a car salesman who would do that?

To these and to other individuals and organizations whose generosity has contributed so much to this book, we express our deep appreciation:

✤ Steven E. Tate, landscape architect in Boca Raton, for the landscape designs using native plants

✤ Dr. Edward F. Gilman, Professor, Environmental Horticulture Department, University of Florida, Gainesville; and Eric Jadaszewski, Apalachee Native Nursery, Monticello, for providing photographs of those trees and shrubs we never managed to locate

✤ Betrock Publishing Co., Hollywood, for the climate map of Florida that appears on page 14

✤ Jim Higgins, resident assistant park manager, Hugh Taylor Birch State Park, Fort Lauderdale

✤ Bonnet House, Fort Lauderdale

❧ J. Roland Lieber, landscape architect, Naples

❧ Barbara Hiaasen, Broward County Cooperative Extension Service

❧ Park naturalists Monica Ribaudo and Judy Sulser of the Broward County Parks and Recreation Division

❧ Donna Leone, Meadow Beauty Nursery, Lake Worth

❧ The Smiths, Native Nursery, Inc., Lake Worth

❧ Chris Griffiths, Runway Growers, Inc., Fort Lauderdale

❧ Pinellas County Extension Service in Largo, and horticulturist Andy Wilson

❧ Linda Smith, Sandhill Native Nursery and Landscaping, Largo

❧ Kristine Hahn, Sanibel-Captiva Conservation Foundation Native Plant Nursery, Sanibel

❧ Wildlife biologist Laurel Schiller, Florida Native Plants, Inc., Sarasota

❧ Florida House Learning Center, Sarasota

❧ Don and Joyce Gann, Gann's Native Tropical Greenery, Miami

❧ Alexander and Donna Sprunt, Florida Keys Native Nursery, Tavernier

❧ William and Nancy Bissett, The Natives, Davenport, and nursery manager Sarah Brooks

❧ The Florida Native Plant Society

❧ David and Marilyn Chiappini, Chiappini Farm Native Nursery, Melrose

❧ Larry Alsobrook, Breezy Oaks Nursery, Hawthorne

❧ The Association of Florida Native Nurseries, whose plant list has been our guide and whose common and botanical names for the most part are used here

❧ And finally, a fond thank you to Hal and Elane Miller of Redington Beach, long-time friends and gracious hosts who provided lodging, sustenance, and more.

INTRODUCTION

$\mathcal{N}$ative plants: Just what are they and why should we be planting them?

Much of Florida was once ocean bottom, which means many plants had to have originated somewhere else. Those we usually call "native" wandered in naturally long ago, brought by wind, sea, birds, animals, or other natural factors. They adapted to conditions here and grew in harmony with each other.

Exotics, on the other hand, are plants that have been introduced, either intentionally or accidentally. Florida botanists sometimes classify native plants as those that were growing here before the middle of the sixteenth century, when the Spanish colonists arrived.

Florida has a vast number of native plants, the third largest number of the 50 states, and while a good many natural plant communities still exist, development has taken a severe toll as housing, farming, logging, and ranching have destroyed huge areas of natural habitat.

Southeastern Florida, especially, has been robbed of the vegetation that once thrived there. Only tiny pockets of mangrove communities remain, and the complex beach community of dunes and shore plants has almost been eliminated, replaced by condo canyons.

At the same time, plants introduced from abroad have come to dominate our landscape. While many of these exotics are beautiful and valuable landscape plants, some fast-growing species have spread and taken over disturbed land, crowding out the natives and creating a genuine menace to native woodlands. Central and south Florida have been most affected, as exotics in these warm regions grow quickly and shade or crowd out the slower-growing natives.

Topping the list of invaders is Brazilian pepper or Florida holly (*Schinus terebinthifolius*). It grows from the seashore to wet interior areas, seeding wherever it goes. Thousands of acres have been lost to this aggressive pest. Close behind it is the melaleuca (*Melaleuca quinquenervia*), revelling in the muck soil of the Everglades and farm areas where it seeds and reproduces prolifically. Interestingly, the melaleuca does not seem to produce seedlings in the sugar sand coastal areas where most of the human population is gathered. Other nonnatives such as the Australian pines, *Casuarina equisetifolia* (the coastal type) and *Casuarina glauca* (the inland windbreak form), are spread by different methods. The tall, open coastal type seeds vigorously in sandy bare spots on the coast and interior, while the tall, dense windbreak form does not seem to set viable seed, but spreads instead by root suckers that cover large areas over time.

We have an army of other exotic invaders: earleaf acacia, bischofia, carrotwood, guava, schefflera, ficus, and more. Especially insidious are schefflera or Queensland umbrella tree (*Brassaia actinophylla*) and Cuban laurel (*Ficus retusa*), which may start life in the tops or the old, rough, leaf bases of date, Canary Island date, sabal, and Washingtonian palms, and send down aerial roots that envelop the host plant over time. (Our native strangler fig has the same unfortunate habit.) An expensive $4,000–$5,000 date palm can be choked out and its place taken by a ficus if an invasive seedling is not removed.

Damage is not restricted to palms. These terrors can root in gutters, roof tiles, chimneys, bridge overpasses, and other rough-barked trees, and the harm their roots cause to plumbing, pools, and paving is legendary.

In other cases, native species have been replaced with ecologically unsound landscaping. Impatiens leads the parade. An annual that struggles to exist for

◀ Florida holly is an aggressive nonnative plant whose seed is often spread by birds.

five months in the south Florida winter landscape, impatiens is incompatible with most other plantings because of its high water requirements. Yet condos, country clubs, cities, and homeowners plant it by the thousands and water it daily to keep it alive, while nearby permanent plantings suffer slow decline from root rot and fungal disease.

You can see many examples of such incompatibility, such as a circle of water-guzzling annuals planted around a date palm from North Africa where rainfall totals 15–20 inches a year. South Florida receives 50–60 inches of rain a year, already pushing the palm's upper limits of water tolerance before the first sprinkler is turned on. Artificial irrigation needed by annuals can dump the equivalent of 182 extra inches of water yearly on top of the natural rainfall.

The destruction of native habitats by invasive plants and the water and fertilization demands made by many otherwise attractive exotics have alerted naturalists and preservationists to the importance of encouraging the use of native plants as well as conserving what natural vegetation we have left. Through the urging of environmentalists, many cities and counties in the state now specify a certain percentage of native plants in new landscaping. Some southeast Florida communities, for example, now require that new landscapes must include 25 percent or more natives.

Are we recommending that landscape designers and gardeners pull up all their nonnative trees, shrubs, and flowering plants and replace them with natives? Of course not. (Although it would be great to get rid of some of those impatiens!) In most cases the two—natives and well-chosen exotics—can coexist quite nicely and blend pleasingly in the landscape. But almost any landscape will benefit when natives are allowed to be a significant part of it.

Generally, natives prove to be tough, low-maintenance plants, resistant to drought, disease, pests, and Florida's changeable weather. Many are beautiful as well and attractive to birds and butterflies.

We are seeing more Florida landscapers and homeowners selecting such well-known species as oaks (live, laurel, and Shumard), maples (red and sugar), elms (Florida and winged), sweet gum and flowering trees such as dogwood and redbud. Southern Florida has a palette all its own: seagrape, buttonwood, gumbo-limbo, mahogany, wild tamarind, bald and pond cypress, fiddlewood, and geiger tree. Pines, although sensitive, have their use throughout the state in parks or naturalized settings where heavy foot traffic is absent and artificial irrigation systems are not used.

◄ *Melaleuca* is an invasive exotic plant.

Increasingly, native nurseries located in every part of the state are providing fine plant material to public and private sectors.

This book, for the most part, deals with native plants that are offered by a reasonable number of nurseries or are otherwise available. In general, it's impractical to recommend rare or endangered plants or those that will not thrive in a home garden, although we do mention a few—native orchids and bromeliads, for example—that hobbyists sometimes grow and share or are being propagated by botanical gardens and may eventually reach the retail market. And for common wild flowers not carried by nurseries, collecting seed is often possible.

We also emphasize central and south Florida in this book, as many species found there grow naturally nowhere else in the country. Northern Florida, on the other hand, has much in common with southern Georgia and the Gulf states.

The important thing is to know your area and to use natives as closely adapted to it as possible. Drive through the neighborhood and see what is already growing there; that may provide a clue to the vegetation suitable to your property. Or better yet, visit the botanical gardens or parks in your area that have sections devoted to native plants.

Then read the plant descriptions in this book. They'll provide you with a guide as to what will grow in your garden.

PLANT COMMUNITIES

*F*orest, flatwood, wetland, seashore—each different, each home to its own particular assortment of vegetation.

Native species have evolved for each of these communities, although in many cases plants and trees uncomplainingly accept being moved about, adapting to a variety of soils, climates, and other conditions. The natural range of some native plants is amazing. Red maple (*Acer rubrum*), for example, grows from Canada to Broward County in southern Florida, a north-south distance of about 2,500 miles.

But the area where a plant first appeared and became dominant may be much more limited.

Florida's native species used in landscaping are, on the whole, upland plants, from parts of the state normally not subject to flooding and therefore best suited for human habitation.

But towns and cities often are established along rivers and near the sea, so we also must consider the types of wet regions that exist. Additionally, in the old days, Florida's wetlands were not immune to development, although in recent years, legislation has helped preserve many borderline environmental areas from the bulldozers. Mangrove swamps on the southeast coast of Florida were destroyed by the creation of a series of finger canals and islands in which the fill from canal dredging was deposited between the canals, creating higher land for expensive housing. (It is interesting to note that some of these former mangrove swamps may be returning to a lowland state because the artificial land is settling and sinking in many areas. High tides in spring and fall bring water up through storm drains, flooding streets and yards. If a hurricane ever hits at the time of the autumn equinox tide, some of Florida's expensive real estate may go under.)

These are the state's upland regions and the plant species that dominate them:

- Beach/dune community, consisting of sea oats, low herbs, vines, and shrubs adapted to the full blast of salt, wind, and sometimes water.

- Maritime forest on the lee side of dunes and mounds of the coast. Tropical evergreens dominate the southern woods, whereas a temperate mix of vegetation is found in northern areas.

- Pine flatwoods, one of the state's major vegetation areas suitable for habitation. Open woods are dominated by longleaf, pond, and slash pine; wildflowers, palmettos, some shrubs, and grasses are found in the understory. These regions are subject to periodic fire, which keeps the vegetation open.

- Rockland, found in extreme southern Florida, with plants growing on porous limestone. Pine rocklands have southern Florida slash pine as a major component with open woodlands of grasses, palms, and shrubs. Rockland hammock vegetation features a thick overstory of tropical hardwoods with a dense understory. The hammock areas are wetter than pine rocklands and rarely are affected by fire.

- Upland mixed forest, on clay uplands in the Panhandle region of the state. Mature woods are dominated by hardwoods but second growth or cut-over areas often have pine as the main component.

- Scrub forest occurring on sandy, well-drained ridges. Plants grow in almost desert-like surroundings, and fire is a major factor.

Pine flatwoods dominated by pines and palmetto. ▶

❧ Sandhill areas, common in the center of the state, with an oak/longleaf pine overstory. The well-drained uplands are subject to frequent fires.

❧ Upland mesic hardwood forests, with a diversity of hardwoods and some evergreens on rich, sandy loam soil.

❧ Cabbage palm forests, rarely flooded, found mixed with oaks or at the edges of grassy prairies.

Florida's wet areas include:

❧ Swamp forest and cypress swamp forest, under water most of the year and dominated by pond and bald cypresses or deciduous trees.

❧ Coastal saline wetlands, including saltwater marshes in the north and western parts of the states and mangrove swamps in the south.

❧ Wet prairies, consisting of seasonally flooded, treeless lowlands, open grassy areas also supporting low herbs and rushes.

Mangroves inhabit southern coastal wetlands. ▶

Cypress swamps are usually under water most of the year.

- ❧ Open scrub cypress with scattered dwarfed pond cypress growing on very thin soil that also supports sedges, low herbs, and grasses.

- ❧ Fresh water marshes, basin areas with a peat soil base, occupied by various rushes and other herbaceous plants.

- ❧ Everglades sawgrass marshes, dominated by sawgrass, although invasive cattails are a problem in some areas.

- ❧ Everglades marshes, sloughs, wet prairies and tree islands, with various grasses and rushes in low areas. On the small isolated tree islands, vegetation varies from bay trees to tropical hardwoods.

- ❧ Prairie/marsh wetland, with sawgrass, wildflowers, and other grasses.

Any of these wetland areas contain many useful native plants, some particularly appropriate for the edges of containment ponds used to collect excess runoff water. Developments and industrial areas may use a system of canals or lakes to catch and store surplus water for flood control, or residents may use water containment areas as a source of irrigation. When dry season lowers water levels, exposing ugly irrigation pipes, native plantings suitable for a pond edge will conceal pipes at low water and still survive when water levels are higher. Some native nurseries now specialize in aquatic plants for this purpose.

These plant communities, both upland and wetland, can be located on the General Map of Vegetation of Florida, published by the Institute of Food and Agricultural Science, University of Florida.

FLORIDA'S CLIMATE

*P*eople have definite preferences as to where they want to live. Some love the heat; others crave a cooler climate. One would choose life in the shady woods; another could sprawl forever on a sandy, sun-drenched dune. Plants are like that, too.

Florida's climate offers its residents, human and otherwise, a good deal of variety. It ranges from cool subtropical in the north to truly tropical in the Keys.

Except for its northern border, the state is surrounded by water, a factor that modifies the climate over most of its area. This close proximity to the water makes for cooler summers and warmer winters. Interior areas away from the water may register 10° warmer in summer and 10° cooler in winter.

The many lakes and rivers of interior Florida offer some micro-climate advantages, particularly in winter. This means the south and southeastern sides of these bodies of water can be a degree or two warmer than the north or west sides, which may make the difference between an injurious freeze and no plant damage during a cold spell.

Hardiness Zone Map

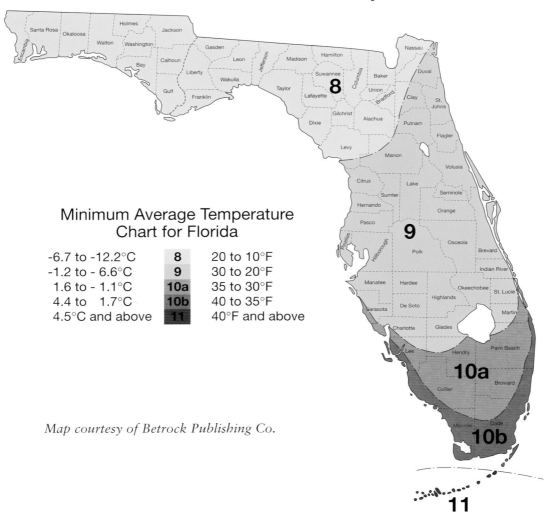

Minimum Average Temperature Chart for Florida

Temperature (°C)	Zone	Temperature (°F)
-6.7 to -12.2°C	**8**	20 to 10°F
-1.2 to - 6.6°C	**9**	30 to 20°F
1.6 to - 1.1°C	**10a**	35 to 30°F
4.4 to 1.7°C	**10b**	40 to 35°F
4.5°C and above	**11**	40°F and above

Map courtesy of Betrock Publishing Co.

The United States Department of Agriculture Plant Hardiness Map of the United States puts northern Florida and the Panhandle in hardiness Zone 8, which corresponds to average lows of 10–20°F. Zone 9 covers central Florida, with average minimums of 20-30°F.

Zones 10a and 10b encompass the southern end of the peninsula. Zone 10a has average minimums of 30–35°F, whereas Zone 10b has lows of 35–40°F. The true tropics are in the Keys, which is Zone 11, with minimum temperatures above 40°F.

In citing the native ranges of plants in this book, you will notice we refer simply to Zone 10, because the minor temperature differences between Zones 10a and 10b seldom are critical when native plants are concerned.

Remember, these are *average* temperatures. A severe cold wave can bring temperatures as low as 15–20°F in the extreme north and around 32°F in the far south. Fortunately, such cold spells seldom last more than three days and usually are followed by a quick warmup. The coldest temperatures often are on the second day of a cold snap, when the wind is calm and radiational cooling drops temperatures to their lowest reading.

Residents can take several steps to lessen or prevent cold damage to their valuable plantings. Individual landscapes can be protected by using windbreaks and locating tender plant material on the south side of a building. A good watering just before a cold spell also will help protect plantings. So will pulling mulch away from the base of a plant so that warmth in the soil can radiate upward.

When, despite your efforts, plants do freeze during a cold night, they should be protected from the morning sun. If allowed to thaw too quickly, their tissues can turn to mush.

Heat also can affect plants adversely, especially in combination with dry weather. A new Plant Heat-Zone Map, published in 1997 by the American Horticultural Society, shows the average number of days per year that various regions of the country experience "heat days," with temperatures higher than 86°F (30°C), the point at which plants may begin to suffer damage. The map divides the country into zones from Zone 1, with no heat days, to Zone 12, with 210 heat days. (Florida ranges from Zone 8 in the Panhandle, with 90 to 120 heat days, to Zone 12, in inland southwest Florida.) Plans are under way to incorporate this coding in publications such as garden catalogs and reference books to indicate various plants' ability to tolerate heat.

In Florida, our summer temperatures usually are modified by frequent afternoon thunderstorms. Most rainfall occurs during the summer wet season, from June to mid-October. Rainfall averages from 48 to 64 inches annually statewide, with the southeast interior areas and the extreme northwest Panhandle having the highest average rainfall.

Hurricanes are the major wind events that plague the state. The southeast coast and Keys are most prone to hurricanes, but the northern Gulf Coast also has been hit in recent years. Fortunately, even a major hurricane's path of destruction usually is only 40–70 miles across, so much of the state is spared.

Tornadoes may accompany a hurricane, causing additional devastation. But even the more severe thunderstorms are capable of producing small tornadoes that can leave tremendous local damage behind them.

CULTURE

*Y*ears ago, Floridians hankering for a native garden had few options when it came to obtaining plants. Most often they went out into the boondocks, collected small trees or shrubs, and brought them home. Some plants lived; a lot more died.

Those days are past. Development has gobbled up once-wild land. Collecting on private property without permission is illegal, and getting such permission, when the land perhaps is owned by a faceless development corporation, is not easy. Besides, many of our most valued species—orchids, bromeliads and more—are protected by state law. No responsible person these days approves transplanting from the wild, unless it is part of a salvage operation to rescue plants from land being cleared for development.

Fortunately, nurseries specializing in natives have multiplied along with the interest in native plants, and even growers who formerly concentrated on fast-growing exotics have added more natives to their listings. Along with commercial nurseries, other sources such as native plant societies often offer container-grown plants at affordable prices. Purchasing from such sources helps guarantee that your plants will be healthy and insect-free.

Native plants often are extolled as being carefree, and to some extent this is true, especially if they are planted in sites similar to their natural habitats. Plants located considerably out of their preferred habitats can have as many problems as exotic species. Knowledgeable nursery personnel can steer you to the plants that will do well in your particular surroundings.

Observing the characteristics of a plant's growth, choosing improved varietal selections, and being aware how big the plant will get at maturity are good ways to assure the success of your native landscape.

Once you've made your choice, it's important to get your tree or shrub off to a good start with proper planting and maintenance.

First, dig a broad, shallow hole no deeper than the depth of the pot or root ball and twice as wide. If you like, you can mix some organic matter such as peat moss or cow manure with the existing soil (one part organic matter to two parts soil), but many horticulturists recommend using the existing soil without improving it.

Position the plant in the hole, fill it two-thirds with soil, and tamp down. Then fill the hole with water. Poke the hose end into the soil to eliminate air pockets, and let the water drain before adding the rest of the soil. Be sure the soil level is no higher than the plant's root ball. Tamp the soil down again. It's a good idea to build a circular dirt "dam" around the plant a little farther out than the root ball; it will help hold water as the plant becomes established. Water again to fill this basin.

One misconception is that natives do not need watering. Once established, correctly located plants can survive nicely without irrigation, but they do need water to get established. Planting in the wet season is practical, as supplemental irrigation may not be necessary. Put your plants in the ground at the start of the rainy season in June or July and they should be well-established before the dry season begins, around mid-October.

Dry season planting, on the other hand, requires a reliable irrigation system or a lot of time spent dragging around the garden hose. Your new plants will need daily watering for the first two weeks, then every three or four days until the wet season arrives.

Fertilizing is another area often misunderstood. For native plants that are well-established, fertilizer is not essential, but a good organic fertilizer can speed their growth. If you choose to use fertilizer, apply it at the rates recommended on the label, in March, June, and October.

If you allow fallen leaves to remain in planting beds, they'll decay naturally and serve as free mulch. An organic layer like this conserves water, suppresses weeds, and acts as a fertilizer as the elements return to the soil. If you use commercial mulch (shredded cypress, pine bark, and the like), keep it a couple of inches away from the plant stem or trunk to avoid bark peeling and rotting.

Pruning is recommended to remove dead wood, crossing limbs, and suckers. While pruning can be done at almost any time, especially in south Florida, early summer is preferable. One time to hold off with the lopping shears, however, is right after a freeze.

As for trimming and shaping to create a hedge, not all species take well to this treatment. Although cocoplum and silver buttonwood are used commonly as hedge plants in south Florida, neither seems able to take repeated pruning to keep them at a specific height. As a hedge, silver buttonwood gets bare and woody at the base and has a short serviceable life, but it is perfect as a small tree. Cocoplum fares better but still does not have a long serviceable life as a hedge. It will be effective longer in a sunny location, but still will have trouble pushing new growth from old wood.

And yes, pests and diseases can attack native plants as well as exotics. For a healthy plant, a problem may be nothing worse than a temporary inconvenience. Much depends on the gardener's tolerance for insects.

Mahogany, for example, is a fine, tough tree, but some are very susceptible to tent caterpillars in the spring. They strip the foliage, and the falling caterpillars and their ugly tents are offensive. Yet the tree survives the attack and quickly puts out fresh green leaves. No spraying is required, but Thuricide or Dipel, a bacillus that acts as a stomach poison to the caterpillars, may be used for control. It is a natural pesticide, safe for the environment.

The introduced Cuban May beetle eats the foliage on many trees, starting to feed in early summer and continuing its nocturnal attacks until early fall. It starts on lower foliage and works its way up the tree. Plants survive, but the loss of leaves is noticeable. Beneficial nematodes will safely control beetle populations while they are in the grub stage in the soil during the winter.

Many gardeners choose to let nature take its course. One gardener we know had a native lysiloma, or wild tamarind, that became infested with thornbugs, an enemy of most members of the legume family. He killed the bugs by spraying, but more were back the next year. The same cycle repeated the following year. He stopped spraying, ignored the bugs, and while the lysiloma may be growing somewhat more slowly, it is still vigorous.

Diversification and good plant health will minimize insect damage. A single specimen in your garden may escape attack entirely, whereas a planting of dozens of the same species may bring in the preying insects from miles around. Besides, diversification replicates nature, makes a garden more interesting, and provides havens for more birds and other predators that will feed on the bad guys without the need for spraying.

And here's a word for those who want to have a native garden but lack the space. Small trees and shrubs such as the various stoppers, pineland privet, and blueberry are fine for container growing. Ferns lend themselves to baskets and pots. Wildflowers will still bring butterflies to your garden even if the garden is a collection of attractive pots arranged on a deck or patio. A commercial, fast-draining potting mix or a blend of peat moss, perlite, and bark, plus sparing use of a good soluble fertilizer, will suit almost any container-grown plant.

Creating a Native Garden

*L*ike any other kind of landscaping, creating a native garden takes some planning. You don't have to be an artist to draw a workable design that will serve as a guide when installing your plants and trees. If you have a professionally prepared survey or architect's drawing of your property, with a bird's-eye view of the house and land, that's a good place to begin. Make a few photocopies and go from there. Or just start with a fresh sheet of graph paper.

Draw your house, driveway, sidewalks, patio, pool, and other features. Your plan must work around and be compatible with all your utilities. They include your septic tank, drain field, sewage lines, underground conduits for water and gas, irrigation lines, and overhead utility wires. So be sure you know where they are located.

During this initial planning stage, you should also locate specific "use areas": the public space at the front of the house, an area for entertaining, utility space for pool pump, clothesline, trash cans and storage, and perhaps hobby areas for a water garden, butterfly or bird gardens, vegetables, or wildflowers.

Meanwhile, try to keep in mind the principles of energy conservation. Properly selected and located native plants can reduce the amount of water needed for irrigation, save money and effort that would be spent on frequent pruning, and provide shade from the hot sun and protection from chilly winds, a major saving on air conditioning and heating bills. Providing a shady canopy for your outdoor air conditioning unit, for example, can increase its efficiency.

Think of your landscape as a series of outdoor rooms, with walls and ceilings fashioned of trees and shrubs.

The first items that should be placed in the landscape are your selected trees, both large and small, and larger palms. Locating a large tree on the southwest side of the house will provide maximum shade. A deciduous tree, providing summer shade and winter sunlight, might give the most beneficial balance in north and central Florida, while an evergreen would be more suitable in the southern region where even winter days often require air conditioning. Evergreen conifers such as red cedar, planted along the north side of the property, could serve as a windbreak, protecting you from cold winter winds.

Nothing needs more careful research than large trees. They're not only expensive at the outset but can prove even more expensive if you must remove them later on. Before settling on a specific tree, be sure you understand its habits. How tall will it grow? Does it have messy leaves and fruit? Are its roots aggressive? A tree with potential growth to 40 or 50 feet should not be located near or under power lines where branches can contribute to power outages and require trimming by the electric company (which may leave your poor oak hacked beyond recognition). Be sure that what you are planting will be a good neighbor.

Shrubs and small palms are useful as accents, for providing screening, blocking unattractive views, and dividing the garden into "rooms." They help direct foot traffic and emphasize focal points, and many add beauty with colorful flowers and interesting textures. Thorny shrubs can provide security as well as cover and nesting sites for birds. Here again, there is an energy factor; shrubs along the east and west sides of the house will reduce the amount of the sun's heat the walls would otherwise absorb.

By their very nature, most of Florida's native plants have a casual look and work well in an informal landscape. But for the tidy type of gardener who loves things clipped and manicured, the native palette has shrubs that will provide this look. The "Schellings" dwarf holly, with its tiny leaves and

tight branching, lends itself to neat little hedges or foundation plantings and requires minimal pruning. Perfect columns are attainable with marlberry, Spanish stopper, or Jamaica caper, which grow naturally in a columnar form and need only an occasional nip and tuck to keep in shape. Even shrubs with natural rounded, squarish, or triangular forms can be found.

Vines on fences and trellises can create vertical walls, or supply shade and shelter when used on an arbor or pergola. Many have attractive, fragrant flowers and are not overly invasive. Be sure to match the size and climbing habit of a vine to its supporting structure. Twining vines are fine on a chainlink fence but could strangle a living tree. A species with hold-fast roots, like Virginia creeper, is excellent for covering an ugly masonry wall along a highway, but when it climbs a wooden structure it can promote decay and harbor insects.

Low-growing flowering plants, ferns, and such should be added last to provide low cover and color and to shade out weeds. Tree leaves will sift into their beds and disappear, making raking unnecessary and will return organic matter to the earth as a natural source of fertilizer.

During this initial planning, it is important to analyze your site to determine what to save and what to remove. Some existing ornamental plants can be blended into the native garden. A shade garden, for instance, can incorporate exotic ferns, camellias, hostas, or other compatible plantings. As long as an exotic plant is not overly aggressive and serves a function, let it remain.

Trees such as ficus and schefflera, with invasive roots or messy habits, usually should be removed. You might also want to eliminate brittle species—willow, poplar, Siberian elm, silver maple, and chinaberry—if they are growing close to the house.

Reducing the size of your lawn as much as possible will save money and energy. While a young family often needs a lawn as a safe play area for children, the garden can be changed and the lawn area reduced as the children grow.

In your planning, you might want to incorporate mini-habitats. A shade garden can mimic the forest on a small scale, with a canopy, understory, and forest floor plants. A small, sunny open meadow can be created with native plants, even on a city or suburban lot. Wherever you live in Florida, there is a palette of native plants and a landscape design that will work for you and your personal lifestyle.

◀ Walter viburnum and wax myrtle in a loose, informal hedge.

1. LARGE TREES
   Oaks
   Pines
   Red maple
   Mahogany
   Hickory
   Sweet gum
   Black gum
   Sugarberry
   Florida elm
   Paradise tree
   Gumbo-limbo
   Southern magnolia
   Wild tamarind
   Green buttonwood
   Jamaica dogwood
   Southern red cedar

2. SMALL TREES
   Winged elm
   Redbud
   Dogwood
   Crabapple
   Plums
   Hollies
   Turkey oak
   Redbay
   Soapberry
   Red buckeye
   Fringe tree
   Sourwood
   Hawthorns
   Geiger tree
   Pigeon plum
   Torchwood
   Fiddlewood
   Sweetbay magnolia
   Loblolly bay
   Stoppers
   Lignum vitae
   Willow bustic

3. ACCENTS
   Saw palmetto
   Yaupon holly
   Wax myrtle
   Buttonbush
   Needle palm
   Swamp lily
   Spider lily
   Fakahatchee grass
   Wild azalea

4. HEDGE
   Florida privet
   Blueberry
   Dwarf yaupon holly
   Viburnum
   Sweetshrub
   Cocoplum
   Bay cedar
   Gallberry
   White indigo berry

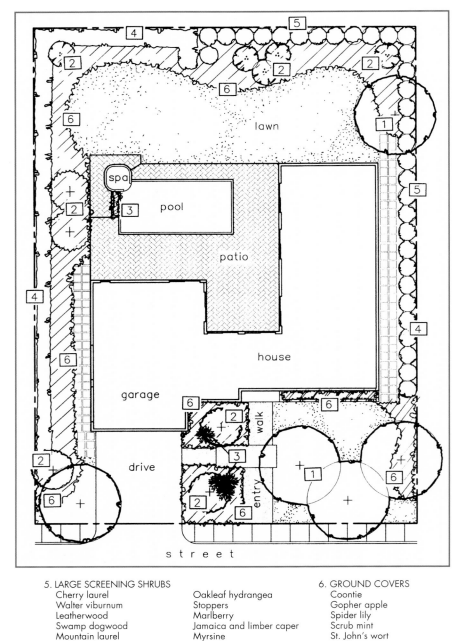

5. LARGE SCREENING SHRUBS
   Cherry laurel
   Walter viburnum
   Leatherwood
   Swamp dogwood
   Mountain laurel
   Wild azalea

   Oakleaf hydrangea
   Stoppers
   Marlberry
   Jamaica and limber caper
   Myrsine
   Cocoplum

6. GROUND COVERS
   Coontie
   Gopher apple
   Spider lily
   Scrub mint
   St. John's wort
   Muhly grass

A native garden for an urban home. The design for this native plant landscape can be adapted to many suburban settings. Use it for ideas in creating your own landscape. The trees and plants listed here are only a few of the possibilities; many others are suitable if they are appropriate for your part of the state. *(Design by Steven E. Tate)*

WATER GARDENS

There was a time when many individual property owners and developers looked upon marshy wetlands and grassy ponds as unattractive places to be cleared and replanted, usually with exotics, or even filled in. Now, appreciation for the value and potential beauty of such sites is emerging.

A case in point is the five-acre Cypress Creek Nature Preserve, only a couple of blocks away from busy I-95 in Fort Lauderdale in Broward County. This bit of preserved wetland is set among the glittering glass and concrete buildings of a large corporate center complex. Cooperation between the developer and the county's parks and recreation division led to the preservation of the stand of old bald cypress, maples, and ferns, along with a large pond inhabited by turtles and fish and visited by egrets, ibises, herons, even ospreys. A simple wood boardwalk and benches along the pond edge make it a restful haven for employees and the public, and at the same time educate them to the beauty and serenity of a natural sanctuary.

If you are the owner of rural, undeveloped property, you may be lucky enough to have a similar freshwater pond, lake, or stream passing through.

Often, all one needs to create an enjoyable water "garden" at such sites is to eliminate undesirable exotics and perhaps thin shrubs or lift the lower branches on trees to open up the view. Flowering shrubs like buttonbush and water-loving wildflowers such as lobelia may be introduced along the bank for color and contrast.

Today, though, it is difficult to find pristine lakes, ponds, or riverfront sites still in a natural condition. Native plantings have disappeared and the original soils are highly disturbed. What we see instead are man-made "lakes" in new developments, where houses are built on elevated pads of soil dug from low areas, thereby creating retention ponds and "waterfront" property.

These ponds catch and hold excess rainwater and may serve as a source of irrigation. All too often they are fitted with drainage and irrigation pipes that are exposed when the water level is low, and the only landscaping is grass planted to the lake edge. Instead of a pleasant water view, residents face a sterile, artificial scene.

J. Roland Lieber, a Naples landscape architect faced with such a challenge, changed a negative to a positive when he added landscaping to a water retention pond in a southwest Florida office building complex. Using water-tolerant bald cypress, red maple, wax myrtle, and Fakahatchee grass, he transformed a sterile pond into a major landscape asset. Like the Cypress Creek Nature Preserve, the restful spot, now furnished with benches and statuary, provides a pleasant lunch and break area for the surrounding business employees and has become the most visited area of the property. Birds and wildlife have returned to the new habitat.

The owner of a home on one of these man-made bodies of water is more likely to have only a few yards of lake edge to work with. Softening the interface of the water and the land can be relatively simple. Be sure to choose trees and shrubs in sizes compatible with the size of the area you are landscaping. Another important factor to consider is your and your neighbors' water view, so that plantings will not block it.

Ideally, whatever you plant should enclose the view at the bottom and sides in the manner of a picture frame. Where space is limited, columnar growers such as bald or pond cypress, red maple, or dahoon holly will fit the bill. Palms are another possibility; sable palms, for example, could be used in a small, tight group of three different sizes so that the fronds do not interfere with each other. Medium-sized shrubs or grasses can be located

◄ Cypress Creek Nature Preserve, Fort Lauderdale, thrives within a modern corporate center.

This retention pond in southwest Florida was turned into a visual asset.
(Photo by J. Roland Lieber)

under the trees or palms to tie them visually to the ground, while grass or low ground covers might be used between the taller plantings.

At water's edge, another group of plants can come into play. This is the place for wildflowers that do not object to wet feet, such as cardinal flower, iris, pitcher plants, and swamp lily; aquatic plants like arrowhead, water lily, alligator flag, canna, and pickerel weed; and ferns.

In planning the water garden, consider the many suitable trees and shrubs that are fragrant, including loblolly bay, sweetbay magnolia, buttonbush, sweetshrub, wild azalea, and water lily. Aromatic foliage is a bonus with red bay, Florida anise, and wax myrtle.

Attracted by such native habitats, wading birds such as herons, egrets, and storks not only will add interest and movement to the landscape but often introduce aquatic life to a new, sterile pond in the form of frog and fish eggs and even small aquatic vegetation that had stuck to their feet and legs.

One caveat: Other critters may be attracted to these watery habitats as well. It's a good idea to keep large plantings at the edges of the "picture frame" described above, not only for the view but to limit the potential habitat for such usually unwelcome visitors as alligators and water moccasins. If a dock, beach, or fishing site is part of your design, make sure a good-sized

Native plants, like duck potato, attract water birds. ▶

open area is available around it. As both alligators and water moccasins are primarily dusk-to-dawn feeders, an open lawn area and appropriate lighting can prevent unpleasant surprises. And it goes without saying: Don't feed the gators and keep pets away from waters they are known to inhabit.

1. LARGE TREES
AND PALMS
Red maple
River birch
Water hickory
Sugarberry
Sweet gum
Southern magnolia
Black gum
Laurel oak
Bald cypress
Florida elm
Sabal palm
Royal palm

2. SMALL TREES
AND PALMS
Pond apple
Pawpaw
Atlantic whitecedar
Fringe tree
Cocoplum
Loblolly bay
Dahoon holly
Sweetbay magnolia
Redbay
Coastal plain willow
Paurotis palm

3. ACCENTS
Needle palm
Florida thatch palm
Saw palmetto
Buttonbush
Oakleaf hydrangea
Wax myrtle
Leather fern
Florida tree fern

4. HEDGE/SHRUBS
Blueberry
Wild azalea
Florida privet
Gallberry
Florida anise
Virginia willow
Elderberry

5. GROUND COVERS
Lizard's tail
Fakahatchee grass
Boston fern

6. EDGE-OF-WATER
PLANTS, AQUATICS
Lizard's tail
Cinnamon fern
Pitcher plant
Cardinal flower

String lily
Spider lily
Yellow canna

Pickerel weed
White water lily
Duck potato

Thalia
Rushes

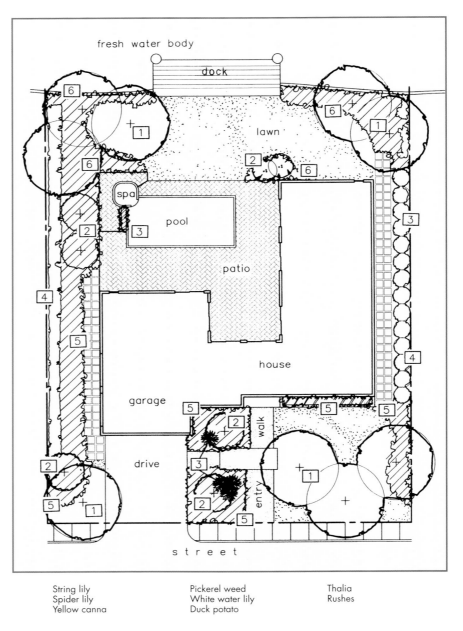

A garden for a fresh water frontage. This waterfront landscape would work along a natural or man-made lake to create an attractive view and help stabilize the bank. Other plants also are suitable. *(Design by Steven E. Tate)*

THE SEASIDE GARDEN

*T*he number of Florida residents who garden next to the sea may not appear great, but with 8,476 miles of coastline (that's the Florida Marine Patrol's figure), landscaping at the ocean's edge or even a block or two from the beach is a challenge facing more than a few of us.

Rough and tough describe the characteristics necessary to confront the elements likely to be tossed at the seaside garden. It's the most hostile environment a plant can face. Punches thrown at it include salt-laden winds, salt water inundation, extreme drought, baking sun, and sterile soil.

The Atlantic coast bears the brunt of strong winter winds; hurricanes can affect all coasts. The Gulf shores suffer most from salt water intrusion, which in major hurricanes may reach far inland. Salt water flooding is less on the Atlantic side because of higher elevations and some protective reefs on the southeast coast. Drought, heat, and sandy soils, of course, create difficulties for plants on all shorelines.

Over thousands of years, some of our native vegetation has adapted to these conditions. Some plants are highly salt tolerant, some less so. Remember that

such plants do not require salt and sand; they simply manage to thrive despite those inhospitable surroundings.

As Laurel Schiller of Florida Native Plants, Inc., a nursery near Sarasota, points out, "salt tolerance" is a relative term. Some plants will endure salt air, she says, and a few will put up with a splash of salt water now and then. But just because a plant—the beach sunflower, for example—grows in high dunes and is tolerant of coastal conditions doesn't mean it can survive being drowned in sea water.

Locating plants is critical, both for practicality and their survival. With seaside gardening, you have to be aware of micro-climates. You can get away with less salt-tolerant plantings on the lee side of a building, away from the water, because the building will give some protection from salt-laden wind.

On the practical side, the picturesque seagrape is great on the beach but not near the swimming pool. Its large leaves take an eternity to decay and the fruit litters and may stain hard surfaces, and the home owner, as he cleans up the constant mess, will curse the landscape designer forever.

As prevailing winter winds come from the northeast, try not to locate any tree on the northeast side of a pool. To avoid blocking water views, use wispy palms or see-through plantings. At a condominium or similar building, locate trees in front of bathroom or bedroom areas so balconies and living rooms have open views of the water.

High-rise buildings such as condominiums, common near our beaches, present special problems. To the uneducated eye, native plantings may take some selling, and the condo owner who is accustomed to impatiens may have trouble appreciating the beauty of a beach sunflower. But an awareness of the value of native plants, community landscape codes requiring the use of a percentage of natives, and the realization by condo boards that they can save on maintenance and irrigation costs are changing the old attitudes.

With high-rises, the list of plant choices narrows sharply. Wind tunnels created between tall walls can double the wind velocity, and wind measuring 30 mph on the beach may reach 60 mph between the buildings. Wind will whip around tall towers and even the protected lee sides may experience unusual air currents. The designer should visit the site on a windy day and take note of the air currents before specifying plantings. The height of such buildings also creates dense shade on the north side, and because most of our native plants require plenty of sunlight, they will languish and die off in the shade.

◄ Sea oats will tolerate a harsh environment.

Sea ox-eye daisy provides color in the beach landscape.

Another potential problem for the seaside garden, especially at condominiums, is the automatic irrigation system, all too often set for daily, lengthy waterings no matter what the weather. Most salt-tolerant natives are not tolerant of excess water, and easily die of root rot. Irrigation is important to get new plantings off to a good start, but should be reduced after the plants are well established. In some respects, this is new territory because some natives have not been tested for a period of time under irrigation. The best advice is to keep a close eye on your plants and use caution and common sense in watering. Less usually is better.

OCEANSIDE:

1. PALMS
   Sabal palm
   Thatch palm

2. DUNE PLANTINGS
   Sea oats
   Railroad vine
   Beach bean
   Seaside goldenrod

3. SHRUBS
   Bay cedar
   Saw palmetto
   White indigo berry
   Scaevola
   Coral bean
   Beautyberry
   Saltbush
   Beach elder

4. ACCENT SHRUBS
   OR PALMS
   Silver palm
   Seven-year apple
   Spanish bayonet
   Spanish stopper

5. GROUND COVERS
   Coontie
   Gopher apple
   Spider lily
   Sea ox-eye daisy
   Dune sunflower

6. HEDGE
   Bay cedar
   Sand cordgrass

7. FLOWERING PLANTS
   Dune sunflower
   Yellowtop
   Blanket flower
   Seaside gentian
   Standing cypress

LEE SIDE:

8. LARGE TREES
   Live oak
   Jamaica dogwood
   Gumbo-limbo
   Sugarberry
   Green buttonwood
   Southern red cedar

9. SMALL TREES
   Torchwood
   Fiddlewood
   Blolly
   Myrtle oak
   Geiger tree
   Pigeon plum
   Seagrape
   Willow bustic
   Lignum vitae
   Wild lime

Stoppers
Hollies
Satinwood
Soapberry
Red bay

10. SHRUBS
    Marlberry
    Beautyberry
    Saw palmetto
    Spicewood
    Wild coffee
    Florida privet
    Coral bean
    Cocoplum
    Jamaica and Limber caper

Wax myrtle
Leather fern
Sparkleberry
Gall berry

11. GROUND COVERS
    Coontie
    Fishtail fern
    Sword fern

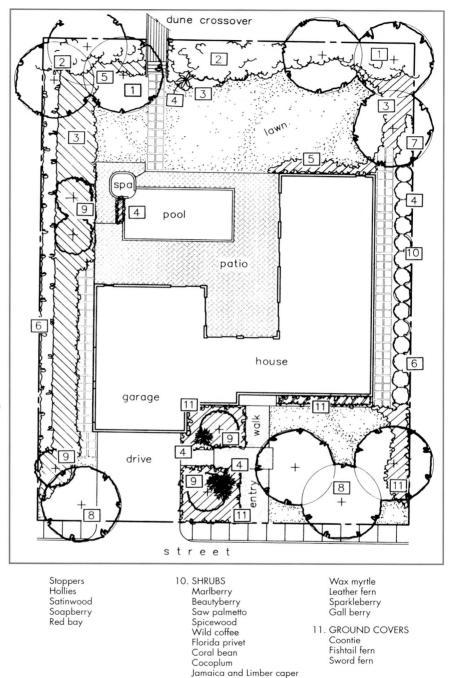

The seaside garden presents a special challenge. This design for an oceanfront landscape emphasizes plants that can tolerate a hostile environment. Note that different plants are suited to the ocean and lee sides of the property. *(Design by Steven E. Tate)*

WILDFLOWER GARDENS AND GRASSY MEADOWS

*I*f, while driving down some back country road, you've ever slammed on the brakes to gawk at a field of purple blazing star and wire grass or yellow drifts of goldenrod, you understand the appeal of these humble but often showy flowers.

Trees and shrubs may be the meat and potatoes of your native landscape, but flowers are the garnish. Of course, your garden can survive without them, but why should it? And if wildflowers take a bit more attention than woody plants, they are well worth the effort.

The north and central parts of Florida generally have a wider palette of attractive wildflowers than the south, but some species cover a large part of the state. Wherever you live, you can find colorful and sometimes fragrant plants suitable for a wild garden.

Some are annuals, living only a year. Biennials live two years, usually blooming the second year. Perennials can live indefinitely. That's in theory, at least. Depending on where in the state they grow, plants behave quite differently. An annual in north Florida may last several years in the south,

Blanket flower, scarlet sage, and Tampa verbena brighten a wildflower bed.

for example. Even annuals that die after blooming often reseed by themselves, so new plants continually replace the old. Some annuals or biennials spread by underground runners or rhizomes, and as plants die away they are replaced by new ones.

Also, a "perennial" in Gainesville, transplanted to south Florida, may hate Miami's heat and humidity so much that it succumbs after a single season, thereby becoming an "annual" as far as its disappointed owner is concerned.

Despite their tough nature, wildflowers transplanted from their natural habitat seldom survive. Native plant nurseries in your area are the best sources of plants.

If you gather seed from the wild (with the landowner's consent) don't be greedy; leave plenty for the plants to reseed in their location. We have found that in most cases, commercial wildflower seed mixes are disappointing.

Few of us are lucky enough to own the rural acreage that can support a natural meadow, but you may be able to duplicate a bit of that ambience, in a border, perhaps, mixing grasses and wildflowers.

Nature is not fond of sharp corners and straight lines, so your wildflower garden should take the form of natural curves with sweeps of color. Plant masses of the same flower, or mix them up as they would appear in a field or along a roadside. Back them with native shrubs or with a large, bold, flowering plant such as spider lily or standing cypress.

Purple liatris accents field of wire grass.

A meadow hardly requires a landscape plan. Simply locate flowers where you can see and enjoy their beauty and observe the butterflies and bees that are sure to visit. But it's important, in an area unlikely to get artificial irrigation, to select the flowering plants and grasses that are suitable for your region and the soil conditions. For boggy sites, look for water-loving plants like lobelia, meadow beauty, or swamp lily; in dry soils, plants such as blanket flower, goldenrod, and Florida paintbrush will do better. Here's the place to stretch your imagination in combining colors. Match goldenrod with black-eyed Susan or create a contrasting combination by adding bright red sage.

Grasses are a natural, graceful addition to the landscape, adding texture. Nancy Bissett, co-owner of The Natives nursery in Davenport, points out that native grasses help stabilize a wildflower planting. Their fibrous, spreading roots fill in empty spaces and don't give weeds a chance to appear. Some species will reseed and fill in bare spots.

Bold blossoms hold their own among heavy-stemmed grasses such as lop-sided Indian grass; fragile-flowered species are better combined with more delicate textures like the love grasses.

Cut grass clumps back now and then. If you cut back your flowering plants at the same time, do it after they have gone to seed. Otherwise, you'll most likely eliminate next season's blooms.

◄ Goldenrod and grasses form a striking combination.

1. TALL GRASSES,
   LARGE FLOWERING PLANTS
   Sand cordgrass
   Fakahatchee grass
   Narrowleaf sunflower
   Goldenrod
   Spider lily

2. MEDIUM GRASSES, WILDFLOWERS
   Lopsided Indiangrass
   Florida gamagrass
   Florida paintbrush
   Standing cypress
   Liatris

3. LOW GRASSES, WILDFLOWERS
   Muhly grass
   Purple coneflower
   Blanket flower
   Ruellia
   Scarlet sage

4. BORDER PLANTS
   Elliott love grass
   White-bracted sedge
   Blue-eyed grass
   Mimosa

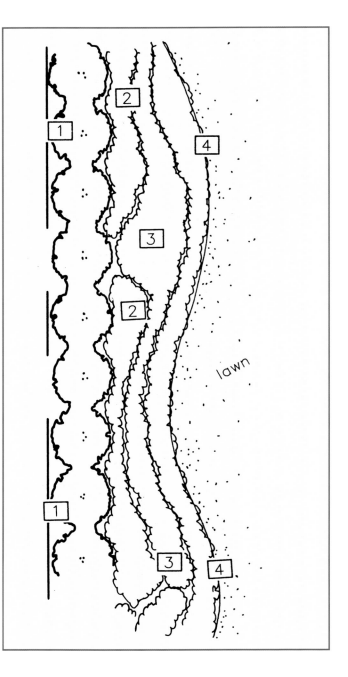

Wildflowers and grasses in a naturalistic border. Even a simple border, as shown in this design, can give the effect of a grassy field with drifts of wildflowers. *(Design by Steven E. Tate)*

WELCOMING WILDLIFE

The pleasure we get from our gardens often is enhanced by sharing them with wildlife, particularly birds. One doesn't have to be a devout bird-watcher to enjoy these visitors, whose beauty, song, and insect-eating activities distinguish them as remarkably welcome guests.

A diverse planting of native trees and shrubs will provide the food, nesting sites, and shelter that birds and other wildlife need. Plants that bear fruit, seeds, or nuts or attract insects will bring a wide variety of birds to your garden. In all likelihood they will also bring squirrels, possums, raccoons, and other small mammals, which many gardeners enjoy or at least accept with a live-and-let-live attitude. If that doesn't describe you, choose plantings that appeal more to birds than to small mammals.

The plantings should be selected for their suitability to your specific site and its climate and for producing a food supply over an extended period of time. Many of our songbirds are migratory and look for food from fall to spring.

Different plants will attract different species of birds. Besides seeking food, birds look for nesting sites and cover. Dense shrubs, the sort you might choose for screening purposes, give birds protection from predators. Thorny shrubs and dense evergreens are particularly valuable for this purpose.

Some species are multipurpose. The southern red cedar, one of the most valuable trees for wildlife, provides both food and shelter. Many members of the holly family have spiny leaves, dense growth, and fruit for winter feeding. Hawthorns and buckthorns are thorny plants, excellent for cover and nesting and bearing fall and winter fruit. Florida privet's twiggy growth is perfect for nesting and cover. The fruit is prized by many birds and other wildlife, and the flowers draw insects for warblers and vireos. Walter viburnum (thicker and more twiggy than other viburnums), wax myrtle, and various species of plum also afford both food and shelter, while good protective cover can be found in acacias and bay cedar.

The greatest number of food plants for birds are the fruit and berry producers, representing many species of trees and shrubs. Among the best are hackberry, southern red cedar, the hollies, red mulberry, tupelo, laurelcherry, black cherry, cabbage palm, blueberry, and elderberry. Here's where you can maintain some control over the sort of wildlife you want to attract. Seedy berries will satisfy the hunger of many kinds of birds, but possums and raccoons are more attracted to fleshy fruits like persimmons, plums, grapes, and blackberries.

Seed-eating birds—and that includes many of our songbirds—will be attracted by various native grasses, sunflowers, magnolia, elms, and redbud. Nut- or acorn-producing trees such as oaks and hickories not only are good shade trees for the landscape but produce food for small animals and larger birds and offer good nesting sites.

Plants provide other food sources. Hummingbirds find nectar in firebush, coral honeysuckle, coral bean, red buckeye, and lobelia, while bug-eating birds will go for the insects attracted to the flower nectar in gumbo-limbo, colubrina, Florida privet, wild tamarind, necklace pod, acacia, and red buckeye.

An important addition to the garden is a good water source such as a bird bath or basin. Locate it fairly close to the house so you can watch the wildlife in action, keeping it indirectly shaded and in the open for clear visibility so that predators such as stray cats can't sneak up unobserved. An open location also means less debris falling into the water. A bird bath or fountain is particularly attractive when the water has a gentle movement, something you can achieve with a small recycling pump.

◄ Fruit-bearing trees like yaupon holly are great for attracting birds.

A raccoon finds shelter in a native strangler fig.

A good-sized bird feeder also adds to the activity and keeps birds coming when your trees are bare of fruit. Find a good feeder that can hold a large supply of high-quality bird seed. Locate it in the open, where it is easy to see, and keep it filled so that birds come to it on a regular basis.

Urban dwellers may find pigeons, starlings, grackles, and other aggressive birds taking advantage of the handout and dominating the food source. Squirrels and rodents will be attracted to the food as well, so look for a feeder designed to discourage such unwanted intruders.

1. SMALL TREE
   Holly
   Southern red cedar
   Redbay
   Hawthorn
   Plum
   Crabapple

2. LARGE SHRUBS
   Elderberry
   Firebush
   Florida privet
   Wax myrtle
   Shining sumac
   Pawpaw

3. MEDIUM SHRUBS
   Fakahatchee grass
   Necklace pod
   Wild coffee
   Beautyberry
   Coral bean
   Gallberry

4. LOW SHRUBS
   Gopher apple
   Darrow blueberry

5. WILDFLOWERS
   AND GROUND COVERS
   Purple coneflower
   Cardinal flower
   Black-eyed Susan
   Coontie
   Sword fern
   Sea ox-eye daisy

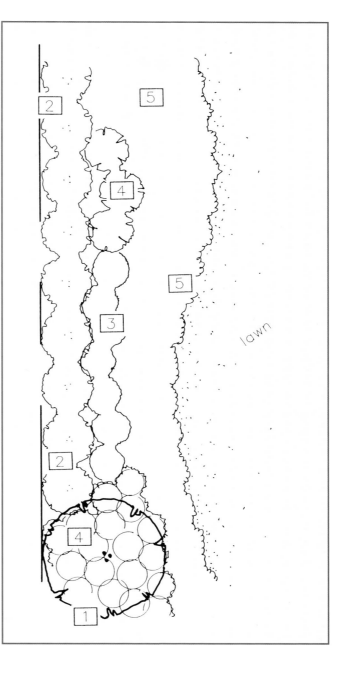

A simple border for birds and other wildlife. The border shown here incorporates plenty of seed- and fruit-bearing trees and shrubs to attract birds and other wildlife to your garden. Many species listed here will provide both food and shelter. *(Design by Steven E. Tate)*

BRING IN THE BUTTERFLIES

*B*utterflies are such desirable garden visitors that whole landscapes have been designed just to attract them to move in and set up housekeeping. They add such ephemeral beauty, color, and movement to a garden that they've been dubbed "flying flowers."

To make butterflies a part of your landscape you'll need to provide two different kinds of plants. One kind is the food sources, the nectar plants on which they feed, such as asters, liatris, and firebush. The other is the larval plants—cassias, passion flower and such—on which butterflies lay their eggs and which provide food for the caterpillars or larvae. Some plants—milkweed, for example—serve both purposes.

Male butterflies also require the alkaloids contained in certain plants, including Spanish needle and wild coffee, in order to mature sexually.

Adult butterflies, which live from a week or two to several months, exist almost entirely on sugars from flower nectar and plant saps. (The zebra

Spanish needle is a favorite of the ruddy daggerwing. ▶

A zebra longwing seeks out firebush blooms.

longwing has a wider appetite: it also eats pollen.) Flower shape and color matters. They seem to prefer flat clusters of tubular flowers in shades of red, pink, or purple.

Butterflies lay eggs; the eggs hatch into caterpillars, and the caterpillars immediately start to chew on their surroundings. But feeding is limited to their particular larval plant, so damage to the landscape usually is minimal. However, if a great many larvae are present they can strip all the foliage from their preferred plants. Consider planting several of each species of larval plant you have chosen and locate them in the background where the chewing damage will be less noticeable.

A swallowtail butterfly finds Florida paintbrush irresistible. ▶

Butterflies are quite specific about the larval plants they choose. Whether you have monarchs, zebras, or sulphurs depends on what is in your landscape, although some plants, like milkweed and passion vine, attract various species. Depending on where you live in the state, you may also play host to skippers, ruddy daggerwings, swallowtails, hairstreaks, malachites, queens, viceroys, julias, atalas, and more.

You may want to devote a specific area of your garden, just off the porch or patio perhaps, where you can sit and enjoy their performance. Large areas, such as parks, often are landscaped this way so that butterfly activity is concentrated in one spot. But butterflies themselves won't care if you cluster their favorite plants together or scatter them throughout the landscape.

There's one other bit of landscaping butterflies appreciate: shelter from the wind and weather. Dense shrubbery, especially planted against a wood or wire fence, will give them the protection they seek.

Keep in mind that butterflies are very sensitive to pesticides. Anything designed to kill insects, whether the product is chemical, organic, or biological, will kill adult butterflies, their eggs, caterpillars, and chrysalis. Try hand-picking pesty bugs first. If you feel that spraying is unavoidable, use a small hand sprayer and spot treat only where you see the unwanted insects. Avoid spraying any larval or nectar plants.

1. SMALL TREE
   Dahoon holly (N)
   Firebush (N)
   Sassafras (L)
   Sweetbay magnolia (L)

2. LARGE SHRUBS
   Necklace pod (N)
   Fiddlewood (N)
   Cassia (N, L)

3. MEDIUM SHRUBS
   Lantana (N, L)
   Wild coffee (N)
   Coontie (L)
   Summersweet (N)
   Bloodberry (N)

4. SMALL SHRUBS
   Beautyberry (N)
   Porterweed (N)
   Blueberry (L)
   Partridge pea (N, L)

5. WILDFLOWERS
   Spanish needle (N, L)
   Milkweed (N, L)
   Florida paintbrush (N)
   False foxglove (L)
   Eryngium (N)
   Coreopsis (N)
   Yellowtop (N)
   Blanket flower (N)
   Liatris (N)

6. VINES
   Coral honeysuckle (N, L)
   Passionflower (L)
   Carolina yellow jessamine (N)

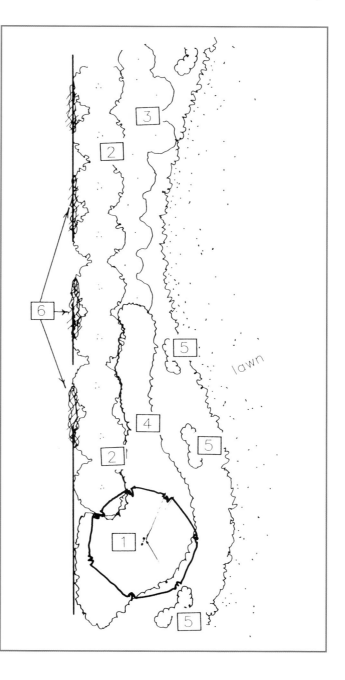

An assortment of shrubs and wildflowers to attract butterflies. This border is designed for butterflies. The following list includes only a few of the many Florida native plants that will attract them. Both nectar plants (N) and larval plants (L) should be included. *(Design by Stephen E. Tate)*

NOT-SO-NICE NATIVES

*N*othing is perfect, and not all native plants are wonderful. Some have such bad habits we don't want them around.

Among the unwelcome few are strangler fig, poisonous and stinging plants like poison ivy, poisonwood and spurge nettle, and aggressive vines such as moonflower and nickerbean.

The strangler fig, *Ficus aurea,* is a major overstory tree in tropical hammocks in south Florida and the West Indies and often reaches a height of 50–60 feet. In older neighborhoods, old strangler figs may be prized because they provide shade and character. The aerial roots and elephantine trunk draw attention, and the red-orange fruit attracts wildlife.

However, the tree has major drawbacks. If it starts life in the ground it usually does not develop aerial roots, but if it begins as an epiphyte, with the seed germinating in a tree canopy, it will drop aerial roots to the ground, enveloping the host plant and eventually killing it. The native cab-

A strangler fig envelops its host. ▶

bage palms (*Sabal palmetto*) and valued and expensive trees such as the date palm (*Phoenix dactylifera*) and Canary Island date palms (*Phoenix canariensis*) often are victims. They are in real danger if a ficus sprouts and grows in the canopy and is not removed quickly.

The strangler fig may also start life in gutters, tile roofs, bridge overpasses, and retaining walls. Like most other ficus, its aggressive roots can puncture pools, clog sewers, septic tanks, and plumbing, and crack pavement.

Poisonwood, *Metopium toxiferum*, grows in tropical hardwood hammocks on upland sites in south Florida and the West Indies, and may reach 30 feet in height. It is common in the Keys but scarcer on the mainland.

Poisonwood is attractive but dangerous.

◄ Strangler fig seedling threatens a sabal palm.

This pretty but poisonous tree has highly irritating sap that can cause a nasty rash, similar to poison ivy, on susceptible persons. The sticky, tar-like sap may leave black patches on the reddish-brown or gray, flaky bark, which is one way of identifying the tree. Other characteristics are open panicles of small, whitish flowers at the ends of the branches, clusters of small orange berries on female trees, and pinnate leaves, usually with five leaflets that may be sprinkled with black dots.

The much rarer machineel, *Hippomane mancinella,* is found mostly in the Everglades National Park in the Cape Sable area. It is a large tree, to 50 feet, with smooth, oval, pointed leaves 2–4 inches long and light gray bark, and while it has an innocent look, it has poisonous, milky sap that causes blisters, swelling, and rash.

The well-known poison ivy, poison oak, and poison sumac also cause blisters and rashes. Poison ivy, *Toxicodendron radicans,* is the familiar three-leaved vine found in woods, fields, waste places and even in residential yards throughout the eastern U.S. Its seeds are spread by birds that eat the small white fruits. Don't confuse it with Virginia creeper, which has five leaves.

Poison sumac, *Toxicodendron vernix,* is found in swampy areas of the eastern U.S., with some in the Panhandle and elsewhere in north Florida. It is a small, fast-growing tree with shiny, compound, deciduous leaves with 7–13 leaflets and open panicles of pale yellow flowers and round, white ½-inch fruits. (True sumacs have red fruit.) Poison oak, *Toxicodendron quercifolium,* is more shrubby than poison sumac but also grows in wet areas. It is not related to oak trees.

Tread-softly or spurge nettle, *Cnidoscolus stimulosus,* has tiny, stinging, needle-like hairs covering all its parts above ground. The stinging sensation these hairs produce is very painful and can last for hours. Swelling and rash often add to the discomfort. This shrubby perennial grows along the beach, in dunes, or in open pinewoods and fields from Virginia through Florida and west to Texas. Its green stems are 3–4 feet tall, and the three- to five-lobed leaves are 3–11 inches long with needles on both surfaces.

Take a hard look at any vine before introducing it into a garden. The moonflower, *Calonyction aculeatum,* is a very aggressive vine native to south Florida and tropical regions. It has lovely 6-inch white, night-blooming flowers, attractive enough that the seed is available in packets. While the white blossoms may be striking, this vine grows fast enough to eat a utility pole for breakfast and power outages have been blamed on it. It also has irritating sap and is very hard to eradicate.

Poison ivy is a familiar pest. ▶

The gray and yellow nickerbeans, *Caesalpinia bonduc* and *C. major,* are two closely related vine-shrubs. They are aggressive, thorny, sprawling, and can cover large areas with an impenetrable thicket of unwanted vegetation. Nickerbeans are found along the seashore and dunes of south Florida.

A number of native plants could be considered borderline: They have both attractive qualities and definite drawbacks. Spanish bayonet, *Yucca aloifolia,* is a dramatic architectural plant with large panicles of beautiful white flowers from May to September. But this big, sprawling plant can be extremely dangerous in the wrong location where its stiff, sharply pointed leaves may cause severe puncture wounds. On the other hand, it is useful for beach plantings and for security purposes if located away from areas where people walk or children play.

Other plants and trees without such obvious liabilities may not suit your landscape for one reason or another, but Florida's vast collection of natives (the Association of Florida Native Nurseries lists more than 550 commercially available species in its 1997-98 directory) provides plenty of choices, as the Plant Profiles later in this book demonstrate.

PLANT PROFILES

There are any number of ways to group plants; here we have arranged them mainly by the way they may be used in the landscape, as large or small trees, shrubs, and so on. Such groupings, of course, are far from exact. A stopper, for example, could be either a shrub or a small tree. A tree that can grow to an impressive size in its ideal habitat may be far smaller when planted at the limit of its natural ranges or where soil and weather are not favorable for its healthy growth. And because a flowering plant such as lobelia sometimes is found growing in shallow water, one might think of it as an aquatic.

So consider these groupings as general guidelines, not as rigid divisions.

Here's how the species we have profiled are arranged:

Palms. When people are asked to visualize Florida, chances are their mental pictures will include palm trees. Palms are wonderful plants, suitable for narrow places, skyline silhouettes, or grouped in masses to provide shade and privacy.

South Florida's skyline was dominated by coconut palms until in the early 1970s a disease called lethal yellowing decimated their population. A more resistant variety of coconut, the Dwarf Malayan, has been planted widely as a replacement. Coconut palms, incidentally, are not considered native. While hundreds of species of palms are grown in Florida, only a handful of them are native. Yet these provide enough choice in size and texture to satisfy most landscape requirements, are resistant to lethal yellowing, and are more tolerant of disease and insects than most exotic species.

Large Trees. In planning a landscape, the designer should site the largest trees first. In choosing a particular tree, it is important to know how tall it will grow, how wide its canopy will spread and whether its roots will be a problem. What is suitable for a large estate or park could become a major pest in a suburban yard.

Small Trees. Homeowners with limited space are wise to stick with smaller trees, and we have many natives to choose from. Some may start life as multi-stemmed shrubs, but good pruning can turn them into single-trunked specimens. A few, particularly those from the north and central parts of the state, are lovely flowering trees.

Shrubs. As understory plants, hedges, and accent plants, shrubs will make up the bulk of your native landscape planting. They'll add interest with their diverse textures and color as well as provide privacy and define separate areas of the yard. Some are attractive flowering plants as well.

Wildflowers. These are wonderful as small accents or to provide sweeps of color. Use them in a casual border, or if you are fortunate enough to have a field or meadow, sow an assortment of flower seeds suitable for your area. Many will attract butterflies.

Vines, Grasses, and Ferns. Here are the details, the embellishments that give your garden its own special character. Vines can cover an unattractive fence or decorate a trellis, grasses can add grace and texture, ferns can fill shady spots, and all add the finishing touches to the garden ensemble.

Aquatics. While residential areas encompassing natural creeks, ponds, and bog areas are limited, developers all over the state have created man-made lakes where banks can benefit from well-chosen plantings. Aquatic plants not only add beauty to the landscape but help prevent erosion and provide habitat, shelter, and food for small fish and birds.

PALMS

PAUROTIS PALM, EVERGLADES PALM
Acoelorrhaphe wrightii

HEIGHT: 20 feet

LIGHT: Sun to part shade

BLOOM: Small white flowers in erect, branching clusters, 3 feet long, appearing in summer

FRUIT: Round, shiny, black ½-inch fruits

LEAVES: 3-foot, fan-shaped, divided fronds with spiny stems; leaves are green above, silvery-green on the underside.

TRUNK: This is a clump-forming, multistemmed palm. The slender individual stems are brown and rough, with old clinging leaf bases.

NATIVE RANGE: South to south-central Florida and the Caribbean; Zones 9–11

HABITAT: Swampy areas in the Everglades

PROPAGATION: Seed, division

This palm is somewhat difficult to grow, but it is beautiful when well-watered and fertilized. The roots produce suckers and the clumps expand with age. When well-cared for, the clump may reach 35 feet in height and width. A damp site is a must for this palm's successful growth. On drier, alkaline sites it may have problems, particularly with manganese deficiency.

SILVER PALM
Coccothrinax argentata

HEIGHT: 15–20 feet

LIGHT: Sun or part shade

BLOOM: Tiny, white, fragrant flowers carried in 2-foot clusters, blooming in spring

FRUIT: Colorful red to black fruit, ½-inch in diameter, maturing in autumn

LEAVES: Smooth, 3-foot petioles carry palmate fronds averaging 2 feet across, shiny green above and bright silver below

TRUNK: Moderately slender, smooth, gray trunk

NATIVE RANGE: West Indies and South Florida; Zones 10–11

HABITAT: Open hammock woodlands, but will tolerate beach exposure

PROPAGATION: Seed, collected in autumn

This is a beautiful, rare, slow-growing palm, which makes it expensive in the nursery trade. The foliage is its chief glory, especially on windy days when the shiny silver alternates with the green. It is superb as a landscape specimen, is salt- and drought-tolerant, and has no major pest or disease problems. It will not take frost, however. Birds are attracted to the fruit.

BUCCANEER PALM, SARGENT'S PALM
Pseudophoenix sargentii

HEIGHT: 10–15 feet

LIGHT: Sun to part shade

BLOOM: Small yellow flowers borne in tight clusters among the leaves

FRUIT: Decorative, round, red berries, ¾-inch across, in tight clusters

LEAVES: Gray-green pinnate leaves average 8–10 feet in length, with smooth petioles

TRUNK: Gray-green trunk is distinctive in young trees; older specimens have a swollen, dark gray trunk topped by a short, blue-green crownshaft.

NATIVE RANGE: Florida Keys and the Caribbean; Zones 10–11

HABITAT: This rare palm is found on Elliott Key in Biscayne National Park and occasionally in other scrubby Key woodlands and forest edges.

PROPAGATION: Seed

Buccaneer palm is an extremely valuable palm, perfect for beachside and other inhospitable locations. It will tolerate salt winds and drought, but it is very slow-growing. Most specimens seen in the landscape have been collected from the wild, but fortunately a few nurseries propagate them for the trade.

NEEDLE PALM
Rhapidophyllum hystrix

HEIGHT: 5–6 feet

LIGHT: Shade to part sun

BLOOM: Clusters of tiny yellow or purple flowers on a foot-long spike

FRUIT: Purple, 1-inch long fruit

FOLIAGE: Deeply divided palmate fronds, 3–4 feet across, dark green above and silvery beneath

TRUNK: Old, black, matted leaf bases form a short trunk, to 3 feet, with black, 10-inch needles; the plant sometimes forms clumps.

NATIVE RANGE: Southeastern United States; Zones 8–9

HABITAT: Deciduous woodlands, rare throughout its range

PROPAGATION: Seed, division

This plant, over-collected in the wild, is considered by many authorities to be the most hardy palm. It has been tested in sheltered locations in Missouri, Tennessee, and Cape Cod and has endured temperatures to -10°F. It is very slow-growing but adds a tropical accent to the landscape. As it is somewhat spiny, it should be planted away from foot traffic.

Royal Palm *Roystonea elata*

Royal palms *Roystonea elata* (Bonnet House, Fort Lauderdale)

ROYAL PALM
Roystonea elata

HEIGHT: To 100 feet

LIGHT: Sun or part shade

BLOOM: Tiny white flowers in drooping clusters up to 2 feet long

FRUIT: Round, ½-inch purplish-black fruit

LEAVES: Huge, dark green, feathery fronds are 15 feet long and 6 feet across, and one can weigh up to 60 or 70 pounds. The leaflets do not have lengthwise veins.

TRUNK: A smooth, cement-gray trunk topped by a bright green, 8-foot crownshaft

NATIVE RANGE: Hammock areas in the Everglades of Monroe County; Zones 10–11

HABITAT: Open, moist muck soil areas on elevated sites

PROPAGATION: Seed

The royal is a spectacular palm, suited to formal plantings on moist sites where it will have plenty of space. It also will grow well on higher, drained sites if given sufficient irrigation. One major mistake made with this palm is planting it where its large, heavy fronds can fall on buildings, vehicles, or even passersby, and many superb specimens have had to be removed because they were badly situated.

The shorter (70-foot) Cuban royal palm, frequently used in Florida landscapes, has oval black fruit and leaflets with pronounced veins. It does better on drier sites. Other royal palm species are found in the West Indies.

Dwarf palmetto *Sabal minor*

Scrub palmetto *S. etonia*

DWARF PALMETTO
Sabal minor

HEIGHT: 4–6 feet

LIGHT: Partial sun to shade

BLOOM: Clusters of small white flowers carried on long branching stems averaging 4–5 feet in length

FRUIT: Round, ⅓-inch black berries borne in open clusters

LEAVES: Bluish-green to green fan-shaped leaves are 3 to 4 feet across. At about midpoint, the leaf splits into many narrow segments. Unlike the saw palmetto, the petiole does not have spines.

TRUNK: Occasionally this palm forms a short trunk, but usually it appears as a trunkless clump.

NATIVE RANGE: Southeastern U.S. into central Florida; Zones 7–10

HABITAT: An understory plant in woods throughout the Southeast

PROPAGATION: Seed

Dwarf palmetto is a very hardy palm, tolerant of drought, salt, shade, and various types of soil. It makes a good accent plant and adds a tropical look to landscapes in the northern parts of its range. The similar but rarer *S. etonia*, called scrub palmetto, has smaller, accordion-like, yellow-green leaves, and is found in dry soils in Zones 9–11. *S. minor* carries its inflorescence above the leaves; the bloom stalks of *S. etonia* recline on the ground.

SABAL PALM, CABBAGE PALM
Sabal palmetto

HEIGHT: 50–60 feet

LIGHT: Sun to fairly deep shade

BLOOM: Small white, fragrant flowers in hanging clusters on 3-foot stems, appearing in early summer

FRUIT: Round, ½-inch, black, edible fruit, ripening in fall

LEAVES: Large palmate fronds are deeply divided and folded in the middle. They are dull gray-green, 3–5 feet across and carried on smooth petioles up to 5 feet in length.

TRUNK: The trunk is smooth and dark gray on old trees; younger trees are covered with cross-hatched "boots," old leaf bases usually considered attractive.

NATIVE RANGE: West Indies, Bahamas, southern coastal Virginia through Florida and along the Gulf Coast to Texas; Zones 8–11

HABITAT: This extremely versatile tree will grow anywhere within its hardiness range, except in standing water or dense shade.

PROPAGATION: Seed germinates very slowly.

Sabal palm is the state tree of Florida and South Carolina. It is widely used in landscaping, transplants easily, and usually is collected from the wild for landscape installation. The flowers are a nectar source and the berries provide food for wildlife. The edible bud, called heart of palm, is considered a delicacy but collecting it kills the plant. Beware of strangler figs, schefflera, Cuban laurel, or clusia rooting in the canopy. They send down aerial roots that will envelop and kill the host palm.

Saw palmetto (blue form) *Serenoa repens*   Saw palmetto *Serenoa repens*

SAW PALMETTO
Serenoa repens

HEIGHT: 6–12 feet

LIGHT: Sun to shade

BLOOM: Long branched clusters of tiny white blooms, favored by bees

FRUIT: Black ¾-inch fruits

LEAVES: Fan-like, 3- to 4-foot divided fronds, either green or silvery blue-green, have vicious spines along the stalks.

TRUNK: Creeping, rough brown stems run along the ground, forming dense thickets.

NATIVE RANGE: Coastal Carolinas to south Florida; Zones 8–11

HABITAT: Coastal secondary dunes and sandy pinewoods

PROPAGATION: Seed

These sprawling palms are a familiar sight in Florida's fields and pine woods and along the coast. The coastal blue form is particularly striking and considered very desirable for native landscaping. The fruit once was used as food by Florida's native Americans, but because the plants provided a good habitat for rattlesnakes, rats, and other varmints, saw palmetto was a scorned native in the early days of Florida settlement. Now it is an appreciated plant, valued as a mass planting, especially in a woodsy setting. The honey produced from its flowers is highly prized.

FLORIDA THATCH PALM
Thrinax radiata

HEIGHT: 20–25 feet

LIGHT: Sun to part shade

BLOOM: Tiny white flowers in 3- to 4-foot long clusters

FRUIT: Round, ½-inch, white fruit, carried in clusters, each with a dark brown seed

LEAVES: Fan-shaped, 3-foot fronds, shiny green above and green-yellow below

TRUNK: Rough, gray, about 6 inches in diameter

NATIVE RANGE: Extreme southern Florida and the West Indies; Zones 10–11

HABITAT: Rocky, open, woodsy areas and shores

PROPAGATION: Seed

This is a tough, small native palm, tolerating salt and alkaline conditions and partial shade. It has no pest or disease problems and deserves wider use. The Key thatch palm, *T. morrisii*, of the Florida Keys and the Caribbean, is very similar except for the bright silvery underside of the foliage. Either of these thatch palms is excellent for seaside locations.

LARGE TREES

RED MAPLE
Acer rubrum

HEIGHT: 60–70 feet in northern Florida; smaller in the south

LIGHT: Full sun to part shade

BLOOM: Small red flowers appearing December through January

FRUIT: Winged fruit, January through February

LEAVES: The three-lobed foliage is deciduous, medium-green above and silvery below, turning bright red, purple, or yellow in the late fall. Leaves are 4–6 inches long with serrated edges and red petioles.

TRUNK: Rough and brown, with upper branches silvery

NATIVE RANGE: Canada south to Broward County in south Florida; Zones 3–10; different forms are found throughout the tree's wide range.

HABITAT: Swampy sites throughout the state

PROPAGATION: Seed, cuttings

Red maple is a valuable native tree, particularly for swampy areas such as drainage swales along streets. It is not well-adapted to dry, sandy sites unless extra irrigation is provided. The winter flowers are moderately showy and the winged fruit that follows is conspicuous, creating a reddish haze through the tree canopy. The foliage color can vary from tree to tree, and in order to add desirable fall hues to Florida's mainly green landscape, work needs to be done to find and propagate specimens with outstanding color.

BLACK MANGROVE
Avicennia germinans

HEIGHT: 40–50 feet

LIGHT: Sun

BLOOM: Small, white, fragrant flowers have yellow centers and grow in spikes at the ends of the branches.

FRUIT: Furry, lima bean-shaped seeds appear all year. They germinate on the tree, a characteristic of all mangroves.

LEAVES: Oval, pointed leaves are dark green above and fuzzy grayish-white below. The petiole is not prominent. Salt is excreted through the upper leaf surface at night or on cloudy days, making them appear whitish.

TRUNK: Rough and dark brown

NATIVE RANGE: South Florida and tropical America; Zones 10–11

HABITAT: Black mangrove is found just behind the pioneering red mangrove on mud flats.

PROPAGATION: Seed

The vertical branching roots, which project just above the highest tide and help the root system "breathe," are a sure way to identify the black mangrove. In the landscape, it may be used for shade or screening along brackish river banks and even on upland areas. It is very cold- and salt-tolerant. This tree and the red mangrove both provide shelter and food at the bottom of the aquatic food chain. The blossoms produce an excellent honey.

River birch *Betula nigra*

River birch *Betula nigra*

RIVER BIRCH
Betula nigra

HEIGHT: 50–60 feet

LIGHT: Sun to part shade

BLOOM: Brown catkins, 2–3 inches long

FRUIT: Small nut appearing in the catkin

LEAVES: The 2- to 3-inch leaves are roughly triangular with edges either coarsely lobed or serrated. They are glossy above, pale below, and turn yellow in the fall.

TRUNK: The trunk may be either single or multistemmed. Young trunks have attractive, exfoliating reddish-brown bark, while old specimens have scaly, dark brown bark.

NATIVE RANGE: Eastern U.S., from Massachusetts to Florida and west to Kansas and Minnesota; Zones 4–9

HABITAT: River banks and other damp areas

PROPAGATION: Seed, cuttings

In the wild, river birch usually is found along streams and the edges of swamps, but it will adapt to upland sites. A common planting error is not allowing it enough space for the spreading canopy. The cultivar 'Heritage' has salmon-white bark on young stems and salmon-brown bark on old stems, along with leaves that are larger and more resistant to leaf spotting than the common form. It also is resistant to borers and is the most heat-tolerant of the birches.

Gumbo-limbo *Bursera simaruba*

Gumbo-limbo *Bursera simaruba*

GUMBO-LIMBO, TOURIST TREE
Bursera simaruba

HEIGHT: 50–60 feet

LIGHT: Sun to part shade

BLOOM: Inconspicuous greenish spikes, blooming in spring

FRUIT: Dark red, angled, ½-inch fruits with white seeds

LEAVES: Pinnate foliage has glossy green leaflets, 1–3 inches long. In nature, the tree is deciduous; when irrigated, it will retain some foliage in winter.

TRUNK: The massive trunk with its smooth, peeling bark and bronze tones, reminiscent of a sunburned, peeling tourist, gives the tree its most common name.

NATIVE RANGE: South Florida through the West Indies, Mexico, and Central America; Zones 10–11

HABITAT: Open hammock woodlands

PROPAGATION: Seed and large cuttings

Gumbo-limbo, a major component of the hammock overstory, is a wonderful character tree. Fast-growing, it will provide quick, open shade, after hurricane damage, for example. To propagate, simply cut off large branches and insert them in the ground. The tree is both salt- and drought-tolerant and not particular about soil conditions. Fruit will attract birds, especially flycatchers, to your garden. Old trees often acquire interesting, contorted shapes that add to their appeal. Gumbo-limbos vary widely in the color quality of the bark, and nurseries should try to select superior forms, some of which have spectacular bark.

WATER HICKORY
Carya aquatica

HEIGHT: 60–70 feet

LIGHT: Sun to part shade

BLOOM: Male flowers have short, three-stemmed catkins; females have short flowering spikes. Flowers appear in spring.

FRUIT: Bitter nuts enclosed in a case that splits away, dropping the nuts

LEAVES: Pinnate leaves have 11–15 lance-shaped leaflets, hairy on the underside and with sawtooth edges. They are similar to pecan foliage, but finer in texture.

TRUNK: Grayish and scaly, separated by narrow cracks

NATIVE RANGE: Southeastern U.S., the Carolinas to central Florida, and Texas; Zones 8–9

HABITAT: Stream banks, flood plains, and other wet sites

PROPAGATION: Seed

Water hickory is a good tree for bank stabilization and a food source for wildlife. It is a big tree; give it plenty of space as well as a damp location. Several other large hickories, native to Florida, take drier soil and are useful as shade trees. Pignut hickory *(C. glabra)* and mockernut hickory *(C. tomentosa)* grow into central Florida, while bitternut hickory *(C. cordiformis)* is found only in northernmost Florida.

Sugarberry *Celtis laevigata*

Sugarberry *Celtis laevigata*

SUGARBERRY, SUGAR HACKBERRY
Celtis laevigata

HEIGHT: 60 feet

LIGHT: Sun

BLOOM: Tiny greenish flowers

FRUIT: Reddish to black sweet fruit, ¼-inch in diameter

LEAVES: Foliage is alternate and deciduous, with oblong, pointed 2- to 4-inch leaves that turn pale yellow in the fall.

TRUNK: Pale gray, smooth, and beech-like in some specimens; others may have numerous wart-like growths.

NATIVE RANGE: Southern Indiana to Texas and Florida and north to Virginia; Zones 5–10

HABITAT: Generally found in low, wet areas, but adaptable

PROPAGATION: Seed, cuttings

Sugar hackberry is a tough tree with a rounded canopy of drooping branches. It is excellent as an urban tree, reasonably wind-tolerant and able to grow in compacted soil areas. Its fruit is a favorite with many birds.

Silver buttonwood *Conocarpus erectus*

Green buttonwood *Conocarpus erectus*

BUTTONWOOD
Conocarpus erectus

HEIGHT: 40–50 feet in green form; silver form is smaller, 20–35 feet

LIGHT: Sun

BLOOM: Insignificant greenish-white flowers appearing most of the year

FRUIT: Round, woody brown cones, to ½-inch in diameter

LEAVES: Oval, pointed leaves, 3½ to 4 inches long, are medium to dark green on the green buttonwood and silvery on the silver form.

TRUNK: Gnarled and twisted on old trees, with rough dark bark

NATIVE RANGE: South Florida and the Caribbean; Zones 10–11

HABITAT: Brackish swamp areas, on higher ground than mangroves

PROPAGATION: Seed, cuttings, air layering

The slow-growing buttonwoods are popular ornamental trees, with interesting trunks and open-spreading canopies. Their ability to withstand wind, salt, and drought makes them invaluable for oceanfront plantings. In the landscape, they frequently are clipped into formal hedges. Green buttonwood is quite upright when young, spreading out with age. It is a little more cold-tolerant than the silver form, which is smaller and more bushy. 'Silver Sheen,' a versatile small-to-medium-sized cultivar, is the best of the lot. It has fuzzy, silver-green leaves and is resistant to scale and mealybug, which cause sooty mold on the common silver form. Because of their rough bark, buttonwoods are a good base for growing orchids and bromeliads.

Persimmon *Diospyros virginiana*

Persimmon *Diospyros virginiana*

PERSIMMON
Diospyros virginiana

HEIGHT: 50 feet

LIGHT: Sun to part shade

BLOOM: Fragrant, greenish-white flowers are dioecious (male and female flowers on separate trees). They are about ⅓-inch long in clusters on male trees, and about ½-inch long and solitary on female trees.

FRUIT: Round, yellow-orange, edible fruits to 1½ inches in diameter, needing frost to ripen

LEAVES: Oval, pointed, alternate, glossy leaves are dark green above and pale green below. Usually they turn yellow-green in autumn, although some trees may color to an attractive reddish-purple.

TRUNK: Bark is dark brownish-gray to black, forming a block-like pattern on the trunk.

NATIVE RANGE: Eastern U.S., from Connecticut to Florida; west to Texas and Kansas; Zones 4–9

HABITAT: Fence rows, old fields, woods, and road edges

PROPAGATION: Seed, or grafting for superior forms of fruit

Persimmon is a tough tree, adapting to many adverse conditions. It usually is found in sandy soils but will do well in most environments, even partial shade. It is at its best in a woodsy, natural setting. The delicious fruit will attract many mammals, and possums or raccoons may beat you to the harvest.

SHORTLEAF FIG
Ficus citrifolia

HEIGHT: 40–50 feet

LIGHT: Sun to part shade

BLOOM: Rounded, open-ended receptacles with flowers inside

FRUIT: Rounded, ¼- to ½-inch fig on a short stalk, turning from yellow to red when ripe

LEAVES: Leaves are oval with a blunted point and rounded base, 2–4 inches long. They are semi-deciduous and have a milky sap.

TRUNK: Large, with some aerial roots; bark is light brown to yellowish brown, becoming scaly with age.

NATIVE RANGE: South Florida, the Bahamas, and the West Indies; Zones 10–11

HABITAT: Usually associated with tropical hammocks

PROPAGATION: Seed, cuttings, air layers

This is considered to be a better-behaved fig than the native strangler fig and many of the exotic species of ficus. It is smaller and less likely to have aerial roots. Nevertheless, it can be an aerial invader like the strangler fig, its seedlings appearing in the canopies of sabal palms and other trees, but it is much less likely to do so. Care still must be taken as to where it is planted because a ficus is a ficus when it comes to aggressive roots. It is fast-growing, will take poor soil and salt air, and has an attractive, spreading canopy, but it needs plenty of space. It will attract many kinds of fruit-eating birds and is a larval plant for butterflies.

RED CEDAR, SOUTHERN RED CEDAR
Juniperus virginiana, J. silicicola

HEIGHT: 45 feet

LIGHT: Sun

BLOOM: Male and female flowers appear on separate trees in spring. The cone-like male flowers are green; females are yellow-green.

FRUIT: Round, ⅛-inch, powdery blue berries

LEAVES: Fragrant, scaly needles, ranging from bluish-green to yellow-green

TRUNK: Exfoliating red to gray bark

NATIVE RANGE: *J. silicicola*, which ranges along the coast from South Carolina to southern Florida (Zones 8–10), usually is regarded as a subspecies of red cedar, *J. virginiana*, which grows east of the Rocky Mountains from Canada to Florida; Zones 2–8.

HABITAT: A pioneer plant, taking over old fields

PROPAGATION: Seed, grafts, and cuttings

Southern red cedar generally is a more open-growing, less conical tree than the northern form and has greater salt-tolerance. It is a versatile tree, useful as a specimen, screen, mass planting, or windbreak. The dense foliage makes a good cover for birds, and the berries are a major food source for wildlife. It is drought-tolerant and will accept a variety of soil types and pH ranges, but needs sun and good drainage to do well. There are many cultivars of *J. virginiana* on the market, offering a wide variety of sizes, shapes, and foliage color.

SWEETGUM
Liquidambar styraciflua

HEIGHT: 80 feet

LIGHT: Sun to part shade

BLOOM: Female trees have ½-inch, ball-like, green flowers on pendulous petioles. Male flowers are 3- to 4-inch upright racemes.

FRUIT: A woody, brown, ball-like fruit, about 1 to 1½ inches in diameter, carried on a long stem

LEAVES: Beautiful glossy leaves are star-shaped, averaging 6 inches in length and width, and turning color in autumn.

TRUNK: The straight trunk has brownish-gray bark, deeply lined into rounded ridges. Twigs may be winged.

NATIVE RANGE: Connecticut to central Florida and west to Texas and Mexico; Zones 6–9

HABITAT: Sweetgum prefers moist to wet acid soil. It is an aggressive tree, taking over fallow fields and swampy areas and turning them into woodlands.

PROPAGATION: Seed, cuttings, grafts

Sweetgum makes a good background or shade tree. It is brilliant in the fall, with colors ranging from yellow to red and apricot to purple. Many cultivars exist, with a wide range of colors. Because of its fleshy root system, the tree is somewhat difficult to transplant. It is not tolerant of air pollution or confined root space. Site it with care: The fruit is spiny and can be messy when it drops through the winter and into spring. The variety 'Rotundiloba' does not bear the objectionable fruit.

TULIP POPLAR
Liriodendron tulipifera

HEIGHT: 60–80 feet

LIGHT: Sun to part shade

BLOOM: Six-petaled, tulip-shaped blooms are yellow-green on the outside with an orange band inside. The striking flowers often are missed because they usually appear at the top of the tree.

FRUIT: Brown, pointed cone, 2–3 inches long, with many winged seeds

LEAVES: The bright green leaves are 3–5 inches long and often wider, being widest at the base. Leaves are two-lobed at the top, with two to four lobes at the lower edges. They turn yellow in fall.

TRUNK: Straight, with dark brown to gray ridged bark; in dense woodlands, there may be no branches on the lower ¾ of the trunk.

NATIVE RANGE: Massachusetts to north Florida and west to Mississippi; Zones 4–9

HABITAT: Tulip tree is found in almost solid stands or mixed with red and white oak, hemlock, white pine, beech, and maple.

PROPAGATION: Seed, cuttings or grafts

This is a big tree, requiring lots of room. It has been reported to reach an astonishing 190 feet in ideal situations. It prefers a moist, well-drained, deep acid soil. Flowers bloom in April in the South, attracting many bees. While attractive, the tree has drawbacks. It can be messy, dropping yellowing leaves and seeds, particularly in dry weather, and is brittle in winds, ice, and sleet. Trees this tall also tend to be lightning targets.

WILD TAMARIND
Lysiloma latisiliqua

HEIGHT: 50–60 feet

LIGHT: Sun

BLOOM: Fragrant, white, ½-inch blooms like miniature powder puffs

FRUIT: A 5-inch long brown pod

LEAVES: Delicate, feathery foliage with tiny leaflets, ⅓ inch long

TRUNK: A tall, light gray to brown trunk supporting a broad, spreading, uneven crown

NATIVE RANGE: South Florida and the Caribbean; Zones 10–11

HABITAT: A dominant tree in native woodlands and particularly common on Key Largo and the Upper Keys

PROPAGATION: Seed

Wild tamarind is a large, fast-growing tree with an airy look to its canopy. While it is very attractive, it tends to drop branches, and the roots are fairly shallow. The foliage is semi-deciduous and stains whatever it falls upon. It could be used on an open lawn, perhaps with native fishtail fern planted underneath.

Southern magnolia *Magnolia grandiflora*

Southern magnolia *Magnolia grandiflora*

SOUTHERN MAGNOLIA
Magnolia grandiflora

HEIGHT: 60 feet

LIGHT: Sun to part shade

BLOOM: Large, white, 8–12 inch, heavily fragrant blooms appearing spring through summer

FRUIT: Rose-red, 4-inch cone splits when ripe, exposing red seeds.

LEAVES: Large, elliptic, evergreen leaves to 10 inches long, glossy, dark green above and often fuzzy and rusty-brown below

TRUNK: A smooth gray trunk that may become rough with age

NATIVE RANGE: North Carolina to central Florida and Texas; Zones 7–9. It often is planted out of its natural range, to south Florida and New York City, and is a major ornamental in parts of the world.

HABITAT: Lowland areas with good drainage

PROPAGATION: Seed, cuttings, and grafts

Southern magnolia is a superb tree where space is adequate. It is a "signature" tree of the Deep South, where in the old days it was a part of plantation landscapes. However, it is quite messy, with old fruits, leaves, and twigs dropping continually. The leathery leaves take a long time to decay. It helps to let the lower branches sweep the ground to conceal the litter. It is fast-growing, which, along with its dense foliage, makes it likely to break in high winds. The tree is subject to scale and mealybug, particularly in south Florida. 'Little Gem' is an excellent small cultivar, reaching 20 feet. 'Edith Bogue' is probably the hardiest, growing as far north as New York City.

Mastic *Mastichodendron foetidissimum*　　　　Mastic *Mastichodendron foetidissimum*

MASTIC
Mastichodendron foetidissimum

HEIGHT: 50–60 feet

LIGHT: Sun

BLOOM: Tiny, yellow, inconspicuous flowers with an odor often considered offensive

FRUIT: Oval, yellow berries up to 1 inch long, appearing in spring

LEAVES: Dark green, oblong leaves, 7–8 inches long, grow in whorls at the ends of the branches. Leaves have wavy edges and, because of their long-leaf stalks, tend to flutter even in a light breeze.

TRUNK: Dark brown and straight, with rough bark

NATIVE RANGE: South Florida and the Caribbean; Zones 10–11

HABITAT: A major canopy tree in tropical hardwood hammocks

PROPAGATION: Seed

Mastic, an important timber tree in tropical America, also serves as an attractive, pest-free evergreen in the landscape. It is salt-tolerant, very resistant to strong winds and not particular about soil conditions. The fruits are edible, if gummy, and attract wildlife such as birds and raccoons.

BLACK GUM, SOUR GUM, SWAMP TUPELO
Nyssa sylvatica

HEIGHT: 50 feet

LIGHT: Sun to part shade

BLOOM: Small greenish-white blooms in clusters on long stems, not showy, appearing in spring

FRUIT: Blue-black, oblong, ½-inch fruit, ripening in fall

LEAVES: Elliptic, 4- to 5-inch leaves, shiny green above and changing from yellow through red to almost purple in early autumn

TRUNK: Rough, checkered, dark reddish-brown bark

NATIVE RANGE: Eastern U.S., from Massachusetts to central Florida; Zones 6–9

HABITAT: Acid, well-drained soils, usually near lake and stream edges, although it is found in a variety of habitats

PROPAGATION: Seed

Black gum is an excellent, slow-growing lawn tree, one of the first to color in the fall with spectacular tints that last a long time. Its fine texture and layered branches add to its appeal. It will accept a variety of conditions, anything from mucky soils to sand. The fruit is relished by birds and mammals.

Slash pine *Pinus elliottii*

Slash pine *Pinus elliottii*

SLASH PINE
Pinus elliottii

HEIGHT: 70–80 feet

LIGHT: Full sun

BLOOM: Insignificant brown flowers in spring

FRUIT: 3–5-inch-long cones with spiny scales

LEAVES: Shiny, dark green needles, 8–12 inches long, in bundles of two or three

TRUNK: Tall, branching only at the top, with plated, dark brown bark

NATIVE RANGE: Southeastern U. S. from North Carolina to east Texas; Zones 8–9. South Florida slash pine is found in south, and coastal central Florida; some populations are located on the Keys; Zones 9–11.

HABITAT: Open woodlands and fields

PROPAGATION: Seed

Slash pine is a dominant tree in pine flat-woods. South Florida slash pine (*P. elliottii var. densa*) was the source of dense, resin-free, long-lasting wood, called "Dade County pine," used in early homes. The tree is drought-tolerant and not fussy as to soils, but is extremely sensitive to disturbance by construction, foot traffic, and artificial irrigation. Borers often attack and kill these weakened trees. The pine seeds provide food for birds and small animals.

Longleaf pine *Pinus palustris*

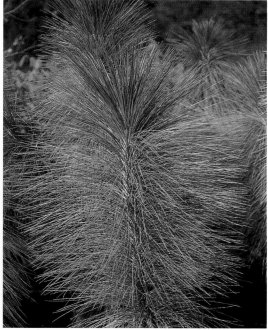

Longleaf pine *Pinus palustris*

LONGLEAF PINE
Pinus palustris

HEIGHT: 60–80 feet

LIGHT: Sun

BLOOM: Purple flowers clustered at the ends of branches in spring

FRUIT: Large, brown cones, 6–10 inches long

LEAVES: Long, glossy, drooping needles, 9–18 inches in length, in groups of three

TRUNK: A tall, straight, brown trunk with branches and foliage at the top; the bark is very thick, protecting it from the periodic fires of its dry habitat.

NATIVE RANGE: A coastal plain tree of the southeastern U.S.; Zones 8–9

HABITAT: Generally found on dry, sandy sites subject to fires, it can tolerate some damper locations such as savannahs.

PROPAGATION: Seed

The longleaf pine is a majestic landscape tree where sufficient space is available. It prefers acid soil. An important timber tree in the south, it goes through an interesting stage in which the young tree resembles a large tuft of grass while it is developing a large root system. After the root system is established, the tree rapidly develops a trunk. Early settlers used the long needles in weaving baskets and similar products.

LOBLOLLY PINE
Pinus taeda

HEIGHT: 50–80 feet

LIGHT: Sun

BLOOM: Small, yellow-brown flowers at branch ends in spring

FRUIT: Medium brown cones, 3–6 inches long with a sharp spine on each scale

LEAVES: Yellow-green needles 6–10 inches long, growing in bundles of three

TRUNK: Rough, reddish-gray bark on a straight trunk

NATIVE RANGE: Eastern U.S. from southern New Jersey to central Florida and east Texas; Zones 6–9

HABITAT: An adaptable species; found in woodlands, it also is an aggressive pioneer species in old fields.

PROPAGATION: Seed

Loblolly pine is a tree of major importance for its valuable lumber. Tolerating heavy clay and poor drainage but preferring acid soil, its wide range of adaptability to marginal sites makes it extremely useful in the landscape. Depending on the light and space available, the tree tends to change character. It is a wide, spreading tree in open fields and a tall tree with its foliage at the top in thick woods. This pine transplants easily as it does not develop a deep root system. It may be used for a fast-growing screen but the lower branches eventually will die off unless it is in full sun.

JAMAICA DOGWOOD, FISHFUDDLE TREE
Piscidia piscipula

HEIGHT: 50–60 feet

LIGHT: Sun to part shade

BLOOM: Pea-like flowers, ¾-inch long with purplish-blue petals, appear before the new leaves, in clusters at the ends of the branches. Delicate but fairly showy, they are a source of honey.

FRUIT: The ¾-inch, light brown pods have four wings and contain reddish seeds, ripening in summer.

LEAVES: Large, compound leaves have seven leaflets, 2–4 inches long; leaflets are oval with pointed tips, coarse and gray-green.

TRUNK: Bark is gray-green, mottled, and scaly on old trees.

NATIVE RANGE: South Florida, West Indies, Mexico; Zones 10–11

HABITAT: Open fields, open tropical hammocks, edges of bays and along roadsides

PROPAGATION: Seed, cuttings

Jamaica dogwood is a fast-growing shade and flowering tree with hard wood. Years ago, when it was more common in Florida, it was a major timber tree. It tolerates drought and salty conditions as well as most soils, both upland and damp. Early pruning of the tree is recommended to correct its tendency to produce narrow, V-shaped crotches that are likely to split in a storm.

In tropical America the leaves, bark, twigs, and roots of this tree sometimes are ground into a powder that is placed in the water to stun fish temporarily, allowing them to be caught easily, a practice now illegal in Florida.

SYCAMORE
Platanus occidentalis

HEIGHT: 80 to 100 feet or more

LIGHT: Sun to part shade

BLOOM: Rounded, 1-inch, ball-like, inconspicuous, greenish-brown flower, blooming in spring

FRUIT: Single, round, 1-inch brown globular fruit on a long stem

LEAVES: Alternate three- to five-lobed, maple-like leaves are as much as 8 inches across and 7–8 inches long. Foliage is medium green in summer, turning brownish in the fall before dropping.

TRUNK: The large, massive trunk, gray-brown at the base, has bark that flakes off the upper trunk and branches, revealing cream to white underbark. This is one of the tree's most identifiable characteristics. In old trees, the huge trunk is often hollow.

NATIVE RANGE: Eastern U.S., Maine to Minnesota, and south to central Florida and Texas; Zones 4–9 (It has been planted infrequently but successfully in south Florida.)

HABITAT: A lowland tree found along riverbanks and other bottomland locations, but quite adaptable to upland situations

PROPAGATION: Seed, cuttings

Sycamore is a good tree for erosion control on stream banks or in parks or schoolyards where it has plenty of space. It prefers rich soil. It is not suitable for the average yard because of its size and the constant shedding of leaves, fruit, and branches. It is subject to anthracnose, a fungal disease causing leaves and branches to die and drop off.

BLACK CHERRY
Prunus serotina

HEIGHT: 50–60 feet

LIGHT: Sun

BLOOM: Drooping 4–5-inch spikes of white flowers in March and early April; individual flowers are ¼-inch in diameter.

FRUIT: Round, ¼-inch fruits ripen in late July and August, changing from red to black as they ripen.

LEAVES: Shiny, dark green, oblong leaves, 3–5 inches long, end in a sharp point and have small-toothed edges. Fall color can be attractive, with a blend of red and yellow on most trees.

TRUNK: Dark brown bark is rough and scaly on old trees. Younger branches are shiny brown, with prominent pores.

NATIVE RANGE: Eastern and central U.S. and southern Canada into central Florida; Zones 3–9

HABITAT: Black cherry is a pioneer species, quickly moving into abandoned fields and along fence rows.

PROPAGATION: Seed

Black cherry is valued for its excellent timber; its fruit is used for wine and jelly and is very attractive to birds. The tree is pretty in spring when in flower and when its leaves turn color in the fall. Tent caterpillars disfigure the foliage in spring, and beetles may feast on the foliage later in the year. It could be used as a background or skyline tree because it may not be all that attractive close up. Sun and well-drained soil are its main requirements.

WHITE OAK
Quercus alba

HEIGHT: 60–80 feet

LIGHT: Sun to part shade

BLOOM: Male flowers are drooping catkins, yellowish, and noticeable; female flowers are in inconspicuous short spikes in the leaf axils.

FRUIT: A deep brown acorn with a light brown, bumpy cup covering one-fourth of the fruit

LEAVES: Oblong leaves are 5 to 8 inches long, with six to nine rounded lobes. They are dark green above and pale green-white below, turning red to purple in the fall.

TRUNK: Gray, scaly, vertically ridged bark

NATIVE RANGE: Maine to central and west Florida and west to Texas; Zones 3–9

HABITAT: Rich, well-drained soils

PROPAGATION: Seed

This is a premier oak, providing excellent shade and a good source of food for wildlife. When not crowded by other trees, it develops a beautiful, wide canopy. It is a slow-grower and not often available at nurseries. The tree has a deep tap root and does not take well to root disturbance or urban areas. Nevertheless, it is a long-lived tree. The Wye Oak, an historical tree in eastern Maryland, is estimated to be about 500 years old.

Eric Jadaszewski

SOUTHERN RED OAK
Quercus falcata

HEIGHT: 70 feet

LIGHT: Sun to part shade

BLOOM: Male trees produce 3- to 4-inch golden catkins in spring; female flowers are inconspicuous.

FRUIT: ½-inch, rounded acorn with a shallow cup, distinctly banded with vertical, alternating dark brown to black and light brown stripes

LEAVES: Oval, alternate leaves, 5–10 inches long, are shiny, dark green above, grayish to brown and hairy beneath, and either deeply lobed with five to seven lobes or with three shallow lobes at the end of the leaf.

TRUNK: Rough, ridged, dark brown bark

NATIVE RANGE: New Jersey to central Florida and west to Texas; Zones 6–9

HABITAT: Dry upland sites

PROPAGATION: Seed

Southern red oak, a common southern species in areas of poor soil, makes a strong, deep-rooted shade tree for a landscape with enough space to accommodate its size. It does not develop the attractive fall color of many other oaks, turning rusty-brown before the leaves fall. The acorns provide a good source of food for birds and wildlife.

LAUREL OAK
Quercus laurifolia

HEIGHT: 60–70 feet

LIGHT: Sun to part shade

BLOOM: Male catkins are pendulous and yellow; female flowers are in small spikes arising from new leaf axils.

FRUIT: Acorns are about 1 inch long, with the cup enclosing about half of the fruit. They take two years to ripen.

LEAVES: Semi-evergreen foliage is 3–4 inches long, shiny green above and pale green underneath. The lance-shaped leaf is widest at the middle, with a pointed tip, narrow base, and usually smooth edges. Leaves fall in late winter or spring.

TRUNK: Deeply furrowed bark is dark brown to almost black. The trunk is straight and may form a single leader to the top of the tree.

NATIVE RANGE: Southern New Jersey to south Florida and west to Texas; Zones 6–10

PROPAGATION: Seed

Laurel oak, also listed as *Q. hemisphaerica*, prefers sandy, moist, well-drained soils. The best locations are along the banks of rivers, lakes, and swamps, but the tree is very sensitive to being planted too deep and many trees decline and die as a result. The tree is pyramidal when young, eventually becoming round-headed. It is fast-growing for an oak, but weaker and shorter-lived than live oak.

SWAMP CHESTNUT OAK
Quercus michauxii

HEIGHT: 70–80 feet

LIGHT: Sun to part shade

BLOOM: Male flowers are borne in catkins in spring; female flowers are inconspicuous.

FRUIT: About one-half to a third of the 1½-inch acorn is covered by a fringed cup.

LEAVES: Oval leaves average 4 to 10 inches in length and are widest near the tips, with shallow, rounded lobes on each side. They are yellow-green, turning yellow to yellow-brown to red in fall.

TRUNK: A straight trunk, covered in scaly, light gray bark

NATIVE RANGE: Maine to central Florida and west to Alabama; Zones 4–9

HABITAT: Wet or flood plain forests and lower mountain slopes

PROPAGATION: Seed

This is a good shade tree, resembling white oak, that does well in damp locations but is rarely found in nurseries. It is valued for its tough, hard wood, and the sweet acorn is a preferred food for many animals.

Water oak *Quercus nigra*

Water oak *Quercus nigra*

WATER OAK
Quercus nigra

HEIGHT: 60 feet

LIGHT: Sun to part shade

BLOOM: Male tree has noticeable pendulous yellow-green catkins in spring; female flowers are inconspicuous.

FRUIT: The ½-inch acorn is banded in black and brown; the cup covers one-third of the base of the fruit.

LEAVES: Foliage is one of the most variable among oaks. Young trees are evergreen with lobed foliage. Older trees are semi-deciduous in the winter, have a spatula-like leaf, narrow at the base and wider at the top, which may be three-lobed near the tip. Leaves are 1–4 inches long and blue-green in color.

TRUNK: Rough, gray-black bark with scaly ridges

NATIVE RANGE: Southern New Jersey to north and north-central Florida and west to Texas; Zones 6–9

HABITAT: Sandy stream banks, flood plains, lake and swamp edges, often in association with sweet gum

PROPAGATION: Seed, cuttings

Water oak is used frequently in the South as a shade and street tree, but it is weaker than most oaks and subject to ice and wind damage. It also seeds aggressively, and sometimes takes over abandoned fields and even residential sites. Its acorns are food for many animals.

Eric Jadaszewski

WILLOW OAK
Quercus phellos

HEIGHT: 50 feet

LIGHT: Sun to part shade

BLOOM: Pendant, yellow-green male catkins are noticeable in spring.

FRUIT: A small acorn, usually ½-inch or less, with vertical brown and black bands and a small, dish-like cup at its base

LEAVES: Lance-shaped or willow-like leaves, 2–6 inches long and less than an inch wide, are medium green, changing to yellow and russet in the fall.

TRUNK: Reddish-brown and smooth when young, becoming dark gray and rough with irregular ridges in older trees

NATIVE RANGE: New York to north-central Florida and west to Texas; Zones 5–9

HABITAT: Moist, well-drained soils near lakes and rivers

PROPAGATION: Seed, cuttings

Willow oak is an attractive, fine-textured tree, excellent as a street tree where there is sufficient space. It also makes a good long-lived shade tree in school yards, golf courses, and large residential lots. It has a fibrous root system, making it easier to transplant than many other oaks.

SHUMARD RED OAK
Quercus shumardii

HEIGHT: 80 feet

LIGHT: Sun to part shade

BLOOM: A brownish, 6-inch catkin in spring

FRUIT: Brown acorn, the basal cup covering one-third of the fruit

LEAVES: Oval leaves are 4–7 inches long and 3–4 inches across, and usually seven-lobed with pointed tips. They are leathery and glossy green above, turning bright red before dropping in the fall.

TRUNK: Straight, with furrowed brown bark

NATIVE RANGE: The Plains states from Michigan to Texas and east to North Carolina and northern Florida; Zone 5–9

HABITAT: Along streams and lakes on well-drained soil

PROPAGATION: Seed

Shumard red oak is a rather uncommon but good-looking tree, with a straight trunk and a broad open canopy. Its foliage is striking: shiny, bright green in the summer and brightly colored in the fall. It's an adaptable tree. In nature it occurs near water, but it has good drought tolerance. Although its natural range is only through Zone 9, a healthy specimen is growing in Mounts Botanical Garden in West Palm Beach, in Zone 10.

Live oak *Quercus virginiana*

Sand live oak *Quercus geminata*

LIVE OAK
Quercus virginiana

HEIGHT: 50–60 feet

LIGHT: Sun to part shade

BLOOM: Pendulous, yellowish catkins to 3 inches long

FRUIT: ¾-inch edible acorn, a major food source for wildlife

LEAVES: The leathery leaves, narrow and oval, can reach 4–5 inches long on vigorous new shoots. They are dark green above, pale green underneath.

TRUNK: Very thick, dividing into many wide-flung branches low on the trunk

NATIVE RANGE: Coastal Virginia into southern Florida and around the Gulf to Mexico; Zones 8–11

HABITAT: Open woodlands, where it is the dominant tree

PROPAGATION: Seed

Live oak is the South's most distinctive tree, especially when draped in Spanish moss. Trees have been reported with a branch spread of more than 150 feet and a trunk circumference of 30 feet or more. It is rather slow-growing but long-lived. Because of its size, it is not a good choice for narrow, confined locations, but is a wonderful tree for big lawns or avenues. The acorns provide food for squirrels and birds. The smaller sand live oak, *Q. geminata,* usually is considered a variety of live oak.

PARADISE TREE, BITTERWOOD
Simarouba glauca

HEIGHT: 40–50 feet

LIGHT: Sun

BLOOM: Yellowish panicle, not showy, appearing in spring

FRUIT: Purplish-black, 1-inch fruits appear on female trees in May; fruit is edible but insipid.

LEAVES: The pinnately compound evergreen leaves are leathery and glossy green above and pale green below. New growth is red and showy. Leaves, which are clumped near the ends of the branches, are 7–15 inches long with oval leaflets 2–4 inches in length.

TRUNK: The single trunk has thin gray bark; twigs are reddish brown.

NATIVE RANGE: Coastal south Florida and the Keys, West Indies, and the Bahamas; Zones 10–11

HABITAT: Tropical hammocks, elevated dry sites with good drainage

PROPAGATION: Seed sown right after ripening in late May

Paradise tree is one of our most beautiful native trees, developing a broad canopy if located in the open. In hammock woods, it is a major canopy tree. Usually found near the coast, it is sensitive to cold and excessive wind. The foliage is the tree's chief attribute, being highly reflective and very lively in a breeze. The red new growth is present through spring and summer and provides good color contrast in the landscape. Birds love the fruit, but fallen berries tend to stain hard surfaces, so be careful where you locate the tree.

MAHOGANY
Swietenia mahagoni

HEIGHT: 60–70 feet

LIGHT: Sun

BLOOM: Inconspicuous clusters of tiny yellow flowers in spring

FRUIT: A brown, cone-shaped pod up to 5 inches long that splits open to let the winged seeds blow away

LEAVES: Pinnate foliage with dark green leaflets, to 3–4 inches long

TRUNK: The dark brown, rough trunk usually divides into several co-dominant trunks 6 to 8 feet above ground level. The bark becomes scaled as the tree grows older.

NATIVE RANGE: South Florida, especially in the Keys, and the Caribbean; Zones 10–11

HABITAT: Open tropical woodlands, where it is a dominant species

PROPAGATION: Seed

For lawn areas, mahogany is a fine shade tree with its broad, dense canopy. It is widely adaptable to almost any site, except for wet locations. Webworms often defoliate the trees briefly in spring but do no lasting damage. Desirable forms should be selected for their resistance to webworms and for their single trunks, which are less prone to splitting.

Pond cypress *Taxodium ascendens*

Bald cypress *Taxodium distichum*

Bald cypress *Taxodium distichum*

BALD CYPRESS
Taxodium distichum

HEIGHT: 70 feet

LIGHT: Sun

BLOOM: Male flowers are small and greenish, in 4- to 5-inch drooping panicles; female flowers are globe-shaped, greenish cones.

FRUIT: Small, round brown cones to 1 inch across

LEAVES: The ½-inch needles fall in winter, giving the tree its "bald" label. New growth is pale green in spring, turning reddish brown in autumn.

TRUNK: The large, straight, buttressed trunk has fibrous, reddish bark. Pointed "knees" can be observed on trees standing in water.

NATIVE RANGE: Delaware, throughout Florida, and west to Texas; also planted as far north as upstate New York; Zones 4–10

HABITAT: Permanently wet swamps and bottomlands

PROPAGATION: Seed, grafts

Bald cypress is a tree with a great deal of character, very stable and strong against high winds and hurricanes. It is one of the signature trees of the deep South, and along with southern magnolia and live oak helps identify the region. Although it normally grows in swampy locations, it is quite adaptable to drier sites. A narrow-growing, closely related form is the pond cypress *(Taxodium ascendens)*, which produces rounded knees and has incurved needles that clasp the stems.

FLORIDA ELM, AMERICAN ELM
Ulmus americana var. floridana

HEIGHT: 60–80 feet

LIGHT: Sun to part shade

BLOOM: Small, greenish-red flowers in clusters of three or four

FRUIT: Green, rounded ½-inch samara

LEAVES: Ovate to oblong dark green leaves are 4–6 inches long with a saw-toothed edge. They turn yellow in fall.

TRUNK: Dark gray bark has deep crossing ridges; the crown often is vase-shaped.

NATIVE RANGE: Southern Canada to central Florida and west to the Rocky Mountains; Zones 2–9

HABITAT: Bottomlands, lake and stream banks, and other damp locations

PROPAGATION: Seed, cuttings

The Florida elm is a smaller version of the American elm. When small, it works well in a garden with an Oriental motif. Dutch elm disease has eliminated the tree in most of its range but does not appear to be active in Florida. Its vase shape and fast growth rate, about 6 feet a year, make this an attractive background or shade tree. It moves easily and even does well south of its range, into Zone 10.

SMALL TREES

CINNECORD
Acacia choriophylla

HEIGHT: 15–20 feet

LIGHT: Sun

BLOOM: Tight, fuzzy, fragrant, bright yellow, ⅓-inch flowers carried in clusters in the leaf axils

FRUIT: Flat, oval, 2-inch brown pods

LEAVES: Leaves are alternate and bipinnate, divided one to three times; individual leaflets are dark green, oval, with smooth margins, fairly thick, and from ¾ to 1 inch long.

TRUNK: Dark brown, multistemmed or single

NATIVE RANGE: Florida Keys (very rare), the Bahamas, and West Indies; Zones 10–11

HABITAT: Open, dry, sunny areas

PROPAGATION: Seed

Cinnecord is a beautiful small tree, easily grown from seed. It stays dark green and healthy looking when the rest of the landscape may be seared by drought. A thornless acacia is a rarity, and this one has only tiny spines in the leaf axils that are unlikely to cause major problems. It is a highly desirable native that deserves a place in the low-maintenance landscape.

SWEET ACACIA
Acacia farnesiana

HEIGHT: 15 feet

LIGHT: Sun

BLOOM: Bright yellow, fuzzy, ¾-inch flowers are highly fragrant. Flowers may appear individually or clustered in groups of two to five, blooming throughout the year.

FRUIT: Cylindrical brown pods, 2–3 inches long, often carried in clusters

LEAVES: Twice-compound, fern-like leaves, 1–4 inches long, made up of tiny bright green leaflets

TRUNK: Shaggy, reddish-brown bark, with narrow ridges and furrows on younger trunks; branches are thorny.

NATIVE RANGE: South Florida, Mexico, and Central America; introduced in the Gulf states, southern California, and other tropical and sub-tropical locations around the world; Zones 9–11

HABITAT: Sunny, dry, well-drained sandy soils in pinelands, disturbed areas, and field edges

PROPAGATION: Seed

This thorny little tree perfumes the air in spring with its bright blooms. The flowers are used in the perfume industry, particularly in France. It has a light, airy appearance, which lends an appealing filigree aspect to the landscape, and its thorny branches provide good nesting sites for birds.

Eric Jadaszewski

FLORIDA MAPLE, SOUTHERN SUGAR MAPLE
Acer saccharum subsp. floridanum

HEIGHT: 25 feet

LIGHT: Part shade

BLOOM: Greenish-yellow, ¼-inch, bell-shaped flowers appear in clusters before new leaves emerge in spring.

FRUIT: Winged 1-inch samara, with the wings at a 60–70° angle

LEAVES: Opposite, medium green, 3–4 inches long, with 3 to 5 lobes

TRUNK: Gray-brown bark, becoming ridged and plated with age; it may be scaly but is variable.

NATIVE RANGE: Virginia to central Florida and west to Texas; Zones 7–9

HABITAT: Moist stream banks and swamp edges, as an understory tree on coastal plain and piedmont regions

PROPAGATION: Seed

The Florida maple, also listed as *A. barbatum*, is a miniature version of the northern sugar maple, minus the maple syrup. It has bright yellow to salmon foliage in the fall, changing about two weeks later than the regular sugar maple and adding a distinctive splash of color to the landscape. The closely related chalk or whitebark maple, *A. leucoderme*, has lighter colored bark, dark green leaves, even better fall color in the orange to red range, and tolerates drier soils. It grows to 30 feet and also is an understory tree.

RED BUCKEYE
Aesculus pavia

HEIGHT: 15–30 feet

LIGHT: Sun to shade

BLOOM: Four- to 8-inch panicles of red, 1½-inch flowers with four or five petals, blooming in April

FRUIT: Rounded, flat capsule containing one or two shiny black seeds, ripening in September or October

LEAVES: Opposite, palmately compound deciduous leaves have five to seven shiny, oval to narrowly elliptic leaflets, each 4–6 inches long with pointed tips and often serrated at the edges.

TRUNK: Single to multistemmed, with dark brown bark

NATIVE RANGE: Virginia to north-central Florida and west to Texas; Zones 4–8

HABITAT: Open deciduous forests of maple, oak, hickory, or beech

PROPAGATION: Seed

Red buckeye is an excellent small tree with a showy flower display and pretty leaves. The flowers attract hummingbirds and butterflies, and the glossy foliage is more attractive than most varieties of buckeye/horse chestnut. Leaves emerge early in spring but often drop early, in late September. The tree will do best in moist, organic soil in part shade.

TORCHWOOD
Amyris elemifera

HEIGHT: 20–40 feet

LIGHT: Sun to part shade

BLOOM: Open clusters of small, fragrant, tan-white flowers blooming in autumn

FRUIT: Black to purple, ½-inch rounded fruit with a single seed surrounded by a narrow band of fragrant black pulp

LEAVES: Compound leaves, which droop on the branches, have three to five opposite leaflets; leaflets are 1–3 inches long, oval, pointed, glossy light green with entire margins.

TRUNK: Light brown single or multistemmed tree or large shrub

NATIVE RANGE: South Florida, West Indies, Central America, and the Bahamas; Zones 10–11

HABITAT: Open hammock woodlands and the edges of old fields

PROPAGATION: Seed

Torchwood's fragrant flowers and shiny foliage add ornamental interest to a landscape. A citrus relative, its leaves have the typical citrus fragrance. The tree is salt- and drought-tolerant, but won't take cold weather, so its use is limited to the southern part of the state. The wood is quite oily and once was used for torches and fuel. The oil has proven useful in the pharmaceutical industry as well.

Pond apple *Annona glabra*

Pond apple *Annona glabra*

POND APPLE
Annona glabra

HEIGHT: 30–35 feet

LIGHT: Full sun

BLOOM: Pale yellow to white 1-inch flowers with six petals, the outer three spotted in red at the base

FRUIT: A 5-inch, conical, edible yellow fruit

LEAVES: Deciduous, leathery, alternate, oval and pointed, to 7 inches in length

TRUNK: A rough-barked trunk that develops character as it ages

NATIVE RANGE: South Florida, the Caribbean, and tropical America; Zones 10–11

HABITAT: Stream banks and swampy areas, but adaptable to drier sites

PROPAGATION: Seed

Pond apple belongs to the annona or custard apple family and is related to such valued fruit trees as cherimoya, sugar-apple, and atemoya. The pond apple fruit, however, is relished more by raccoons than humans. In their native habitat, the trees often are draped with native epiphytes such as bromeliads, orchids, and ferns, and in the landscape the branches provide a good place to naturalize such plants. The trunks also may become gnarled and distorted with age, taking on a movie-set quality like the evil trees in *The Wizard of Oz*.

Dr. Edward F. Gilman

PAWPAW
Asimina triloba

HEIGHT: Variable, from 2 to 20 feet

LIGHT: Sun to shade

BLOOM: Three-lobed flowers, deep purple-red in some species, white in others

FRUIT: Aromatic yellow-green berry, round to elongated and 1–6 inches long, turning black when ripe

LEAVES: Alternate, oblong leaves, 7–12 inches long, have pointed tips. Pawpaws are deciduous, with leaves turning yellow in autumn.

TRUNK: Usually multistemmed, with rough, dark brown bark on older trees

NATIVE RANGE: New York to central Florida, west to Texas; Zones 5–9

HABITAT: Pine woods, coastal hammocks, dunes, lowlands along stream banks

PROPAGATION: Seed, suckers

Several species of pawpaw are found in Florida. The large, drooping foliage of these small trees or shrubs is quite decorative, adding a tropical touch along the edges of woods or other naturalistic setting. They produce suckers, often forming thickets. Pawpaws will take quite a bit of shade. They usually form a dense leaf canopy in full sun; in a shaded area the crown will be more open. The purple flowers of *A. triloba* have a rather unpleasant aroma, but the fruit is edible. *A. parviflora* is similar but shorter and with smaller leaves and flowers. *A. reticulata* is a shrubby species with fragrant white flowers.

BAHAMA STRONGBARK
Bourreria ovata

HEIGHT: 20 feet

LIGHT: Sun to part shade

BLOOM: Terminal clusters of fragrant, ½-inch white, funnel-shaped flowers that bloom most of the year

FRUIT: Showy clusters of red-orange, ½-inch fruit

LEAVES: Alternate leaves are 2–4 inches long, oval with a rounded or notched tip, evergreen, smooth, and deep, glossy greenish-yellow.

TRUNK: Reddish-brown and scaly

NATIVE RANGE: South Florida, the Bahamas, and West Indies; Zones 10–11

HABITAT: Pinelands and hardwood hammocks, especially in the Keys

PROPAGATION: Seed

Strongbark is a decorative, shrubby tree with a modest flower display and striking fruit, largely problem-free, and not fussy about soils or occasional drought. It's a good choice for an evergreen dooryard or specimen tree, especially if it is limbed up a bit. The flowers will attract hummingbirds and butterflies.

Tough bumelia *Bumelia tenax*

Alachua buckthorn *B. anomala*

TOUGH BUMELIA, TOUGH BUCKTHORN, IRONWOOD
Bumelia tenax

HEIGHT: 20 feet

LIGHT: Sun to part shade

BLOOM: Tiny clusters of white flowers appearing in the leaf axils in spring

FRUIT: Round, black, ½-inch edible fruit, appearing in the leaf axils and ripening in autumn

LEAVES: Alternate, oblong, evergreen, 1- to 3-inch leaves with rounded tips have rusty to coppery-gold hairs on the lower surface, a significant feature in identification.

TRUNK: Thick, reddish-brown bark is deeply lined and sharp, stout spines appear along the stems.

NATIVE RANGE: Coastal South Carolina to south Florida; Zones 8–10

HABITAT: Open maritime woodlands among dunes where scrub oak and sand pine are the major components

PROPAGATION: Seed

This is a tough, drought- and salt-tolerant plant suitable for a hostile environment. It will grow in poor, dry soil and needs little care. As it is very thorny, it is useful as a security screen or to control unwanted traffic. Its fruit also provides food for wildlife. Several other bumelias, also armed with thorns and ranging from small trees to ground covers, are propagated for landscape use. Among them, saffron plum *(B. celastrina)*, slender buckthorn *(B. reclinata)*, and Alachua buckthorn *(B. anomala)*.

SPICEWOOD, PALE LIDFLOWER
Calyptranthes pallens

HEIGHT: 20 feet

LIGHT: Sun to part shade

BLOOM: Fuzzy, fragrant, pale green to white flowers are borne in loose clusters in late spring.

FRUIT: Round ¼-inch berry with edible dry flesh, turning from green to orange to black as it ripens

LEAVES: Oval, opposite, pointed leaves average 3 inches in length, are glossy above and slightly fuzzy below. Pink when they open, gradually changing to green. They have a pleasant spicy aroma.

TRUNK: Multi-trunked, with pale bark, gray to almost white

NATIVE RANGE: South Florida, the Caribbean, Mexico, and Guatemala; Zones 10–11

HABITAT: Edges of hammocks, open understory, fields

PROPAGATION: Seed

These rounded shrubs or small trees serve well for hedges, screening, or, if limbed up, as small shade trees. The colorful fruit, fragrant foliage, and subtle fuzzy flowers make this an interesting tree year-round. The fruit attracts birds, which also use the tree for shelter. While it is adaptable, it does best in damp soil.

The related Myrtle-of-the-River, *C. zuzygium*, is very similar although rare in Florida. It grows in low elevations and is useful for landscaping wet areas. The flower buds and fruit sometimes are used as a spice for flavoring.

CINNAMON BARK
Canella winterana

HEIGHT: 30 feet

LIGHT: Sun to part shade

BLOOM: Terminal clusters of ⅛-inch orange-red (occasionally white or purple) flowers, blooming year-round

FRUIT: Soft, round, red, ½-inch fruit, appearing from late winter through early fall

LEAVES: Leaves are 3 to 5 inches long and have an extended oval shape with a narrow base and a rounded tip. They are semi-glossy, dark green above and pale green below, with a leathery texture. Bruised leaves have a wintergreen fragrance.

TRUNK: The straight trunk has gray, checkered bark. The yellow, inner bark, known as wild cinnamon bark, has been used in drinks and condiments and medicinally.

NATIVE RANGE: South Florida, the Caribbean, Bahamas, and northern South America; Zones 10–11

HABITAT: Hardwood hammocks, edges of woods

PROPAGATION: Seed

Cinnamon bark is a tidy little tree with an open growth, valued for its delicate flower display and colorful fruits and useful as a specimen plant or for informal screening. The fragrant foliage adds to its attraction. It is salt- and drought-tolerant, and while it will accept a wide range of soils, it needs good drainage and protection from wind and cold.

SCRUB HICKORY, FLORIDA HICKORY
Carya floridana

HEIGHT: 30 feet

LIGHT: Sun to part shade

BLOOM: Tiny, yellow-green male flowers are carried on clustered, 1- to 2-inch catkins in spring; female flowers on short spikes are inconspicuous.

FRUIT: Globe-shaped, 1- to 1½-inch brown husks split to reveal round brown nuts.

LEAVES: Pinnately compound, 5–8 inches long, with three to five pointed, lance-shaped leaflets; leaflets are 2–4 inches long, lightly serrated and yellowish green above and paler below.

TRUNK: The tree is often shrubby, with gray-brown bark becoming slightly rough and with shallow interconnecting ridges.

NATIVE RANGE: Central and northern Florida; Zones 8–9

HABITAT: Coastal dunes and sandy ridges in association with sand pine and scrub oak

PROPAGATION: Seed

One of the smaller members of its family, this attractive hickory produces edible sweet nuts, attracting birds and animals. Its drought tolerance makes it ideal as a small tree for unirrigated sites.

EASTERN REDBUD
Cercis canadensis

HEIGHT: 20–30 feet

LIGHT: Sun to light shade

BLOOM: Rosy-pink flowers, ½-inch long, in short racemes of four or more flowers, bloom on bare branches from February to April and last two to three weeks. Trees blossom when quite young; in rare cases flowers are produced directly on the old trunks.

FRUIT: Short 2- to 3-inch brown pod ripening in October

LEAVES: Dark green, rounded leaves, somewhat heart-shaped and pointed, are 3–5 inches across, sometimes shiny, and sometimes wider than they are long. New leaves are reddish when unfolding; foliage is deciduous and may turn yellow in autumn.

TRUNK: Dark brown to black bark with hints of orange inner bark perceptible through fissures in the trunk

NATIVE RANGE: New Jersey to north Florida and west to New Mexico; Zones 4–9

HABITAT: Edges of woods or understory in light shade, but very adaptable to various soils except wet locations

PROPAGATION: Seed, grafting

Redbud is one of our most beautiful flowering trees that, along with dogwood, welcomes spring. It is a popular street and specimen tree everywhere in its range, although relatively short-lived. If the tree has a heavy crop of pods, it may have an untidy appearance in fall. Several cultivars are on the market, some with white or clear pink flowers and variegated or purple foliage.

ATLANTIC WHITE CEDAR, SOUTHERN WHITE CEDAR
Chamaecyparis thyoides

HEIGHT: 30–40 feet

LIGHT: Sun

BLOOM: Male blooms are oval and red or yellow, appearing at branch tips; their sheer numbers can make a showy display. Female blooms are small, round, green, and inconspicuous.

FRUIT: Small, round, ¼-inch blue-purple cones on outer branchlets, containing winged seeds

LEAVES: Tiny blue to gray-green leaves are awl-shaped on young trees and scale-like on older trees, occurring on fine, irregular branches.

TRUNK: Light gray to reddish-brown, thin, lightly peeling bark

NATIVE RANGE: Coastal plains from Maine to central Florida; Zones 3–9

HABITAT: Freshwater swamps near the coast, stream banks, bogs and lakesides, usually in colonies by itself

PROPAGATION: Seed, cuttings

This is one of the few evergreens that will tolerate wet feet, and while it is not the most ornamental cedar, it has a place in a landscape with moist soil. A narrow, conical tree, it prefers sun and is best grown by itself, as it does not compete well with hardwood trees. It is best known, perhaps, for its close-grained wood, widely used for shingles that turn a beautiful silvery gray as they age.

Pygmy fringe tree *Chionanthus pygmaeus*

Fringe tree *Chionanthus virginicus*

FRINGE TREE
Chionanthus virginicus

HEIGHT: 20 feet

LIGHT: Sun

BLOOM: White, slightly fragrant flowers bloom from late March to May through its range. The blossoms, with 1- to 1½-inch petals, hang in dense drooping clusters and create an airy, shimmering appearance.

FRUIT: Ovoid, dark-blue, ⅔-inch fruit ripening in August and September; although the berries often are half-hidden by the leaves, birds quickly find and eat them so the showy display is brief.

LEAVES: Opposite, 4–8 inches long, oblong with a pointed tip and a coarse texture, medium green and sometimes quite glossy

TRUNK: Usually multi-trunked and somewhat shrubby, with gray, slightly rough bark on old trees

NATIVE RANGE: Southern New Jersey to central Florida and west to Texas; Zones 3–9

HABITAT: Swamp edges and stream banks, usually in full sun

PROPAGATION: Seed, grafts, and, with difficulty, cuttings

When in bloom, the fringe tree has such an ethereal appearance that it has become a highly popular landscape tree, and a number of commercial varieties have been developed. It adapts well to urban sites and can be used as a specimen, in a group planting, or as a screen.

COCOPLUM
Chrysobalanus icaco

HEIGHT: 15–20 feet

LIGHT: Sun or part shade

BLOOM: Spikes of tiny, fragrant white flowers, blooming all year

FRUIT: Off-white to purple edible fruits, round to oval, 1½-inch or larger, with a single seed

LEAVES: Shiny, rounded, alternate, leathery leaves to 3 inches; new growth is yellow-green on the coastal form and reddish on the inland variety.

TRUNK: Usually multistemmed with brown bark

NATIVE RANGE: South Florida and the Caribbean; Zones 10–11

HABITAT: Open tropical hammock woodlands

PROPAGATION: Seed, cuttings, air layering

Cocoplum is a valuable, pest-free shrub for hedges or screens in full sun, forming a dense mass of foliage. In shady sites, however, it quickly thins out and becomes leggy. The coastal form is salt-tolerant but seldom available commercially. The 'Red Tip' variety is seen most often in nurseries; it is an inland form that is not salt-tolerant. Cocoplum fruit may be eaten fresh or used for jelly.

SATINLEAF
Chrysophyllum oliviforme

HEIGHT: 25–30 feet

LIGHT: Sun to part shade

BLOOM: Small yellowish-white flowers appear in autumn. Buds have a downy covering.

FRUIT: Oblong, edible, purple fruit, 1 inch long, ripening in spring

LEAVES: Oval and pointed, 5 to 6 inches long, glossy green above and with a satiny, copper-colored down on the underside

TRUNK: Dark brown, sometimes with multiple stems

NATIVE RANGE: South Florida and the Caribbean; Zones 10–11

HABITAT: Openings in hardwood hammocks

PROPAGATION: Seed

Satinleaf is one of our most beautiful native trees, absolutely stunning when the wind reveals the coppery underside of the foliage. Its fruit will bring birds to your garden. The tree is difficult to establish, but is worth the effort. It may be that it needs organisms that exist in hammock soil to grow successfully.

FIDDLEWOOD
Citharexylum fruticosum

HEIGHT: 15–20 feet

LIGHT: Sun to part shade

BLOOM: Fragrant white flowers, tubular and five-petaled, are carried in 2- to 4-inch clusters emerging from the leaf axils.

FRUIT: Round, ⅜-inch, reddish-brown fruits

LEAVES: Pointed, oblong foliage averages 4 to 5 inches in length and is very glossy green above, dull green below. Leaves are leathery with smooth margins; leaf stalks are pinkish or orange.

TRUNK: Trunk may be single or multistemmed, with smooth light brown bark that develops fissures as the tree ages.

NATIVE RANGE: South Florida and the West Indies; Zones 10–11

HABITAT: Dry, open woodlands through the Keys and coastal South Florida

PROPAGATION: Seed

Fiddlewood is a beautiful small tree, one of the more delightful natives, with spring-to-fall, delicately scented flowers that attract butterflies and glossy leaves that catch the sunlight. Its berries also attract birds and other wildlife. In some cities, including Fort Lauderdale, a few specimens have been trained as standards and used as street trees.

Clusia *Clusia rosea*

Clusia *Clusia rosea*

CLUSIA, AUTOGRAPH TREE, PITCH APPLE
Clusia rosea

HEIGHT: 30 feet

LIGHT: Sun to part shade

BLOOM: Showy, drooping, 3-inch flowers with thick white and pink petals and yellow stamens, blooming during the warmest months

FRUIT: A woody, 3-inch green pod that turns brownish and splits to reveal black seeds in red flesh

LEAVES: Thick, oval and leathery, 5–7 inches long, notched at the tip and with a thick mid-vein

TRUNK: Smooth gray bark covers a stout trunk with spreading branches. Aerial roots often appear on the tree, which may start as an epiphyte in the top of a palm, in the manner of the strangler fig.

NATIVE RANGE: Florida Keys, Bahamas, tropical America; Zones 10–11

HABITAT: Formerly the Florida Keys; probably no longer exists outside of cultivation. Botanists disagree if it is truly a native.

PROPAGATION: Seed, cuttings

Clusia is a dense tree that looks neat and attractive year-round and provides excellent shade. As it is very salt- and wind-tolerant, it is a good candidate for beachfront plantings. Nevertheless, it has aggressive roots and should be used with care. Seedlings should never be allowed to remain in the canopies of palms and other trees where the seeds sometimes germinate.

Why the name autograph tree? When the smooth leaf surface is scratched, the markings will remain, and it's not unusual to see a tree with its lower leaves bearing initials and other "graffiti."

PIGEON PLUM
Coccoloba diversifolia

HEIGHT: 30–40 feet

LIGHT: Sun to shade

BLOOM: Small whitish flowers in spikes, appearing in early spring

FRUIT: Narrow clusters of purple, edible, acid fruit about ½-inch across

LEAVES: Thick, oval, alternate leaves normally are 3–4 inches long. New growth is much larger, and leaves vary greatly in shape as the species name, meaning "diverse foliage," indicates.

TRUNK: The trunk may be single or multiple. The bark is light gray on young trees and the upper branches of older trees; mature trees have multicolored, peeling bark.

NATIVE RANGE: South Florida and the Caribbean; Zones 10–11

HABITAT: Tropical woodlands

PROPAGATION: Seed, cuttings

Pigeon plum, a close relative of seagrape, is a useful tree where space is at a premium. The narrow, upright growth makes it a good choice for formal entries, hedges, avenues, or narrow spaces between houses where shade is desired. It also may be used as a large container plant. It has some problems with insects attacking the foliage.

SEAGRAPE
Coccoloba uvifera

HEIGHT: 30 feet

LIGHT: Sun to part shade

BLOOM: Tiny white blooms in spikes to 10 inches long

FRUIT: Edible, purple, ¾-inch fruit is carried in grape-like clusters. The fruit can be eaten fresh or used for making jelly.

LEAVES: Large, round, leathery leaves, 6–8 inches across, are very distinctive. New growth is glossy bronze; old leaves turn red or yellow before falling.

TRUNK: Usually a multistemmed tree with peeling bark in varying shades of brown

NATIVE RANGE: South Florida and coastal Caribbean; Zones 10–11

HABITAT: Coastal beaches, dunes, and tropical hammocks

PROPAGATION: Seed, cuttings

Seagrape is an excellent seaside tree with a broad, spreading, rounded canopy. In harsh, windy conditions, it often has a dwarfed appearance. In landscaping, it sometimes is used as a hedge plant, but eventually becomes woody and leggy. It tends to be messy as well, a drawback when used in formal landscapes or near pools. Leaf drop is constant and leaves take a long time to decay. Nevertheless, it has a great deal of character and is extremely salt-tolerant. Birds and animals are attracted to the fruit.

COFFEE COLUBRINA
Colubrina arborescens

HEIGHT: 20 feet

LIGHT: Sun to part shade

BLOOM: Small, fragrant yellowish flowers, clustered in the leaf axils, bloom most of the year.

FRUIT: Round, purple-brown fruits about ¼-inch in diameter are carried in small clusters in the leaf axils.

LEAVES: Oval, 2- to 4-inch leaves are shiny, dark green above, slightly fuzzy and brownish below, and have smooth margins.

TRUNK: Single or multistemmed trunk with flaking brown bark

NATIVE RANGE: South Florida, Mexico, the Caribbean, and Central America; Zones 10–11

HABITAT: Most common in hammocks and pinewoods in the Keys

PROPAGATION: Seed

Here is an attractive, fast-growing small tree with glossy leaves that catch the light in a cheerful way. The shrubby growth of coffee colubrina makes it suitable for screening or other informal plantings, and its tough nature makes it useful where salt or drought rules out more delicate plants.

SOLDIERWOOD
Colubrina elliptica

HEIGHT: 20 feet

LIGHT: Sun to part shade

BLOOM: Tiny, clustered, greenish-yellow flowers appear in the leaf axils most of the year.

FRUIT: Orange-red fruit, ¼-inch across, is clustered in the leaf axils. On warm, sunny days, the ripe fruit explodes with a popping sound, scattering the seed.

LEAVES: Alternate, 2- to 4-inch leaves are thin, medium green, and rather glossy above and may be rusty below. The shape is variable, from oval to lanceolate, with a blunt, pointed tip.

TRUNK: Multistemmed or single trunk has orange-brown, scaly bark, divided by deep, irregular furrows.

NATIVE RANGE: The Florida Keys, the Bahamas, West Indies, coastal Mexico, and Guatemala; Zones 10–11

HABITAT: Hammocks in the Keys

PROPAGATION: Seed

Soldierwood is variable; it may be shrubby or, in more favorable locations, develop into a good-sized tree. It is tolerant of adverse conditions such as drought, poor soil, and some salt—a good choice for difficult sites.

GEIGER TREE, GERANIUM TREE
Cordia sebestena

HEIGHT: 20 feet

LIGHT: Sun

BLOOM: Very showy tubular orange flowers to 1½ inches across, in terminal clusters, scattered over the tree most of the year

FRUIT: White, 1–1½ inches long, oval to pear-shaped, in clusters; edible but of poor flavor

LEAVES: Oval, pointed evergreen leaves, coarse textured and rough to the touch, average 7–8 inches in length and 4 inches in width.

TRUNK: A single trunk with rough brown bark

NATIVE RANGE: The Keys, coastal south Florida, and West Indies; Zones 10–11

HABITAT: Warm coastal areas

PROPAGATION: Seed, air layering

Geiger tree is one of our few really showy flowering native trees. An excellent small tree for coastal locations, it tolerates drought, wind, and salt but is very cold-sensitive and can freeze to the ground in inland locations in Zone 10. The flowers, which attract hummingbirds, have enough carrying power to be visible for a good distance, and the tree is best located at some distance as the foliage is routinely attacked by the geiger beetle. The chewed foliage is unattractive when viewed up close, so locating the plant in the background of a landscape may eliminate the need for spraying. The tree will continue to grow despite the beetles.

FLOWERING DOGWOOD
Cornus florida

HEIGHT: 20–30 feet

LIGHT: Sun to part shade; in Florida, best in part shade with protection from the hot afternoon sun

BLOOM: The showy structure, 3–4 inches across, is formed by four white bracts that surround the true, tiny, greenish-yellow flowers. They appear in Florida in March and April, with the display lasting 10–14 days.

FRUIT: Oval bright red fruit, ⅓-inch long

LEAVES: Opposite, oval, pointed leaves, often with wavy edges, are 4–6 inches long and deciduous, turning purplish-red in autumn.

TRUNK: Gray-green and smooth on young trees; the checkered gray bark is distinctive on older trees.

NATIVE RANGE: Eastern U.S. from Massachusetts to north Florida and west to Texas; Zones 6–9

HABITAT: Open woodlands

PROPAGATION: Seed, cuttings, grafts

Dogwood is one of our best-known and most-beloved flowering trees. Its fruit is a favorite of many birds. Acid, well-drained soil is essential, and adding mulch helps retain some moisture and keeps roots cool. Many cultivars exist, including pink or red forms, variegated leaf types, weeping forms and double flowering types. Lately, particularly in the northern states, dogwood has been troubled with anthracnose, a fungal disease that can kill the tree.

Parsley haw *C. marshallii*

Green hawthorn *Crataegus viridis*

May haw *C. aestivalis*

HAWTHORN, HAW
Crataegus spp.

HEIGHT: 20–30 feet

LIGHT: Sun to part shade

BLOOM: White, five-petaled, ½- to 1-inch flowers carried in flat clusters, blooming in spring

FRUIT: Bright red, ⅓-inch berries (haws), ripening in the fall and carried through the winter

LEAVES: Depending on species, leaves are 1–4 inches long and 1–2½ inches wide, oval and pointed, with shallow lobes and serrated edges. Often glossy green above and paler below, they turn red and purple in autumn.

TRUNK: The small tree or multistemmed shrub has silvery-gray stems and exfoliating old bark, exposing orange bark underneath. Stems may have thorns up to 1½ inches long.

NATIVE RANGE: Eastern U.S.; Florida species range from Maryland south through central Florida and west to Texas; Zones 6–9

HABITAT: Edges of woodlands, damp areas, old fields

PROPAGATION: Seeds, cuttings

Many species and cultivars of native hawthorn exist in the U.S. Florida has about a dozen species, including green hawthorn, *C. viridis*. Native to central and southeastern U.S., it is a colorful tree that seems more resistant to insects and disease than most other hawthorns. Attractive flowers, good fruit display, exfoliating bark, and excellent fall color are among its many attributes. The very ornamental parsley haw *(C. marshallii)* has deeply cut leaves and tiny red fruit that attracts birds. May haw *(C. aestivalis)* is an thorny, early spring bloomer in north Florida. Cockspur haw *(C. cruz-galli)*, has a flat crown and long limbs that often touch the ground.

WILLOW BUSTIC
Dipholis salicifolia

HEIGHT: 25–30 feet

LIGHT: Sun to part shade

BLOOM: Small white flowers, usually in heavy clusters, appear in spring along the young stems and in leaf axils near the ends of the branches.

FRUIT: Round, ¼-inch fruits, clustered at the ends of branches, change from red to black as they ripen.

LEAVES: Alternate, lance-shaped leaves, 3–5 inches long, are shiny dark green above and paler green below. They occur mainly at the ends of branches and tend to droop.

TRUNK: Rough, scaly, light brown or light gray

NATIVE RANGE: South Florida, the Bahamas, and the Caribbean coast from Mexico to Guatemala; Zones 10–11

HABITAT: Hammock areas near the coast

PROPAGATION: Seed

Willow bustic is a small, pretty tree, suitable as a street tree or to shade a townhouse or other small property. The wood is hard and strong, and breakage in a windstorm is unlikely. The glossy leaves are shiny in the sunlight, and the tree is open-growing, making it suitable for planting in lawn areas. It also is listed as *Bumelia salicifolia*.

WHITE STOPPER
Eugenia axillaris

HEIGHT: 20 feet

LIGHT: Sun to part shade

BLOOM: Small, fuzzy, fragrant white flowers are borne in the leaf axils.

FRUIT: The round, ¼- to ½-inch fruit is edible and changes from red to black as it ripens.

LEAVES: Oval, 1- to 3-inch leathery leaves are dark green and have pointed tips; new growth is pinkish. The foliage has a distinctive skunk-like odor, which a breeze can carry throughout the garden.

TRUNK: Bark is smooth and brownish-gray.

NATIVE RANGE: South Florida, the Caribbean, and the Bahamas; Zones 10–11

HABITAT: Understory of tropical hardwood hammocks

PROPAGATION: Seed

The tall, narrow growth makes the white stopper suitable for borders or for screening narrow areas. It will endure considerable shade. Some people, however, find the odor of the foliage "skunky" and offensive, and it may be best to use it as a background plant. Like the other stoppers, its fruit attracts many kinds of birds.

REDBERRY STOPPER
Eugenia confusa

HEIGHT: 20 feet

LIGHT: Shade to part sun

BLOOM: Fuzzy white flowers, ¼-inch across, appearing in leaf axils

FRUIT: Bright red, ¼-inch berries in leaf axils

LEAVES: Stiff, glossy, 2-inch tapered, elliptic leaves that hang downward

TRUNK: Straight, with light gray exfoliating bark

NATIVE RANGE: South Florida, West Indies, and the Bahamas; Zones 10–11

HABITAT: Tropical hardwood hammocks, but only scattered populations remain.

PROPAGATION: Seed

This is one of the prettiest and least common of the stoppers, with showy red berries and glossy foliage. It makes a good screening, background, or understory specimen, and, because of its narrow crown, can be used in constricted growing areas.

SPANISH STOPPER
Eugenia foetida

HEIGHT: 15–20 feet

LIGHT: Tolerates most conditions except for dense shade

BLOOMS: Tiny white, barely noticeable flowers

FRUIT: Round, black, ¼-inch fruit containing one or two seeds

LEAVES: Oval evergreen leaves, 1½ to 2 inches long and blunt-tipped

TRUNK: Slender gray-brown trunk

NATIVE RANGE: South Florida, Mexico, Central America, and the West Indies; Zones 10–11

HABITAT: Common as an understory plant in tropical hammocks

PROPAGATION: Seed

Spanish stopper is a tall, narrow shrub or small tree, good for narrow hedges where height is required. It is not a dense grower but can create a filigree effect, forming a visual barrier.

RED STOPPER
Eugenia rhombea

HEIGHT: 15 feet

LIGHT: Sun to shade

BLOOM: Fuzzy, white, ½-inch flowers in the leaf axils

FRUIT: Small, round berries turning from orange to red to black as they ripen

LEAVES: Oval, pointed, 2- to 3-inch leaves are dark green above and paler below; new growth is red.

TRUNK: The single or multistemmed trunk has smooth, light gray bark.

NATIVE RANGE: South Florida, West Indies, and Central America; Zones 10–11

HABITAT: Usually an understory plant in hardwood hammocks

PROPAGATION: Seed

This is another pretty stopper, supplying some color in the dark understory of the tropical hammock. Similar in appearance to the white stopper, it also provides food for birds and other wildlife.

INKWOOD, BUTTER-BOUGH, IRONWOOD
Exothea paniculata

HEIGHT: 40–50 feet

LIGHT: Sun to part shade

BLOOM: Open panicles of fragrant, white, ¼-inch, five-petaled flowers with yellow stamens blossoming in spring in leaf axils or at the branch tips.

FRUIT: Round, ½-inch fruit containing one seed, borne in open panicles and turning from red to purple as it ripens

LEAVES: Pinnately compound leaves are composed of two to four oval to oblong leaflets with rounded tips. Leaflets are glossy dark green, 4–5 inches long, and grow at the ends of the branches.

TRUNK: A single or multistemmed trunk with dark gray bark

NATIVE RANGE: South Florida, Central America; Zones 10–11

HABITAT: Elevated hammock areas in alkaline soil

PROPAGATION: Seed

Glossy leaves and tiny fragrant blooms make inkwood a valuable addition to the landscape. The tree provides good shade and is resistant to hurricane winds. The strong wood, which is bright red with lighter sapwood, has been used in boat construction and for tool handles, and is prized by woodworkers for making bowls, candlesticks, and such.

LOBLOLLY BAY
Gordonia lasianthus

HEIGHT: 30–40 feet

LIGHT: Sun to part shade

BLOOM: Fragrant, white, 3- to 4-inch flowers have five petals and a central cluster of yellow stamens. Individual flowers, on red stalks, are scattered over the tree in spring and summer.

FRUIT: An oval, ½-inch woody capsule containing winged seeds

LEAVES: Alternate, elliptic, pointed leaves, 4–5 inches long, have a leathery texture. They are evergreen, turning bright red before they fall.

TRUNK: Straight, with dark gray furrowed bark

NATIVE RANGE: Virginia to central Florida to Texas; Zones 7–9

HABITAT: Hammocks, wetland areas of acid soil

PROPAGATION: Seed, cuttings

Loblolly bay is a sensitive tree that with some help, such as adding native soil or peat moss to its new location when it is transplanted, can adapt to a more upland setting. It is not adaptable to alkaline soils, however. The flower display is showy and the red leaves scattered over the tree colorful. The tree is definitely worth trying in the landscape, where its columnar form does not require much space.

LIGNUM VITAE
Guaiacum sanctum

HEIGHT: 10–20 feet

LIGHT: Sun to part shade

BLOOM: Blue, star-shaped, five-petaled flowers, ¾-inch across, appear singly or in clusters at the ends of the branches. Young plants and those growing in the wild usually flower in April, but older or fertilized plants in the landscape may continue blooming all summer.

FRUIT: Yellowish fruits split to expose red flesh and black seeds.

LEAVES: Evergreen leaves are pinnately compound, with three to five pairs of shiny, dark green, oval, pointed leaflets, each about 1 inch long.

TRUNK: A short, gnarled trunk with rough, whitish bark

NATIVE RANGE: South Florida, the Bahamas, and the Caribbean; Zones 10–11

HABITAT: Originally found in open, tropical hammock woodlands in the Florida Keys, lignum vitae now is rare and endangered. It is protected in a few areas, such as Lignum Vitae Key.

PROPAGATION: Seed

Lignum vitae—the name means "tree of life"—is slow-growing, with extremely hard, heavy, resinous wood with many specialized uses, such as bearings and other machine parts. At one time it was considered a medicinal plant as well. The collecting of this valuable and endangered plant has led to its disappearance in most parts of its original habitat but it is being propagated in cultivation. It is drought- and salt-tolerant, and its clear blue flowers are a rare and esteemed color in the landscape. Cold-sensitive, it will grow as far north as coastal Palm Beach County but needs some protection in chilly weather. Good fertilization lengthens the blooming season and encourages the growth rate. A similar species, *G. officinale*, from the Caribbean area, grows in Florida but is not native.

Blolly *Guapira discolor*

Blolly *Guapira discolor*

BLOLLY, LONGLEAF BLOLLY
Guapira discolor

HEIGHT: 30 feet

LIGHT: Sun to part shade

BLOOM: Inconspicuous clustered yellow-green to purple flowers without petals, blooming in spring and summer

FRUIT: Decorative clusters of red, ⅓-inch, oval berries

LEAVES: Oblong, opposite, light green leaves, 1–2 inches in length and half as wide

TRUNK: The trunk, with pale, reddish-brown bark, may be either single-stemmed or shrub-like.

NATIVE RANGE: South Florida and the Caribbean; Zones 10–11

HABITAT: Usually found in hardwood hammocks back from the ocean, but sometimes mixed in with pine trees.

PROPAGATION: Seed

Blolly is an attractive small tree for coastal locations. It has a rounded canopy when grown in the open and a vertical growth that makes it suitable for backgrounds and screening purposes. The red fruit is very decorative and a favorite with wildlife. It also is listed as *G. longifolia*.

CRABWOOD, OYSTERWOOD
Gymnanthes lucida

HEIGHT: 20–30 feet

LIGHT: Sun to part shade

BLOOM: Tiny, fragrant, greenish-yellow flowers appear on 1- to 2-inch spikes in the leaf axils. Male flowers are abundant on spikes; female flowers occur individually on separate stalks.

FRUIT: Dark brown to black, round, ½-inch capsules, carried individually on 2-inch stems

LEAVES: Dark green, elliptical, 2- to 4-inch leaves are semi-glossy on the upper surface, alternate, with entire edges, a tough texture, and pronounced veins on the top surface. New growth is reddish.

TRUNK: Single or multi-trunked, with reddish-brown to gray fissured bark

NATIVE RANGE: South Florida, West Indies, and Mexico; Zones 10–11

HABITAT: Coastal areas, hammocks, and low woodlands

PROPAGATION: Seed

Crabwood is an attractive small evergreen shade tree, and its compact, narrow-growth habit makes it suitable for a site between buildings. It will withstand salt, drought, wind, and chilly weather. The sapwood is light yellow and the heartwood very dark. The hard, contrasting wood is a favorite with woodturners for bowls and other items. It also is listed as *Ateramnus lucida*.

Mahoe *Hibiscus tiliaceus*

Mahoe *Hibiscus tiliaceus*

MAHOE
Hibiscus tiliaceus

HEIGHT: 20–30 feet

LIGHT: Sun

BLOOM: Showy five-petaled, cupped, 2- to 3-inch flowers, yellow when they open in the morning and turning orange-pink through deep red as the day progresses

FRUIT: Long, greenish, pointed capsules that split to reveal small brown seeds

LEAVES: Heart-shaped, 4–6 inches across and glossy green

TRUNK: A dense multistemmed or single trunk with brown bark

NATIVE RANGE: South Florida and the Caribbean; Zones 10–11

HABITAT: Beachfront, low coastal areas, often associated with mangroves

PROPAGATION: Seed, cuttings

The fast-growing, salt-tolerant mahoe can provide shade on a beach, which is a rare commodity, or form a privacy barrier between beach properties where there is enough space. It will do just as nicely in inland situations. It is a very dense, sprawling, messy tree with weak wood. The flowers and leaves are edible when young.

EAST PALATKA HOLLY
Ilex X attenuata

HEIGHT: 25 feet

LIGHT: Sun to part shade

BLOOM: Small, white, inconspicuous flowers, typical of holly

FRUIT: Bright red, ¼-inch fruits, showy in late fall and winter, are often so numerous that they weigh down the branches. A male American or yaupon holly is needed nearby for the female tree to produce fruit.

LEAVES: Yellow-green to dark green, alternate, entire, 1½–3 inches in length, with occasional leaves toothed near the apex

TRUNK: Single trunk with pale to medium gray bark

NATIVE RANGE: The original tree, a natural hybrid of American and dahoon hollies, was found in the wild near East Palatka, Florida, and has since been grown throughout many of the southeastern states; Zones 8–10

HABITAT: Open woodlands

PROPAGATION: Cuttings, grafts

This is an attractive southern holly with an open growth habit, making a good hedge or small specimen tree. It is fairly drought-tolerant, prefers acid soil, and is more tender than other related hybrid hollies, such as Savannah and Fosterii, because of its southern origin. The fruit display is typical of most hollies and is a great favorite with birds.

DAHOON HOLLY
Ilex cassine

HEIGHT: 35 feet

LIGHT: Sun to part shade

BLOOM: Small white flowers with male and female blooms on different trees

FRUIT: Female trees bear bright red, ¼-inch berries that make a colorful display in fall and winter. For good fruit set, a male tree should be nearby.

LEAVES: Oblong, 5-inch-long, glossy dark green leaves are leathery and may have toothed edges.

TRUNK: A single or multiple trunk with light gray bark

NATIVE RANGE: Coastal Virginia to Louisiana, throughout Florida and the Bahamas; Zones 7–11

HABITAT: Usually found near streams or swamps

PROPAGATION: Seed, cuttings

Dahoon holly is an attractive small- to medium-sized tree with decorative red fruit and an erect growth habit that makes it suitable for small spaces. Although it occurs naturally in damp habitats, it will survive nicely on drier sites if irrigated. All holly berries are poisonous to humans, although birds feed on them without harm.

KRUG'S HOLLY, TAWNYBERRY HOLLY
Ilex krugiana

HEIGHT: 25 feet

LIGHT: Sun to part shade

BLOOM: Small white flowers, in clusters in the leaf axils, appear in winter; male and female flowers occur on separate trees.

FRUIT: Round black berries, up to ¼-inch across, ripening in summer

LEAVES: Alternate, oval, simple leaves are 1½–3 inches long, flat, leathery, and shiny with smooth edges and are unusual for a holly in having long pointed tips.

TRUNK: Single or multistemmed; bark is smooth and pale brown, turning darker as the tree ages.

NATIVE RANGE: Extreme southeastern Florida and the West Indies; Zones 10–11

HABITAT: Hammocks and pinewoods

PROPAGATION: Seed

This is an attractive small holly that may be used as an understory tree or as a specimen. It is salt-tolerant and problem-free. The glossy foliage is quite ornamental and the black fruit is unusual in an American species of holly.

AMERICAN HOLLY
Ilex opaca

HEIGHT: 30–50 feet

LIGHT: Sun to shade

BLOOM: Tiny white flowers appear in the leaf axils in summer; male and female flowers are on separate trees.

FRUIT: Orange-red berries, averaging ½-inch in diameter on female plants, appear from fall to spring.

LEAVES: Evergreen foliage is spiny, leathery, elliptic, yellow-green to dark green, 2–4 inches long and half as wide.

TRUNK: The tree can be multi- or single-stemmed. The smooth light gray trunk often is covered with lichens.

NATIVE RANGE: Coastal eastern United States into north Florida; Zones 6–9

HABITAT: A versatile tree found on acid soil sites varying from wet to fairly dry

PROPAGATION: Seed, cuttings

American holly is a cheerful tree in winter, when the female trees are in full fruit. A male tree is needed nearby for good fruit set. The showy display can last from October to spring, and the fruit is a major food source in winter for birds, which also use the tree for nesting and shelter. This popular holly is useful in the landscape as a specimen, screen or tall grouping, and as an understory tree, tolerating shade well. It has a wide range, and many improved cultivars are available for local conditions.

Yaupon holly *Ilex vomitoria*

Dwarf yaupon holly *Ilex vomitoria*

YAUPON HOLLY
Ilex vomitoria

HEIGHT: 20–25 feet

LIGHT: Sun to part shade

BLOOM: Tiny white flowers in spring and summer

FRUIT: Female trees bear heavy crops of red to orange translucent fruit. Male trees are needed nearby for pollination.

LEAVES: Small, glossy, ½-inch oval foliage

TRUNK: A single to multistemmed whitish-gray trunk with lighter twigs

NATIVE RANGE: Coastal New Jersey south to central Florida and west to Texas; Zones 7–10

HABITAT: Wet to dry areas, in woodlands and near the coast

PROPAGATION: Seed, cuttings

Yaupon is a very adaptable holly, tolerant of cold, salt spray and dense shade, and its colorful fruit is ornamental from fall to spring. It takes well to being shaped for hedges. Weeping and dwarf forms are available for foundation and specimen use. The 'Schellings Dwarf' is a fine, compact variety with reddish new growth and is used frequently in south Florida landscaping. 'Jewel' is prized for its heavy production of berries, while 'Nana,' another dwarf form, bears no fruit.

JOEWOOD
Jacquinia keyensis

HEIGHT: 15 feet

LIGHT: Sun to part shade

BLOOM: Fragrant, ½-inch, star-shaped flowers carried in terminal spikes, blooming throughout the year

FRUIT: Red to yellow, ½-inch fruits carried in drooping clusters

LEAVES: Oval to paddle-shaped, thick, light green, to 4 inches long

TRUNK: Usually seen with a multistemmed trunk with light gray bark, joewood sometimes develops a single stem and becomes more tree-like.

NATIVE RANGE: South Florida and the Bahamas, with closely related forms in the West Indies; Zones 10–11

HABITAT: Edges of tropical hammocks and near beaches

PROPAGATION: Seed

Joewood is a beautiful evergreen native that is tolerant of sun, salt, and drought, making it a good choice for seaside locations. Foliage, flowers, and fruit are all attractive. It is very slow-growing; small plants may be used as bonsai specimens. The fruit and other plant parts are poisonous if eaten.

Black ironwood *Krugiodendron ferreum*   Black ironwood *Krugiodendron ferreum*

BLACK IRONWOOD, LEADWOOD
Krugiodendron ferreum

HEIGHT: 25 feet

LIGHT: Sun to part shade

BLOOM: Greenish-yellow flowers clustered in the leaf axils, blooming in spring

FRUIT: Rounded, ¼-inch black fruit with little flesh

LEAVES: Thin, shiny green, oval to rounded opposite leaves, 1–1½ inches long

TRUNK: The trunk may be single or multistemmed, with rough, furrowed, light gray bark. The trunks of old trees tend to be gnarled.

NATIVE RANGE: South Florida, the Bahamas, West Indies, east coast of Mexico and central America; Zones 10–11

HABITAT: Tropical hammocks, open woodlands, coastal areas

PROPAGATION: Seed

This small, attractive evergreen tree has the heaviest wood of any American tree, weighing in at more than 80 pounds per cubic foot. It will sink in water. In the landscape, black ironwood is slow-growing but hardy under adverse conditions. Given fertilization, it will respond with faster growth than you might expect. Its glossy leaves reflect the light and give an airy quality to an otherwise heavy tree.

WHITE MANGROVE
Laguncularia racemosa

HEIGHT: 30–40 feet

LIGHT: Sun

BLOOM: Tiny, fragrant, white flowers in spikes arising from the leaf axils and blooming most of the year

FRUIT: Oblong, green to brownish pods to ¾-inch long, containing a single seed

LEAVES: Oval, opposite leaves, ¾-inch long, have a prominent mid-vein and are rounded at both ends. They are green on both sides and have two noticeable glands, located on the petiole below the leaf, whose purpose is to remove excess salt.

TRUNK: A light brown trunk, often multistemmed, with vertical ridges in the bark

NATIVE RANGE: South Florida, the Caribbean, and tropical America; Zones 9–11

HABITAT: Coastal and brackish water sites on the landward side of the red and black mangroves

PROPAGATION: Seed

White mangrove is an interesting small tree closely related to buttonwood. It has a massive root system that helps stabilize and hold soil, but the roots are not invasive in the landscape. Used as an evergreen hedge or windbreak, it can help protect waterfront property from erosion.

SWEETBAY MAGNOLIA
Magnolia virginiana

HEIGHT: 30 feet

LIGHT: Sun to part shade

BLOOM: Fragrant, 2- to 3-inch white flowers with up to 12 petals, appearing in spring through summer

FRUIT: A 2-inch reddish cone which opens to expose red seeds

LEAVES: Elliptic 4-inch leaves, deep green above and silvery below, are very distinctive on windy days when the silvery undersides are exposed. The tree is evergreen in the South and deciduous in the North.

TRUNK: Sweetbay magnolia generally is multistemmed in the North and single-stemmed in the South. The thin, light gray bark is exceptionally delicate.

NATIVE RANGE: Massachusetts to Florida and Texas, with a few trees found as far south as Key Largo; Zones 5–10

HABITAT: Wet, swampy areas, usually near the coast

PROPAGATION: Seed, cuttings

Sweetbay is a small, narrow-growing tree with attractive flowers and foliage and colorful fruit. It requires acid soil for best growth. Because of its thin bark, the tree should be located in a bed of ground cover or shrubs for protection against lawn mowers and weed trimmers. Several named varieties are in cultivation.

SOUTHERN CRABAPPLE
Malus angustifolia

HEIGHT: 20 feet

LIGHT: Sun to part shade

BLOOM: The extremely fragrant flowers, blooming usually in February or March in Florida, are pink in bud and pale pink to white when they open. Single blooms are about 1 inch across.

FRUIT: Yellowish-green, ¾-inch berries, ripening in early fall, are not very showy.

LEAVES: Simple, alternate, glossy, dark green leaves are narrow, 1 to 1½ inches long and ½ inch wide, terminating in a blunt point. There is little fall color.

TRUNK: Single or multistemmed, with scaly, ridged, reddish-brown bark

NATIVE RANGE: Maryland south to northern Florida and west to Texas; Zones 5–9

HABITAT: Open woodlands, river banks, often growing in thickets in moist, rich soil

PROPAGATION: Seed, suckers

This short-lived tree is spectacular in spring when the flowers perfume the air. It is susceptible to tent caterpillars in spring and cedar-apple rust that affects the foliage later in the growing season. The sour fruits are useful for making cider and preserves and are a favorite with wildlife.

RED MULBERRY
Morus rubra

HEIGHT: 30–40 feet

LIGHT: Sun

BLOOM: A catkin with tiny whitish flowers, blooming in spring

FRUIT: The 1½-inch oblong, edible fruit ripens in late spring, turning from red to black as it ripens.

LEAVES: Soft, fuzzy, variable heart-shaped leaves with toothed edges, to 6 inches long

TRUNK: A medium brown trunk with thin, ridged bark

NATIVE RANGE: Eastern North America from Massachusetts south into south Florida; Zones 4–10

HABITAT: Moist bottomlands; populations widely scattered in the wild

PROPAGATION: Seed, cuttings

Red mulberry is highly cold-tolerant. In the north, the tree is deciduous; in south Florida it loses its leaves for a brief period in winter. It is somewhat valued as a fruit tree in south Florida, and everbearing cultivars are available at nurseries. It is best used in an orchard setting or as a background tree because of the messiness and odor of fallen, decaying fruits, although birds and other wildlife usually eat most of them before they drop.

SIMPSON STOPPER
Myrcianthes fragrans

HEIGHT: 20 feet

LIGHT: Sun to shade

BLOOM: Fuzzy, white, fragrant, ¼-inch flowers blooming in summer

FRUIT: Red-orange, ⅓-inch berries

LEAVES: Opposite, deep green, fragrant, oval, ½–1 inch long, somewhat glossy

TRUNK: A slender single or multistemmed trunk with light tan, exfoliating bark

NATIVE RANGE: South Florida and West Indies; Zones 10–11

HABITAT: Scattered populations found in tropical hammocks and near the coast

PROPAGATION: Seed

This is one of our best small trees, with ornamental bark, fragrant flowers and decorative orange fruit that attracts birds. It is dense and shrub-like in a sunny location, taller and looser when grown in shade. Outstanding specimens may be seen at the north entrance to the Broward General Medical Center in Fort Lauderdale.

LANCEWOOD
Nectandra coriacea

HEIGHT: 30–35 feet

LIGHT: Sun to part shade

BLOOM: White, ½-inch flowers borne in open panicles, mainly in spring

FRUIT: Blue-black, ½-inch berries carried in orange, cup-like bases

LEAVES: Smooth-edged, fragrant, evergreen leaves have a yellow midrib, vary from elliptical to oval in shape, and tend to droop.

TRUNK: Reddish-brown and sometimes corky

NATIVE RANGE: South Florida, tropical America, and the West Indies; Zones 10–11

HABITAT: Tropical woodlands close to the coast

PROPAGATION: Seed

The moderate size of lancewood and its undemanding character make it a potentially valuable shade tree for today's smaller residential yards. Its flowers are a good source of honey and the wood is prized for cabinetry.

OGEECHEE LIME, OGEECHEE TUPELO
Nyssa ogeche

HEIGHT: 15 feet

LIGHT: Sun to part shade

BLOOM: Inconspicuous greenish male flowers appear in spring in round clusters; female flowers are carried individually on short stalks.

FRUIT: Red to purplish, 1½-inch, plum-shaped edible fruit ripening over the summer

LEAVES: Heart-shaped to oval, 3- to 6-inch alternate leaves, smooth above and softly fuzzy beneath, with rounded tips

TRUNK: Scaly, dark brown bark on a shrubby or single-stemmed trunk

NATIVE RANGE: Coastal South Carolina to central Florida; Zones 7–9

HABITAT: Wetlands, often found with other water lovers such as bald cypress, red maple, and sweetbay magnolia.

PROPAGATION: Seed

A wetland situation suits this small tupelo best. The tree has a rounded canopy and the fall color, ranging from red to purple, can be striking. In the wild it may form dense thickets. The fruits sometimes are used as a substitute for limes and for making preserves and beverages; they also are enjoyed by wildlife. The flowers produce a superior honey.

Dr. Edward F. Gilman

SOURWOOD, LILY-OF-THE-VALLEY TREE, SORREL TREE
Oxydendrum arboreum

HEIGHT: 30 feet

LIGHT: Sun to part shade

BLOOM: Drooping panicles of fragrant, white, bell-like flowers, ¼-inch across appear in early summer (usually June or July) after most other trees are finished blooming. The panicle is up to 10 inches long and resembles a spray of lily of the valley.

FRUIT: A yellow to brown capsule that hangs on the tree through the winter

LEAVES: Oblong, 4–8 inches long with a pointed tip; shiny, dark green above and paler beneath, they turn red, yellow, or even purple in autumn.

TRUNK: Single- or multi-trunked, with dark reddish brown to black, deeply cut bark

NATIVE RANGE: Virginia to western Florida and coastal Louisiana; Zones 5–9

HABITAT: Acid, well-drained soils on steep stream banks or ridges

PROPAGATION: Seed

Sourwood is a beautiful, drought-tolerant, slow-growing native tree with showy, fragrant flowers, brilliant, long-lasting fall color, and an attractive pyramidal form. Flowers are a nectar source for high-quality honey. In its yellow stage, the fruit has the visual effect of flowers. The common name comes from the sour taste of the foliage.

Redbay *Persea borbonia*

Redbay *Persea borbonia*

REDBAY
Persea borbonia

HEIGHT: 40 feet

LIGHT: Sun to part shade

BLOOM: Small, inconspicuous, clustered, whitish flowers in spring

FRUIT: Blue-black, ½-inch fruit on a red stem

LEAVES: Fragrant, evergreen, lance-shaped to oblong, pointed 2- to 4-inch leaves, whitish on the underside, often infected with prominent black or brown nipple galls

TRUNK: A single or multistemmed tree with gray-brown, scaly, ridged bark

NATIVE RANGE: Delaware to south Florida; Zones 7–10

HABITAT: Coastal lowlands and interior swamps

PROPAGATION: Seed

Redbay, which is drought- and salt-tolerant, prefers sandy, acid soil but is adaptable. This avocado relative is best used in a background planting because of disfiguring galls caused by insects. The foliage is fragrant and may be used in cooking in the manner of bay leaves, and the purple fruit is attractive to birds.

BITTERBUSH
Picramnia pentandra

HEIGHT: 10–15 feet

LIGHT: Sun to part shade

BLOOM: Open clusters of inconspicuous, greenish-white flowers blooming in summer, with male and female flowers on separate plants

FRUIT: Fleshy, ½-inch, oblong fruit, turning from red to black as it ripens

LEAVES: Alternate, pinnately compound leaves are 8–14 inches long, with five to nine leaflets and a terminal leaflet. Individual leaflets are oval and pointed, 2–4 inches long, shiny dark green above and somewhat leathery, with conspicuous veins. The foliage is somewhat similar to that of its relative, the paradise tree.

TRUNK: Yellow-brown bark is smooth and thin and bitter to the taste.

NATIVE RANGE: South Florida, the Caribbean, and tropical America; Zones 10–11

HABITAT: Along the seacoast in sandy, well-drained soil

PROPAGATION: Seed

The slender form and narrow canopy of this large shrub or small tree makes it suitable for confined spaces. Its blossoms attract bees, which make a good honey from the nectar, and the bark and leaves are used in the Caribbean to treat fever.

SAND PINE
Pinus clausa

HEIGHT: 30–40 feet

LIGHT: Sun

BLOOM: Inconspicuous, brownish male flowers appear at the branch tips; female flowers, which are brownish and globe-shaped, appear lower on the branch, below the male blooms.

FRUIT: Brown, 2- to 3½-inch clustered cones open slowly over a four-year period, releasing flat brown, winged seeds.

LEAVES: Dark green needles, 2–3½ inches long, flexible and soft, and carried in bundles of two

TRUNK: Straight, single trunk has dark brown, plated bark; young branches may be gray or reddish. The trees have a tendency to lean after wind storms.

NATIVE RANGE: Florida and extreme southern Alabama; Zones 8–10

HABITAT: Sandy, well-drained ridges and hills near coastal areas, often in association with oaks in mixed stands

PROPAGATION: Seed

The sand pine is one of the major components in the sand-scrub habitat favored by the gopher tortoise and other endangered species. It does best when not disturbed and left unirrigated. The root system is very sensitive to any sort of traffic. Choctawhachee pine *(P. clausa* var. *immuginata)* is a variety of sand pine found mainly on Florida's west coast.

BLACKBEAD
Pithecellobium guadalupense

HEIGHT: 20 feet

LIGHT: Sun to light shade

BLOOM: Fuzzy, rounded flowers, carried individually or in clusters, are pink or white and average an inch across.

FRUIT: Reddish-brown, 2- to 4-inch pods are curving and spiralled, opening when ripe to expose a red interior with glossy black seeds.

LEAVES: Leaves are pinnately compound, with two pairs of rounded 1- to 3-inch leaflets. The leaf stalks are longer than those of the leaflets. New growth is pinkish.

TRUNK: Generally a multistemmed shrub or small tree with rough, brown bark

NATIVE RANGE: South Florida, the Caribbean, Mexico and northern South America; Zones 10–11

HABITAT: Hammock edges, dunes, fields in coral or sandy, dry soil

PROPAGATION: Seed

Blackbead is an attractive, small evergreen tree or large shrub, useful where little else will grow. It's easy to establish and needs little care. It attracts butterflies, which lay their eggs on its leaves, and the seed pods are colorful when ripe and open. The closely related catclaw, *P. unguis-cati,* has greenish-yellow flowers and two thin, sharp spines at the base of each leaf. It will serve the same landscape purposes as blackbead but is less user-friendly, although its thorny nature makes it a particularly efficient property barrier.

AMERICAN PLUM
Prunus americana

HEIGHT: 15–20 feet

LIGHT: Sun to part shade

BLOOM: Small clusters of two to five white, very fragrant flowers, about ⅓-inch across, blooming in early spring

FRUIT: Rounded to elongated ¾- to 1-inch long fruits, turning orange to red in late summer to fall

LEAVES: Deciduous 2½- to 4-inch leaves are alternate, oval and pointed, sometimes with double serrations along the margin.

TRUNK: Single or shrubby, with dark reddish-brown bark that initially is smooth but forms plates with age

NATIVE RANGE: Throughout the eastern and midwestern states and into northern Florida; Zones 3–8

HABITAT: Sandy or rocky soils in old fields, edges of woodlands, and along fences and streams

PROPAGATION: Seed, cuttings, suckers

Its flowers and fruits make this small tree attractive in two seasons. It is thorny and might be used effectively as a barrier or to control foot traffic, but it is fairly short-lived. The fruits are excellent for jam, jelly, and pies and also have great value for attracting birds and other wildlife.

Chickasaw plum *Prunus angustifolia*   Chickasaw plum *Prunus angustifolia*

CHICKASAW PLUM
Prunus angustifolia

HEIGHT: 10 feet or more

LIGHT: Sun to part shade

BLOOM: Fragrant, ½-inch, white, five-petaled flowers carried in small clusters in the leaf axils, blooming in spring

FRUIT: Shiny red to yellow edible fruit, about ½-inch across

LEAVES: Glossy green, lance-shaped, 1–3 inches long, with a pronounced tip

TRUNK: Single- or multi-trunked; old stems have reddish-brown bark with long furrows. The plant tends to sucker and can form thickets.

NATIVE RANGE: Delaware, south to central Florida and west to Texas; Zones 5–9

HABITAT: Open fields, edges of woods, bottomlands, roadsides, and fence rows

PROPAGATION: Seed, division of suckers

Chickasaw plum's showy early spring flowers produce a brief but attractive display. This large shrub or small tree offers shelter for wildlife and its fruit is a favorite with animals and birds. The plant's suckering habit makes it useful for soil stabilization and erosion prevention. The foliage often is attacked by webworms, which do no permanent damage but are unattractive.

CAROLINA LAURELCHERRY, CHERRY LAUREL
Prunus caroliniana

HEIGHT: 20–30 feet

LIGHT: Full sun to part shade

BLOOM: Heavily fragrant white flowers, five-petaled and about ¼-inch wide, are borne in the leaf axils on short, 2- to 3-inch racemes in February or March.

FRUIT: Shiny, black, ½-inch fruits

LEAVES: Shiny, dark green, 2–3 inches long, oblong with a pointed tip, usually with smooth edges although leaves on young plants may be serrated

TRUNK: Single or multistemmed, dark gray, brown, or black trunk

NATIVE RANGE: Virginia to central Florida and west to Louisiana; Zones 7–9

HABITAT: Hedgerows, edges of woods or fields, untended landscapes

PROPAGATION: Seed, cuttings

Carolina laurelcherry is a small, decorative evergreen tree sometimes used for hedges and screening, although, as a foundation planting, it soon outgrows its usefulness. Flowers are ornamental, but the fragrance does not appeal to everyone. The tree prefers well-drained, moist soil, either acid or alkaline. Its excessive seeding is the main drawback; the fruit is a favorite with birds, which disseminate seeds widely, causing seedlings to appear everywhere. It also is soft-wooded and may break up in snow, ice, or wind.

WEST INDIAN CHERRY, MYRTLE LAURELCHERRY
Prunus myrtifolia

HEIGHT: 20–30 feet

LIGHT: Sun to part shade

BLOOM: Racemes, 1–3 inches long, of small white flowers with yellow centers, blooming in autumn

FRUIT: Open clusters of round, ½-inch fruits, orange-brown when ripe in the summer

LEAVES: Alternate, evergreen leaves, glossy light green above and paler green below, oval, pointed, 2–5 inches long with wavy edges

TRUNK: Reddish-gray, with shallow cracks

NATIVE RANGE: South Florida and the West Indies; Zones 10–11

HABITAT: Open woodlands and the edges of streams and ponds

PROPAGATION: Seed

This is a nice accent or specimen plant with a modest flower display, decorative fruit, and glossy foliage that adds interest throughout the year. The fruit is a food source for many birds and small animals. Leaves and seeds are poisonous to humans.

POP ASH, HOP TREE, WAFER ASH
Ptelea trifoliata

HEIGHT: 15–20 feet

LIGHT: Sun to dense shade

BLOOM: Clustered, fragrant, greenish-white flowers to ½-inch in diameter blooming in spring

FRUIT: A round, flattened, winged samara, to 1 inch in diameter

LEAVES: Deciduous, alternate, trifoliate leaves are glossy green above and smooth below; leaflets are oval and average about 3½ inches in length. When bruised, they have an aromatic scent.

TRUNK: Shrubby or tree-like, with smooth, dark gray bark; sometimes warty growths, like those on hackberry, are present. The tree may send out suckers, forming clumps.

NATIVE RANGE: Eastern U.S., from upstate New York west to Minnesota and south into central Florida; Zones 3–9

HABITAT: Usually found as an understory plant in open woodlands

PROPAGATION: Seed, root cuttings

Pop ash is a dense shrub or small tree suitable for screening along property lines. It is very adaptable and tolerant of a wide variety of cultural and light conditions, but prefers well-drained sites. The clustered flat seeds are an attractive feature, and once were used like hops in beer brewing.

BLUEJACK OAK
Quercus incana

HEIGHT: 20–30 feet

LIGHT: Sun to part shade

BLOOM: Male catkins are 2–3 inches long and yellowish-green, appearing near the branch tips; female flowers are inconspicuous.

FRUIT: Globe-shaped acorn, ½-inch long, is held by a shallow, bright brownish-red cup that just covers the base of the fruit.

LEAVES: Deciduous leaves, 2–5 inches long and lance-shaped, are fuzzy, blue-green to gray-green above, with distinct veining below.

TRUNK: The dark gray to blackish bark develops distinctive rough plates as it ages. The trunk is low-branching and may be multistemmed or shrub-like.

NATIVE RANGE: Southeastern Virginia to north Florida and central Texas; Zones 7–9

HABITAT: Sandhills, in association with other oaks, longleaf pine, and persimmon

PROPAGATION: Seed

Bluejack oak, a shrubby tree, is valuable for wildlife cover and is a reliable producer of small acorns, which are a good food source for many birds and animals. It is drought-tolerant, will do well in most kinds of soil, and needs little attention.

TURKEY OAK
Quercus laevis

HEIGHT: 30–40 feet

LIGHT: Sun to part shade

BLOOM: Yellowish male catkins, 3–5 inches long, are noticeable in early spring; female flowers are inconspicuous.

FRUIT: 1-inch long, light brown acorn, with the cup enclosing a third of the nut

LEAVES: Glossy, greenish-yellow leaves, 4–12 inches long, have three to five deeply cut lobes and are sharply pointed at the tip. Normally the leaves are wider above the middle and downy on the underside.

TRUNK: Rough, dark gray to black bark, furrowed and ridged

NATIVE RANGE: Coastal South Carolina through central Florida to southern Alabama; Zones 8–9

HABITAT: Sandy ridges, bluffs, and hills near the coast

PROPAGATION: Seed

This is a fast-growing tree with spreading branches and an open crown, and often is found growing with sand pine. It is useful for stabilizing sandy areas and providing food and cover for birds and other wildlife. Turkey oak will grow under extremely dry, sterile conditions.

MYRTLE OAK
Quercus myrtifolia

HEIGHT: 25–30 feet

LIGHT: Sun to part shade

BLOOM: Typical yellow-green oak catkins

FRUIT: Tiny, ⅓-inch acorns with the cup covering a third of the nut

LEAVES: Leaves are oval, 1–2 inches long, with rounded ends and entire margins. They are evergreen and somewhat leathery, shiny and dark green above and paler below.

TRUNK: Shrubby and often multistemmed, with dark brown, rather smooth bark

NATIVE RANGE: Southern South Carolina to central coastal Florida; Zones 8–9

HABITAT: Found mainly along the coast with sand pine and turkey oak in very dry, sandy soils

PROPAGATION: Seed

As a small tree or large shrub, myrtle oak is useful for stabilizing drifting sand and is tolerant of extreme drought and poor soil. It can spread to form dense colonies that provide excellent cover for wildlife. The acorns are a valued food source for many animals.

Red mangrove *Rhizophora mangle*

Red mangrove *Rhizophora mangle*

RED MANGROVE
Rhizophora mangle

HEIGHT: 30 feet

LIGHT: Sun to part shade

BLOOM: Pale yellow, four-petaled flowers, about 1 inch across, appearing most of the year

FRUIT: A brown berry germinates on the tree, producing a long pod with a new plant sprouting from the top; this falls into the water, floating until it reaches a muddy bottom where it takes root.

LEAVES: Thick, oval, dark green and glossy, 2–6 inches long and 1–2 inches across, narrower near the base

TRUNK: Prop roots grow from the smooth brown trunk to the mud below. These roots expand, catching soil and debris and gradually building up land.

NATIVE RANGE: South Florida, throughout the tropics; Zones 10–11

HABITAT: Red mangrove prefers brackish, shallow bays, forming thickets and sometimes even islands.

PROPAGATION: Seed

Red mangrove is an extremely valuable tree, serving as a nursery for small fish and crabs, a natural shock absorber against storms, and a builder of land. On waterfront properties, its prop roots and dense foliage offer good protection from wind and storm surges. While red mangrove is not on the state's endangered species list, it is of such importance to the environment that removal from its natural habitat usually is regulated by law.

SHINING SUMAC, FLAMELEAF SUMAC
Rhus copallina

HEIGHT: 15–20 feet

LIGHT: Sun

BLOOM: A stiff panicle, 4–8 inches long and 3–4 inches across, of small, five-petaled, whitish-green flowers, blooming at the branch ends in summer

FRUIT: Female trees produce small, fuzzy, bright red fruit that ripens in fall.

LEAVES: Alternate compound leaves have nine to 21 oblong, pointed leaflets, 2–4 inches long, glossy dark green above and fuzzy beneath. The petioles are winged, an identifying feature.

TRUNK: Medium brown, thin-barked, with younger stems reddish and fuzzy; the open growth and suckering habit are typical of sumac.

NATIVE RANGE: Maine to Minnesota, south to central Florida and Texas; Zones 4–9

HABITAT: Open, sunny, well-drained areas such as banks, hillsides, railroad beds, and other pioneering locations

PROPAGATION: Seed, suckers

Shining sumac is an aggressive shrub or small tree, useful for erosion control or suitable in large, naturalized garden areas where the persistent suckering is not a problem. Individual plants vary from upright to spreading. Sumac tolerates heat and cold, but not salt. Its beauty is in its brilliant red fall color. Birds also are attracted by the long-lasting fruit. This is a non-poisonous relative of poison ivy.

COASTAL PLAIN WILLOW
Salix caroliniana

HEIGHT: 25 feet

LIGHT: Sun

BLOOM: Small greenish catkins at the ends of the branches, blooming in spring

FRUIT: Elongated capsule that opens, releasing silky, hairy seeds that are distributed by the wind

LEAVES: Lance-shaped, deciduous green leaves to 4 inches in length

TRUNK: Rough, dark brown trunk, often multistemmed

NATIVE RANGE: Southeastern U.S. to south Florida; Zones 6–10

HABITAT: Swamps, river and stream banks, and other moist locations

PROPAGATION: Seed, cuttings

Carolina willow is a small, fast-growing tree that provides nesting and cover in open areas like the Everglades. It is a pioneer tree, stabilizing stream banks and helping to control erosion. In the landscape, it can be used as a background plant for wet sites or as a vertical element along waterways. Give it full sun and a moist but well-drained soil.

Wingleaf soapberry *Sapindus saponaria*

Wingleaf soapberry *Sapindus saponaria*

WINGLEAF SOAPBERRY
Sapindus saponaria

HEIGHT: 20–30 feet

LIGHT: Sun to part shade

BLOOM: Open clusters of small white flowers, appearing at the ends of branches in winter and spring

FRUIT: Yellow, ½-inch fruit are carried in clusters; the black seeds are poisonous.

LEAVES: Leaves are pinnately compound, with distinctive winged petioles. Each leaf usually has three to six pairs of 2- to 4-inch leaflets, smooth-edged and light green, darkening to medium green as they age.

TRUNK: Gray bark, dividing into scaly plates with age

NATIVE RANGE: Central and south Florida, the Bahamas, West Indies, and tropical America; Zones 9–11

HABITAT: Usually found in coastal hammocks

PROPAGATION: Seed

This is a nice, quick-growing small shade tree, both salt- and drought-tolerant. The foliage is deciduous in the northern part of its range, evergreen in the south. The fruit, when rubbed in water, produces a lather that can be used as a soap substitute.

SASSAFRAS
Sassafras albidum

HEIGHT: 40 feet

LIGHT: Sun to part shade

BLOOM: Yellow racemes of flowers, averaging 1–2 inches long, appear in early spring; male and female flowers usually are on separate trees.

FRUIT: Female trees produce ½-inch, oval, blue-black fruit, ripening in late summer. The stalk bearing the fruit is bright red and very showy.

LEAVES: Foliage is quite variable in shape, with three-lobed, oval, and mitten-shaped leaves appearing on the same tree. They are 4–7 inches long and 2–4 inches across, with an aromatic odor.

TRUNK: Reddish-brown bark is deeply indented, with flat ridges between the indentations. The tree may be clump-forming or have a single trunk.

NATIVE RANGE: Maine to north Florida and west to Texas; Zones 4–9

HABITAT: A pioneer tree that often appears in abandoned fields and along fence rows and the edges of woods

PROPAGATION: Seed, root cuttings

Sassafras, a deciduous tree, is noted for its spectacular fall color, with leaves turning shades of yellow, purple, orange, and red. Its flowers are small but attractive close up. The tree prefers acid, well-drained soils but is quite adaptable. It can be invasive because it spreads readily by root suckers, which should be removed as they appear. The extract from the roots has long been used for tea and flavoring, but its use has been discouraged lately as sassafras oil is reported to be a carcinogen. It also is a host plant for butterflies.

FLORIDA BOXWOOD
Schaefferia frutescens

HEIGHT: 15–20 feet

LIGHT: Sun to part shade

BLOOM: Greenish-white, ½-inch flowers with four petals, borne in small clusters in the leaf axils in spring

FRUIT: Red, ¼-inch fruit with two seeds

LEAVES: Oval, alternate leaves, 2–4 inches long, wavy and pale green, have smooth margins.

TRUNK: A multistemmed large shrub or small tree; older bark is light gray and warty.

NATIVE RANGE: South Florida, the Caribbean, and tropical America; Zones 10–11

HABITAT: Near or on the coast, on sandy soil above the high tide line; edges of coastal hammocks

PROPAGATION: Seed

Because of its salt tolerance, Florida boxwood is a good choice for seaside landscaping, but it looks best when it is given some shelter from salt winds. The bright yellow wood is hard and heavy, and sought after by woodcarvers.

FLORIDA TREMA
Trema micranthum

HEIGHT: 20–25 feet

LIGHT: Sun to part shade

BLOOM: Clusters of yellow-green flowers in the leaf axils, blooming all year

FRUIT: Round, orange, ¼-inch berries clustered in the leaf axils

LEAVES: Oval, alternate, dull green, ¾-inch leaves with fine-toothed margins

TRUNK: Single or multistemmed, with brown bark

NATIVE RANGE: Coastal south Florida, West Indies, tropical America; Zones 10–11

HABITAT: Coastal hammocks and edges of woods

PROPAGATION: Seed

This small, sprawling tree or large shrub is useful as a large screening plant for the edge of a property. The colorful fruit contrasts well with the dull leaves, and attracts birds and other wildlife.

WINGED ELM
Ulmus alata

HEIGHT: 30–40 feet

LIGHT: Sun to part shade

BLOOM: Small clusters of inconspicuous, reddish-green flowers in late winter

FRUIT: Winged, ⅓-inch long, rounded and flattened, dry brown fruit covered with hairs

LEAVES: Small, lanceolate leaves are 1–2½ inches long, alternate, and with double-toothed edges. They are dark green above and paler green below, turning yellowish in the fall.

TRUNK: Gray to red-brown bark, shallowly furrowed

NATIVE RANGE: Southeastern and south-central U.S. into central Florida; Zones 6–9

HABITAT: Stream banks, fence rows, low hillsides, and bluffs

PROPAGATION: Seed

Winged elm is a nicely rounded, smallish shade or street tree whose main characteristic is the corky wings appearing along the twigs. The delicate texture of the foliage makes it an attractive alternative to many coarser shade trees. Its seeds provide food for birds. The tree is fast-growing, drought-tolerant, and adaptable to many soil types, but some specimens are prone to powdery mildew, which turns the foliage almost white late in the growing season. Select a mildew-resistant form.

SPARKLEBERRY, FARKLEBERRY
Vaccinium arboreum

HEIGHT: To 20 feet

LIGHT: Sun to part shade

BLOOM: Clusters of fragrant, white, urn-shaped flowers, ½-inch long, blooming in early spring

FRUIT: Shiny, round, black, seedy, ¼-inch berries, ripening in fall

LEAVES: Evergreen, shiny, alternate, round to oval, to 2 inches long

TRUNK: Multistemmed or single trunk; bark is brown and flaking.

NATIVE RANGE: Virginia west to Illinois, south to northern and central Florida and Texas; Zones 6–9

HABITAT: Hammocks, sandy wooded areas

PROPAGATION: Seed, cuttings

The largest of the native blueberries, sparkleberry is grown more as an ornamental tree than for its fruit, prized for its glossy foliage, attractive bark and small but attractive flowers. It is slow-growing, and requires moist but well-drained acid soil; otherwise, it is very undemanding and needs little care. In cool climates the leaves turn red to purple in the fall, when birds feed on the small berries.

WALTER VIBURNUM
Viburnum obovatum

HEIGHT: 20 feet

LIGHT: Sun to shade

BLOOM: Small white flowers in a flat-topped cluster carried on a very short stalk, appearing in early spring

FRUIT: Berries, ⅛-inch in diameter, in open clusters, ranging from red to black and ripening over the summer.

LEAVES: Oval, evergreen, 1- to 1½-inch-long leaves have rounded tips and smooth edges and are widest near the center. They are glossy dark green above, pale green and spotted on the underside.

TRUNK: Rough, reddish-brown bark, divided into plates as the tree ages

NATIVE RANGE: Coastal South Carolina through south Florida; Zones 8–10

HABITAT: Wet forests, coastal swamps and hammocks near the coast, less frequently in upland sites

PROPAGATION: Seed, cuttings

Walter viburnum is a small, neat, colorful tree or large shrub with a rich, if short-lived, flower display and show of fruit, and a favored food of birds and small animals. Birds also like its dense, shrubby branches for nesting and shelter. It will serve as a small shade tree or, if left unpruned, as a tall, loose screen; it may send out suckers, forming a thicket. It takes well to being sheared and will withstand dry conditions. Various forms, both upright or spreading, are available commercially.

WILD LIME
Zanthoxylum fagara

HEIGHT: 25 feet

LIGHT: Sun to part shade

BLOOM: Insignificant green, clustering flowers, blooming most of the year

FRUIT: Round brown fruit to ⅛ inch across, ripening in summer and fall

LEAVES: Shiny, pinnate evergreen foliage, with fine-textured 1-inch leaflets and winged petioles

TRUNK: Usually multistemmed, with rough, dark, gray-brown bark with recurved spines

NATIVE RANGE: South Florida, tropical America, the Caribbean and Bahamas; Zones 10–11

HABITAT: Understory or edges of woods

PROPAGATION: Seed, cuttings

Wild lime, related to citrus, is easily recognized by its winged petioles and zig-zag branches. It is a small tree or large shrub whose spiny branches serve well for security purposes or as an effective property line barrier to discourage unwanted traffic. In the West Indies, the leaves, twigs, and bark are used in medicine, especially to relieve toothache.

SATINWOOD, YELLOW-HEART, YELLOWWOOD
Zanthoxylum flavum

HEIGHT: 15–20 feet

LIGHT: Sun to part shade

BLOOM: Terminal, open-branched clusters of many tiny, greenish-white flowers appear on both male and female trees in summer.

FRUIT: Small, brown, oval fruit opens to expose a single black seed.

LEAVES: Evergreen leaves, 4–10 inches long, are alternate and pinnately compound, with five to nine leaflets; the oval, shiny green leaflets are 1–3 inches long.

TRUNK: The multistemmed, light gray trunk is smooth or lightly roughened, and not spiny like many of its prickly ash relatives.

NATIVE RANGE: Florida Keys, the Bahamas and West Indies; Zone 11

HABITAT: Open woodlands, edges of fields

PROPAGATION: Seed

Satinwood is an attractive, small shade tree with delicate foliage. In its native habitat, it is rare and endangered because of its valuable wood, sought for use in fine cabinetry, inlay work and paneling. The yellow to orange wood is beautifully figured and develops a smooth finish after polishing.

A related species, *Zanthoxylum clava-herculis*, called Hercules' club, southern prickly ash, or toothache tree, grows from Virginia into southern Florida. It is deciduous, coarse-textured and salt-tolerant, but is very thorny and tends to sucker.

SHRUBS

PIPESTEM, FETTERBUSH
Agarista populifolia

HEIGHT: To 12 feet

LIGHT: Semi-shade

BLOOM: Heavy clusters of small, white, urn-shaped flowers similar to blueberry and other members of the heath family, blooming from spring to early fall

FRUIT: Small brownish berries

LEAVES: Oval to lance-shaped, alternate, 2- to 4-inch leaves are bright, glossy green; young leaves have a reddish tint.

TRUNK: Arching green stems

NATIVE RANGE: South Carolina through north and central Florida; Zones 7–9

HABITAT: Hammocks, damp sites, creek banks

PROPAGATION: Seed, cuttings

Also listed as *Leucothoe populifolia*, pipestem is a graceful evergreen shrub for shady areas, especially along the banks of a river or pond. A good screening plant, it does best in sandy, rather acid soils with good irrigation. Cutting back the old stems helps keep it vigorous.

MARLBERRY
Ardisia escallonioides

HEIGHT: To 20 feet

LIGHT: Part to full shade

BLOOM: Clusters of ¼-inch, fragrant white flowers, streaked with red or purple, appearing from spring to fall

FRUIT: Rounded, shiny, purplish-black, ¼-inch fruits

LEAVES: Oblong or lance-shaped, dark green and glossy, up to 6 inches long

TRUNK: Thin trunk with gray bark

NATIVE RANGE: South Florida and the West Indies; Zones 10–11

HABITAT: Hammocks, where it is a common understory plant

PROPAGATION: Seed, cuttings

Marlberry, which may be used as an evergreen shrub or small tree, makes a beautiful screening or background plant for shady sites; it will not be at its best if planted in full sun. It is salt-tolerant and generally undemanding, and its fruits will bring birds to your garden.

SALTBUSH, GROUNDSEL
Baccharis halimifolia

HEIGHT: 10–12 feet

LIGHT: Sun

BLOOM: Small, white to yellowish, rayless flowers carried in large clusters at the ends of the branches

FRUIT: White fruits with silky hairs, blooming in late summer and fall

LEAVES: Gray-green, oblong leaves, 2 to 3 inches long, are toothed near the ends. The tree is deciduous in the North, but from central Florida southward it tends to retain its leaves.

TRUNK: Multistemmed, brown trunk

NATIVE RANGE: Massachusetts to Texas, including all of Florida; Zones 5–11

HABITAT: Salt water marshlands and roadsides near the coast

PROPAGATION: Seed, cuttings

Baccharis is an extremely hardy plant, able to grow in almost any soil and tolerating salt, heat, and cold. The fluffy seed clusters produced by the female plants make quite a showy display; while lovely to look at, they can be messy when wind blows them about the neighborhood.

LOCUSTBERRY, KEY BRYSONIMA
Brysonima lucida

HEIGHT: 15 feet

LIGHT: Sun to part shade

BLOOM: Small, ¼-inch flowers are borne in elongated clusters of 6 to 12 blooms in spring and early summer; white and pink when they open, they change to yellow and deep pink as they age.

FRUIT: Rounded, brown, ¼-inch fruits, ripening in summer

LEAVES: Opposite, 1- to 2-inch leaves are spatulate with rounded tips, shiny dark green above and pale green underneath.

TRUNK: Multistemmed and spreading, with smooth, light brown bark

NATIVE RANGE: South Florida, the Caribbean, and the Bahamas; Zones 10–11

HABITAT: Open pine woods, edges of hammocks

PROPAGATION: Seed

Locustberry is one of those in-between-sized plants that can function either as a large specimen or small tree. Its wide-spreading branches make it a useful small shade tree, and removing the lower branches will allow the attractive trunk to be displayed. Its colorful flowers and shiny leaves also contribute to a pleasing picture, and birds are attracted to its fruit.

Beautyberry *Callicarpa americana*

Beautyberry (white form)
Callicarpa americana

BEAUTYBERRY
Callicarpa americana

HEIGHT: 5–6 feet

LIGHT: Part sun to full shade

BLOOM: Small, clustered, pale purple blooms, appearing in spring and summer

FRUIT: Small, round, bright purple fruits clustered along the stems and lasting throughout the year

LEAVES: Oval, pointed, opposite, somewhat rough, light green leaves to 6 inches in length

TRUNK: Multistemmed with light brown, open-growing, arching stems

NATIVE RANGE: Southeastern U.S., throughout Florida; Zones 8–11

HABITAT: Pine woods, open hammocks

PROPAGATION: Seed, cuttings

A colorful plant when in flower or fruit, beautyberry is useful for shady sites and dry areas. Tolerant of drought and cold weather, it is one of the best ways to attract birds, which love the fruit. Butterflies also are attracted to the flowers. Plant it in front of all-green shrubs for its bright color, and trim the plant back in late winter to keep it from sprawling untidily. There is a less common form of beautyberry, also native, with white berries; planting the two forms together creates a striking display in the garden.

Dr. Edward F. Gilman

SWEETSHRUB, CAROLINA ALLSPICE, STRAWBERRY-BUSH
Calycanthus floridus

HEIGHT: 7–8 feet

LIGHT: Sun to shade

BLOOM: The 2-inch, reddish-brown flowers are not particularly showy, but have a strong and distinctively sweet strawberry fragrance. They bloom in late March in north Florida, but may appear as late as June or July in the northern parts of the plant's range.

FRUIT: An urn-shaped capsule ripening in late summer to early fall

LEAVES: Deciduous leaves are elliptic, 3–5 inches long and pointed, fuzzy below and somewhat rough-textured above. Dark green on the upper surface and gray-green beneath, they turn yellow in fall.

TRUNK: Multistemmed, brownish-gray bark; stems have a camphor-like odor when crushed.

NATIVE RANGE: Virginia to central Florida; Zones 5–9

HABITAT: Varying; it prefers moist, rich soils but adapts to poorer conditions.

PROPAGATION: Seed, cuttings

Sweetshrub is a valuable landscaping choice for north and central Florida, particularly if you have a shady spot. It tolerates a wide variety of environments, from sun to shade and alkaline to acid soils, but does not do well in a dry situation. The plant is pest-free and would be ideal for a mixed border or near a seating area where the spring fragrance can be enjoyed. Buy the plant when it is in bloom to check the strength of the flower fragrance, as some individuals have little or no fragrance.

Jamaican caper *Capparis cynophallophora*   Limber caper C. *flexuosa*

JAMAICAN CAPER
Capparis cynophallophora

HEIGHT: 15 feet

LIGHT: Sun to part shade

BLOOM: Fragrant flowers have four white petals and many ½-inch-long drooping stamens, and appear in April and May. The stamens are white when they open, turning purple as they age.

FRUIT: A brown pod, to 1 foot long, that splits open to reveal glossy brown seeds

LEAVES: Leathery, oval, 2- to 3-inch leaves, rounded at the tips, shiny light green above and slightly rusty-colored below

TRUNK: Smooth, straight trunk with reddish-brown bark

NATIVE RANGE: South Florida, the Caribbean, and tropical America; Zones 10–11

HABITAT: Edges of tropical hammocks

PROPAGATION: Seed, cuttings

Jamaican caper is one of Florida's finest ornamentals, serving as a specimen, screen, or accent plant. The columnar growth and rounded crown mean minimal pruning to maintain a neat, regular shape. It is salt- and drought-tolerant, but needs some protection from wind and cold in the northern part of its range. Limber caper *(C. flexuosa)* is similar but has a more sprawling shape and leaves that are green on the underside. Its fruit also is more conspicuous, the pods splitting open to expose a red interior with white seeds. Both species are related to the Mediterranean plant that produces edible capers, which are pickled flower buds.

SEVEN-YEAR APPLE
Casasia clusiifolia

HEIGHT: 8–10 feet

LIGHT: Sun to part shade

BLOOM: Single, 1½-inch, white, fragrant five-petaled blooms similar to species gardenias, which are closely related, and blooming year around

FRUIT: Oval fruit is green, blackening as it ripens. The fruit averages 2½–3 inches in length (and it doesn't take seven years to ripen).

LEAVES: Shiny, leathery, opposite, 6-inch leaves, clustered at the branch ends in whorls

TRUNK: Normally the plant has a shrubby habit but sometimes forms a single trunk, becoming tree-like.

NATIVE RANGE: South Florida and the Caribbean; Zones 10–11

HABITAT: Coastal hammocks, ocean front, dunes

PROPAGATION: Seed, cuttings

Seven-year apple is a slow-growing but decorative seaside plant that tolerates salt spray and dry, sandy soil. It does, however, respond well to good care, including fertilization. The fragrant blooms would be an asset near a seaside swimming pool, but a fungus may occasionally disfigure foliage and fruit. The fruit, which may stay on the tree for a year or more, is eaten by birds and mammals.

BAHAMA CASSIA, BAHAMA SENNA
Cassia chapmanii

HEIGHT: 6–8 feet

LIGHT: Sun

BLOOM: Golden-yellow flowers, 1 inch across, carried in the leaf axils in clusters of four to nine blooms, from October to July

FRUIT: Flat, brown 1- to 3-inch pods holding several seeds

LEAVES: Evergreen, pinnately compound leaves are 1–2½ inches long; oval, light green leaflets are carried in pairs with up to 10 leaflets per leaf.

TRUNK: Multistemmed, shrubby trunk, with smooth, dark brown to black bark

NATIVE RANGE: South Florida, tropical America, and the Caribbean; Zones 10–11

HABITAT: Open, sunny, dry fields and edges of woods

PROPAGATION: Seed

This cassia, also listed as *C. bahamensis*, is a fast-growing, salt-tolerant shrub that supplies cheerful color during the dry winter season. In a sunny location it will seed freely and be smaller and denser than when growing in partial shade. Unfortunately, the plant is short-lived, lasting only about eight to ten years. It is both a larval and nectar plant for several kinds of butterflies, especially sulphurs. There is some disagreement about its status as a true native.

PRIVET CASSIA
Cassia ligustrina

HEIGHT: 6–8 feet

LIGHT: Sun

BLOOM: Yellow flowers, carried in open clusters at the ends of the branches all year

FRUIT: Flat, brown seed pod

LEAVES: Fine-textured pinnate leaves with long, slender, pointed evergreen leaflets, 1–2 inches long

TRUNK: An open, sprawling shrub with dark brown bark

NATIVE RANGE: Central and south Florida and the Caribbean; Zones 9–11

HABITAT: Roadsides, open fields, edges of woods

PROPAGATION: Seed

Like Bahama cassia, this is a colorful shrub with the same disadvantage of a somewhat short life span. Blooms can appear any time of the year but are more likely in the dry season. The delicate texture of the foliage contrasts nicely with large-leaved background plantings, and it is a very desirable plant for the butterfly garden. It is also listed as *Senna ligustrina*.

BUTTONBUSH
Cephalanthus occidentalis

HEIGHT: 4–15 feet

LIGHT: Sun to part shade

BLOOM: Round, white, fuzzy, fragrant flowers, 1–1½ inches across, are carried in clusters. They usually bloom between May and September, although flowering starts later in the northern part of the plant's range.

FRUIT: Dense, rounded heads, splitting in half over the winter and revealing small seeds

LEAVES: Oval, pointed, 2- to 6-inch leaves are dark green and glossy, emerging late in spring on this deciduous shrub.

TRUNK: Buttonbush is a shrubby grower with very dark gray to black bark; old bark has flat, rough ridges and fissures.

NATIVE RANGE: Eastern U.S. from Maine to south Florida, west to central Texas, and scattered through Arizona, California, and Mexico; Zones 5–10

HABITAT: Swamps, floodplains, banks of ponds, lakes, and streams

PROPAGATION: Seed, cuttings

Buttonbush is an attractive and versatile shrub with fragrant flowers that attract bees and butterflies. It has shiny foliage that glistens in the sun, but it is suitable only for wet locations. As it will grow with its roots in water, it is a good choice for a natural landscape with a poorly drained area, or along a lake or pond. It is open-growing and leafs out later than many plants.

Snowberry *Chiococca alba*

Pineland snowberry *C. parvifolia*

SNOWBERRY
Chiococca alba

HEIGHT: 10 feet

LIGHT: Sun to part shade

BLOOM: Drooping clusters of dainty, fragrant, yellow or white bell-shaped flowers, ¼- to ½-inch long, blooming all year

FRUIT: Round, bright white fruits, ¼–½ inch long

LEAVES: Shiny green, leathery, opposite, 2–4 inches long, oval in shape and terminating in a sharp point

TRUNK: Older trunks of this sprawling, almost vine-like shrub have yellow-gray bark. Growth is very variable; the plant may even creep along the ground.

NATIVE RANGE: South Florida and the Caribbean; Zones 10–11

HABITAT: An understory plant in hardwood hammocks

PROPAGATION: Seed

This gardenia relative offers delicate flowers with a pleasant fragrance, as well as ornamental fruit that stands out distinctly against the dark foliage. It will need occasional trimming to keep it from climbing into other plants. The pineland snowberry, *C. parvifolia*, is a close relative but smaller in size; it reaches only 3–4 feet and behaves more like a high ground cover. Its leaves are only 1–2 inches long, and flowers are white to whitish purple, with smaller white fruit.

Dr. Edward F. Gilman

SUMMERSWEET, SWEET PEPPERBUSH
Clethra alnifolia

HEIGHT: 4–7 feet

LIGHT: Sun to shade

BLOOM: White, very fragrant ⅓-inch flowers in 3- to 6-inch vertical spikes, bloom in July and August. Some cultivars have pink blooms.

FRUIT: Small, dry capsules that remain on the spikes through the winter

LEAVES: Alternate, broad, pointed, oval leaves are 2–4 inches long, either smooth or slightly fuzzy on the underside, turning yellow to orange in fall.

TRUNK: Erect, sometimes suckering, with brown stems

NATIVE RANGE: Maine to central Florida; Zones 3–9

HABITAT: Damp, acid soils in pinelands and coastal areas

PROPAGATION: Seed, cuttings

Summersweet is a wonderful shrub for the water's edge, or located near a patio, dock, or gazebo where its summer fragrance can be enjoyed. The flowers attract bees and butterflies. It is valuable for a perennial border where some height is required, and its suckering habit can help hold a stream bank, preventing erosion. The plant will take fairly deep shade and salt air.

BLOODBERRY, BUTTERFLY SAGE
Cordia globosa

HEIGHT: 6–8 feet

LIGHT: Sun

BLOOM: Small (¼-inch), funnel-shaped white flowers, carried in clusters at the ends of the branches, and blooming most of the year

FRUIT: Small, red, globe-shaped fruit in terminal clusters

LEAVES: Rough, hairy, gray-green, 1–1½ inches long, elliptic with pointed tips and coarsely toothed edges

TRUNK: Usually multistemmed, medium brown in color

NATIVE RANGE: South Florida and the Caribbean; Zones 10–11

HABITAT: Disturbed fields, open areas, edges of hammocks

PROPAGATION: Seed

This rounded shrub, which is both drought- and salt-tolerant, is an important element of the butterfly garden, drawing many species—malachite, atala, and dagger wings among them—to its nectar. Birds appreciate the small fruits. Use it as a background shrub, as it is not the garden showpiece that its relative, the orange geiger tree, is considered to be.

SWAMP DOGWOOD
Cornus foemina

HEIGHT: 10 feet

LIGHT: Sun to part shade

BLOOM: Flat-topped, branching clusters, 1–2 inches across, of four-petalled white flowers, blooming in spring

FRUIT: The ¼-inch blue fruit is showy in late summer, but usually short-lived as it is eaten quickly by birds.

LEAVES: Variable, opposite leaves, 2–4 inches long, ranging from oval to lance-shaped, with little change of color in autumn

TRUNK: Multi-trunked; shrubby stems are gray and twigs may be reddish. The plant tends to sucker.

NATIVE RANGE: Delaware to central Florida and west to Texas; Zones 6–9

HABITAT: Wet areas such as edges of lakes, swamps, slow-moving rivers and streams, and floodplains; usually found as an understory plant or at the edge of woods

PROPAGATION: Seed, cuttings

Swamp dogwood is a good shrub for bank stabilization along rivers and streams and could be used in an informal setting or as a shrub border. It is fairly tolerant of light shade and, while it prefers damp soil, it is adaptable. The small white flowers are fairly decorative, but the blue fruit is its best attribute in the landscape.

RHACOMA
Crossopetalum rhacoma

HEIGHT: 15 feet

LIGHT: Sun to part shade

BLOOM: Tiny clusters of yellow-green flowers bloom in the leaf axils most of the year.

FRUIT: Bright red oval fruit, ¼-inch in diameter, with one seed

LEAVES: Oval, about 1 inch long, light green above and very pale beneath, with a rounded tip and smooth edges, carried on the stem in a whorled, opposite or alternate pattern

TRUNK: Usually tree-like, with smooth pale brown bark

NATIVE RANGE: South Florida and the Caribbean; Zones 10–11

HABITAT: Hammocks, as an understory or edge-of-woods plant, and near beaches

PROPAGATION: Seed

Rhacoma is a pleasing shrub or small tree with an upright growth habit that makes it suitable as a screen in a narrow location. It tolerates both drought and salt well. The red fruit is its main feature, but the leaves also are interesting in that they may be arranged on the stem in several different ways. Another related species, called quail berry *(C. illicifolium)*, inhabits the same region but reaches only 2 feet in height, making it a good border plant. It has small leaves with spiny edges and bright red berries.

LEATHERWOOD, TITI
Cyrilla racemiflora

HEIGHT: 10–15 feet

LIGHT: Full sun to part shade

BLOOM: Flowers are white, fragrant and about ¼ inch across, carried on graceful spikes 4–5 inches long. They bloom in June and are quite showy.

FRUIT: Round, ½-inch capsules born along the raceme

LEAVES: Oblong leaves, about 3 inches long, are glossy on the upper surface. In Florida, the plant is evergreen to semi-deciduous; in cold weather the leaves may turn orange and scarlet.

TRUNK: Stringy, brownish-gray bark covers the stems of this large and sometimes sprawling shrub. Branches are twisted and spiralling.

NATIVE RANGE: Virginia to Texas and into southern Florida, the West Indies, and eastern South America; Zones 6–10

HABITAT: Swampy, acid soil areas

PROPAGATION: Seed, cuttings, root cuttings

Cyrilla is a beautiful native plant offering attractive flowers and foliage. It is excellent for plantings along the edges of water in damp, acid soils, although it is also salt- and drought-tolerant. Left unpruned, it can form a thicket.

VARNISHLEAF
Dodonaea viscosa

HEIGHT: 10 feet

LIGHT: Sun to part shade

BLOOM: Tiny, not showy, yellow-green to reddish terminal flowers

FRUIT: Clusters of ½-inch round, greenish fruit with three or four rounded purple or red wings

LEAVES: Foliage is 2–6 inches long, with an elliptical or sometimes spatulate shape. They are glossy, as though they are covered in varnish. New foliage is particularly shiny, becoming less so as the season progresses.

TRUNK: A multi-trunked plant with brown bark

NATIVE RANGE: Pan-tropical; Zones 9–11

HABITAT: Open dry fields and the edges of hammocks; shell ridges in association with sabal palms

PROPAGATION: Seed

Varnishleaf is a useful, drought-tolerant plant for hedges, ocean-front landscaping, and for binding sand dunes. It is variable according to its habitat; leaves may be large and soft, small and leathery, or long and narrow. One form, with leaves that turn purple during cold weather, is used in southern California landscaping.

BLACK TORCH
Erithalis fruticosa

HEIGHT: 7–8 feet

LIGHT: Sun to shade

BLOOM: Delicate panicles of small, star-shaped white flowers emerging from the leaf axils, blooming most of the year

FRUIT: Shiny, black, ⅓-inch round fruit

LEAVES: The 1- to 2-inch rounded, slightly pointed leaves are medium green, growing opposite each other on the twigs.

TRUNK: The single or multistemmed trunk has smooth, dark-brown bark with lighter brown streaks.

NATIVE RANGE: South Florida; Zones 10–11

HABITAT: Open fields or edges of tropical hardwood hammocks

PROPAGATION: Seed

Black torch is a nice, neat evergreen shrub, attractive as an informal screen or privacy barrier. In full sun, it is dense and rounded; in a shaded area, it will have a looser, more open growth.

GOLDEN CREEPER, ERNODEA
Ernodea littoralis

HEIGHT: 2 feet

LIGHT: Sun to light shade

BLOOM: Small, tubular, white to pinkish flowers, blooming all year, followed by small round or oval golden fruit

LEAVES: Shiny green to yellow, narrow, somewhat fleshy leaves, 1½ inches long, clustered on arching stems

NATIVE RANGE: South Florida and the West Indies; Zones 10–11

HABITAT: Beaches, coastal dunes

PROPAGATION: Seed, cuttings, layering

Beach creeper is a low, sprawling shrub found on the most inhospitable dry, sandy soils, making it a practical choice for ocean-front gardens or arid rocky areas such as road medians. As a ground cover, it forms attractive, spreading mats of arching stems, and helps control sand erosion. It is drought- and heat-tolerant but, being a tropical species, cannot take severe cold. Nor should it be overwatered. A threatened species, it is being propagated by some native plant nurseries.

CORAL BEAN, CHEROKEE BEAN
Erythrina herbacea

HEIGHT: 3–5 feet

LIGHT: Sun to part shade

BLOOM: Tubular, curving, 2-inch red flowers on a foot-long spike, appearing in late spring to early summer

FRUIT: Constricted pods, splitting in the fall to expose bright red poisonous seeds

LEAVES: Deciduous, alternate, compound leaves divided into three triangular, pointed leaflets

TRUNK: Soft, woody growth that dies back in cold weather

NATIVE RANGE: North Carolina to south Florida and Texas; Zones 8–10

HABITAT: Elevated sites in open woods or clearings

PROPAGATION: Cuttings, seed

This is a showy plant, good for partly shaded sites in well-drained soil, although it blooms better in full sun. The vivid red blooms are a favorite with hummingbirds. Because the stems are bare in the winter, it could be planted among other shrubbery where its barren branches will be less noticeable. In very cold weather it may die back to the roots, but new growth will reappear in spring. It is salt- and drought-tolerant. The bright, poisonous seeds can attract children's attention; use the plant with caution.

FLORIDA PRIVET
Forestiera segregata

HEIGHT: 10–15 feet

LIGHT: Sun to part shade

BLOOM: Tiny, fuzzy, yellowish-green flowers, blooming in clusters along the branches in spring

FRUIT: Oval, olive-like, ¼- to ½-inch black fruit

LEAVES: Small, opposite, oval leaves, 1–3 inches long, are glossy dark green above and lighter green below, with smooth edges and either rounded or pointed tips.

TRUNK: Usually multistemmed, with smooth, pale gray bark

NATIVE RANGE: Coastal Georgia through Florida, the Caribbean, and Central America; Zones 8–11

HABITAT: Coastal regions, at the edges of woods or in open fields

PROPAGATION: Seed, cuttings

Florida privet is a tidy, fine-textured shrub suitable for screening or hedges like its near relative, the common privet, seen in northern states. Drought- and salt-tolerant, it will accept moist to dry conditions. Birds are attracted to the fruit and to the insects that visit the flowers; the plant's dense, shrubby structure also provides good cover and nesting sites. Pineland privet, *F. segregata var. pinetorum,* is a more compact relative, reaching only 5 feet in height. This dainty plant has smaller, gray-green leaves and would be a good candidate for bonsai, with its delicate foliage, fine branching, and ability to withstand shaping.

GARBERIA
Garberia heterophylla

HEIGHT: 3–6 feet

LIGHT: Sun to part shade

BLOOM: Flat clusters of tubular pink to lavender, rayless flowers, blooming summer through late fall.

LEAVES: Aromatic leaves are oval, alternate, gray-green, cupped and wavy-edged, up to 2 inches long and dotted with tiny glands that give them a sticky feel.

TRUNK: Woody, branching shrub

NATIVE RANGE: Gulf Coast into north and central Florida; Zones 8–9

HABITAT: Pinelands, dunes, edges of woods

PROPAGATION: Seed, cuttings

An evergreen shrub in the aster family, garberia prefers acid soil, will withstand drought after it is well established, and is fairly salt-tolerant. Use it in a border or wherever a small, low-maintenance but showy flowering shrub is desired. If you fertilize it, do so very lightly. A nectar source for butterflies, the plant also is listed as *G. fruticosa.*

Firebush *Hamelia patens*

Firebush *Hamelia patens*

FIREBUSH
Hamelia patens

HEIGHT: 10 feet

LIGHT: Sun to part shade

BLOOM: Clustered, tubular, orange-red flowers, to 1½ inches long, blooming year around

FRUIT: 1/4-inch, dark purple, rounded fruit

LEAVES: Oval, pointed pale green leaves, 5–8 inches long, often with reddish tints

TRUNK: Multistemmed and shrublike; sometimes single-stemmed in woodsy locations

NATIVE RANGE: South Florida, Central and South America; Zones 10–11

HABITAT: An understory or edge-of-woods plant

PROPAGATION: Seed, cuttings

Firebush is a superb wildlife plant, a major nectar plant, and one of the best for attracting butterflies and hummingbirds. It will take either damp or dry soil. In partial shade it stays green; while it will grow well in full sun, the leaves may bleach out. Cold weather may kill it back to the ground, but it will regrow quickly. Because it is prone to aphids and lubber grasshoppers, it probably is best used as a background plant.

OAKLEAF HYDRANGEA
Hydrangea quercifolia

HEIGHT: 5–6 feet

LIGHT: Part shade to shade

BLOOM: Upright panicles of 1–1½-inch flowers bloom in summer, changing from white, through shades of pink, to brown. The sterile outer flowers produce the showy effect; the inner fertile flowers are not prominent.

FRUIT: An inconspicuous capsule

LEAVES: Opposite, 3- to 8-inch oak-like leaves with three to seven lobes and some serrations. They are dark green above; undersides are fuzzy and white to brown in color. Fall color is striking as foliage turns shades of red, purple, and orange. Leaves, ordinarily deciduous, will stay on the plant in areas with a mild climate.

TRUNK: An upright, multistemmed, suckering shrub with few branches and attractive exfoliating, dark brown bark

NATIVE RANGE: Georgia to north Florida and Mississippi; Zones 5–9

HABITAT: Shady woods with rich, moist soil; along streams

PROPAGATION: Seed, root division, cuttings

Oakleaf hydrangea is a coarse-leaved plant prized for its large, dramatic flowers and intense fall color. It is effective as a mass planting or a naturalistic border in a shady setting, or as a specimen surrounded by a fine-leaved ground cover such as liriope. Rich, acid soil and moisture suit it. It is not salt-tolerant and is subject to powdery mildew. Many cultivars are available, with even better blooms and more colorful foliage.

St. Andrew's cross *Hypericum spp.*

St. John's wort *Hypericum spp.*

ST. JOHN'S WORT, ST. ANDREW'S CROSS
Hypericum spp.

HEIGHT: 1–2 feet or more

LIGHT: Sun

BLOOM: Bright yellow four- or five-petaled flowers, usually in clusters at the branch ends and with many yellow stamens

FRUIT: Inconspicuous

LEAVES: Dark green, needlelike, or narrow to oval, to 2 inches in length

TRUNK: Multistemmed, some species erect, others with branches leaning or trailing on the ground

NATIVE RANGE: The Carolinas through Florida to Alabama; Zones 8–10

HABITAT: Open disturbed areas, open sandy woodlands, damp areas, coastal dunes

PROPAGATION: Seed

About 16 species of this small shrub grow throughout the state, many difficult to tell apart. Most are low-growing, although sandweed, *H. fasciculatum*, can reach 7–8 feet. All have similar four- or five-petaled yellow flowers that bloom most of the year. Hypericums are suitable for almost any sunny area, from wet to dry, depending on the species. They produce a colorful flower display and make attractive, but short-lived, additions to a garden.

Dr. Edward F. Gilman

GALLBERRY, INKBERRY
Ilex glabra

HEIGHT: 6–7 feet

LIGHT: Sun to part shade

BLOOM: Small greenish-white flowers, carried in the leaf axils, are not particularly ornamental. Male and female blooms are on separate plants; male flowers are in clusters and female flowers are single.

FRUIT: Rather showy, ¼-inch round black fruit usually remains on the shrub throughout the winter and is a food source for birds.

LEAVES: Lance-shaped foliage, evergreen and glossy dark green on the upper surface, 1–2 inches long and arranged alternately on the stem

TRUNK: Bark is smooth and gray. This shrubby grower often produces suckers to form colonies.

NATIVE RANGE: Nova Scotia to central Florida and west to Mississippi; Zones 4–9

HABITAT: Usually found in wet, swampy, acid soils

PROPAGATION: Seed, cuttings, division

Gallberry is a valuable holly with a loose, informal growth habit. Its combination of moisture, salt, and shade tolerance is not easy to find in landscaping plants. It is very useful as an open screen or foundation planting, and if it is satisfied with its location it tends to produce suckers. A number of dwarf selections are on the market.

FLORIDA ANISE
Illicium floridanum

HEIGHT: 8–10 feet

LIGHT: Part to dense shade

BLOOM: Fragrant, drooping, ½-inch maroon flowers with about 25 strap-like petals, carried on 2-inch stems, and appearing in March and April

FRUIT: Brown, star-shaped fruit, 1 inch across

LEAVES: Fragrant, elliptic, 3–6 inch-long foliage is shiny green above and smooth below, with reddish-purple petioles; leaves tend to droop on the branches.

TRUNK: This shrubby plant has a brown trunk and branches and an upright growth habit.

NATIVE RANGE: Low, swampy areas from central Florida to Louisiana; Zones 7–9

HABITAT: Moist to wet locations

PROPAGATION: Seed, cuttings

This is an excellent evergreen for screening or background in a wet, shady spot, and will grow well quite a bit south of its natural range. Its fragrant foliage projects a pleasant licorice scent to the garden. The related *I. parviflorum*, with yellow petals, is rare but equally attractive. In Florida, it occasionally is found along the edges of swamps.

VIRGINIA WILLOW, VIRGINIA SWEETSPIRE
Itea virginica

HEIGHT: 3–7 feet

LIGHT: Sun to part shade

BLOOM: Fragrant, white, ½-inch flowers on 3- to 6-inch spikes appear in late spring or early summer.

FRUIT: Brown, ¼-inch capsules carried on the old flower spikes

LEAVES: 2- to 4-inch elliptic leaves are semi-evergreen in Florida, and in a chilly autumn can produce spectacular and long-lasting color, when the glossy dark green foliage may turn to scarlet, crimson, or purple.

TRUNK: Upright brownish stems, which, in natural conditions, branch near the top of the plant

NATIVE RANGE: New Jersey to central Florida and west to Louisiana; Zones 5–9

HABITAT: Moist lowlands near rivers and creeks

PROPAGATION: Seed, cuttings, division of suckers

The attractive flowers and winter color are Virginia willow's main assets. Although it is found in damp areas, it is drought-tolerant under cultivation. However, it has a tendency to produce suckers and is best grown in an area where its growth can be contained. 'Henry's Garnet' is a selection that is better than the original form, as it has brighter fall color and larger flowers.

Marsh elder *Iva frutescens*

Seacoast marsh elder *Iva imbricata*

MARSH ELDER, SEACOAST MARSH ELDER
Iva frutescens, I. imbricata

HEIGHT: 3–6 feet

LIGHT: Sun

BLOOM: Panicles of small green flowers, fragrant when crushed, growing at the ends of the branches

FRUIT: Inconspicuous

LEAVES: Lanceolate, fuzzy, fleshy, 2-inch leaves with toothed margins

TRUNK: Multistemmed and upright with pale gray bark, woody at the base

NATIVE RANGE: Virginia to southern Florida, west to Texas; West Indies; Zones 8–11

HABITAT: Dunes, beachfronts

PROPAGATION: Cuttings, layering, division

These two closely related shrubs share the same damp, salty environment and are good companion plants for sea oats and other coastal pioneers, needing little care. Seacoast marsh elder *(I. imbricata)*, the smaller of the two, reaches only about 3 feet and has finer leaves. It also has suckering roots that help stabilize dunes and make the plant better able to withstand high winds than its taller relative.

MOUNTAIN LAUREL
Kalmia latifolia

HEIGHT: 10–15 feet

LIGHT: Part shade to shade

BLOOM: Broad, cupped flowers, 1 inch across and carried in terminal clusters 5–6 inches across, ranging from white through deep pink to almost red, and blooming in May and June

FRUIT: A brown, ¼-inch capsule with small seeds

LEAVES: Evergreen, oval, pointed, dark green, 2–6 inches long

TRUNK: Single or multi-stemmed; rough brown bark and a gnarled appearance are characteristic of old specimens.

NATIVE RANGE: Northern New England west to Ohio and south into northern Florida; Zones 4–9

HABITAT: Woodlands and well-drained stream banks with acid soil

PROPAGATION: Seed, cuttings, tissue culture

Mountain laurel is considered one of America's most beautiful native plants. It is superb when in bloom in the spring but difficult to grow in Florida, except for the northern areas, in acid soils. Plant it in a shady, raised bed with mulch and light soil, and remove seed heads to encourage future bloom. The plant is subject to leaf spot, sunburn, borers, lacebugs, and flower blights. Many cultivated varieties have been developed and are on the market.

SALTMARSH MALLOW
Kosteletzkya virginica

HEIGHT: To 3 feet

LIGHT: Sun

BLOOM: Distinctive hibiscus-like, pink, five-petaled flowers, 3 inches across, with showy yellow stamens, blooming from spring to fall and each lasting only a single day

FRUIT: Flat pod, divided into segments, with one seed per segment

LEAVES: Alternate, triangular or lobed, 2–5 inches long, gray-green, rough or fuzzy

TRUNK: Fuzzy, woody stem

NATIVE RANGE: Coastal New York south to southern Florida and along the Gulf Coast; Zones 6–11

HABITAT: Fresh water or brackish marshes

PROPAGATION: Seed

This small perennial shrub is somewhat coarse for landscape use, but might have a place in brackish, wet areas where the choice of flowering plants is limited. Other Florida mallows being grown commercially for landscape use in Florida include the bright red-flowered scarlet hibiscus *(Hibiscus coccineus)* and the swamp hibiscus *(H. grandiflorus)*, with large pink flowers; they'll grow just about anywhere in the state in a wet location.

LANTANA, WILD SAGE
Lantana involucrata

HEIGHT: 4–5 feet

LIGHT: Sun

BLOOM: Clusters of small white or yellow flowers

FRUIT: Dark blue berry, to ¼-inch across

LEAVES: Rough, oval, fuzzy leaves to 1¼ inches long, with a pungent odor when crushed

TRUNK: Shrubby and brown

NATIVE RANGE: Southern United States, tropical America, and the Caribbean; Zones 8–11

HABITAT: Open clearings in woods, along roadsides and coastal dunes

PROPAGATION: Seed, cuttings

Lantana is a woody shrub with small flowers that attract a number of butterfly species. Wild sage, *L. involucrata*, is an upright plant with clusters of white flower, while *L. depressa*, or pineland lantana, is low, sprawling, and has bright yellow flowers. It is found in pinewoods and other dry areas. Lantanas are drought-tolerant and particularly good when used near the coast. They tend to become leggy as they age, so prune them back now and then to keep them bushy. Several species of lantana grow wild in Florida, and there is some disagreement over which truly are natives. The weedy *L. camara*, with bright yellow and red flowers and poisonous fruit, is common to waste areas but is not native.

DOGHOBBLE, COAST LEUCOTHOE
Leucothoe axillaris

HEIGHT: 3–4 feet

LIGHT: Part shade to shade

BLOOM: Short racemes of bell-like white flowers hang from the leaf axils, appearing in April at the southern end of its range.

FRUIT: Inconspicuous brown capsule

LEAVES: Lance-shaped, dark green and glossy with a leathery texture, 2–4 inches long and sharply pointed at the tip

TRUNK: A low suckering or layering shrub with brown bark, creating large thickets in a suitable environment

NATIVE RANGE: Virginia to north Florida and west to Mississippi; Zones 6–8

HABITAT: Shady lowland, moist areas

PROPAGATION: Seed, cuttings

Doghobble makes a good low to mid-sized evergreen ground cover, if space is provided for its spread. Leaf spot sometimes affects the plants quite severely. It can be fussy but is very attractive when the right location is found for it, such as a stream bank or other damp, but well-drained, site with acid soil.

GOPHER APPLE
Licania michauxii

HEIGHT: 1 foot

LIGHT: Sun

BLOOM: Tiny clusters of yellow-green flowers, blooming at the branch tips in early summer

FRUIT: Oval fruits, 1 inch long, white with a purplish tinge when ripe

LEAVES: Glossy, evergreen, 2- to 4-inch leaves are alternate, long and narrow with rounded tips and prominent veining.

TRUNK: Low, shrubby plant with dark brown underground stems

NATIVE RANGE: Georgia through Florida and tropical America; Zones 9–11

HABITAT: Sunny beaches, dunes, and coastal ridges

PROPAGATION: Seed

Because of its tolerance to salt, drought, wind, and poor soil, gopher apple is a valued addition to the coastal landscape. It spreads, forming a good ground cover even in the worst of soils. Its fruit is a favorite of wildlife, including the gopher tortoise. Despite its tough qualities, it is very difficult to transplant or propagate from the underground stems, and seed is the most practical means of propagation.

RUSTY LYONIA
Lyonia ferruginea

HEIGHT: 10–15 feet

LIGHT: Sun to part shade.

BLOOM: Fragrant, white to pink, bell-shaped ½-inch flowers, appearing in spring and carried in racemes in the leaf axils

FRUIT: Rounded, brown, ⅓-inch capsule

LEAVES: Elliptic, shiny green leaves, 1–2 inches long, fuzzy and rusty-red on the underside, with a leathery texture

TRUNK: Multistemmed reddish-brown trunk

NATIVE RANGE: Southeastern U.S. into south Florida; Zones 8–10

HABITAT: Acid, wet areas along the edges of swamps, ponds, and wet forests

PROPAGATION: Seed

Rusty lyonia is a beautiful native and a good choice for a damp shrub border, although it tolerates dry sandy soils as well. It is not salt-tolerant, however. It does best without supplemental care except for pruning. Good foliage and attractive flowers add to its appeal as a low-care native.

SHINY LYONIA, FETTERBUSH
Lyonia lucida

HEIGHT: 3–5 feet

LIGHT: Sun to part shade

BLOOM: Fragrant, white to deep pink, ½-inch bell-shaped flowers, appearing in spring and carried in racemes in the leaf axils

FRUIT: Rounded, brown, ⅓-inch capsule on raceme

LEAVES: Oval, alternate, 1- to 2-inch, sharp-pointed, smooth-edged leaves are coppery when young; when mature they are deep, shiny green and have a leathery texture.

TRUNK: Multistemmed, reddish-brown trunk

NATIVE RANGE: Virginia to Louisiana and to south central Florida; Zones 7–9

HABITAT: Acid, wet soil areas along the edges of swamps, bogs, ponds, and wet forests

PROPAGATION: Seed or cuttings

Shiny lyonia is a delicate plant that is at its best in its natural setting in damp, acid soil. While the flowers and evergreen leaves are quite attractive, the sensitive foliage is subject to leaf spotting when the plant is under cultivation.

WAX MYRTLE
Myrica cerifera

HEIGHT: 20 feet

LIGHT: Sun

BLOOM: Insignificant greenish-white flowers in spikes

FRUIT: Blue-green, waxy, ⅛-inch round berries on spikes

LEAVES: Narrow, ¾-inch, fragrant, notched leaves that may be used like bay leaves in cooking

TRUNK: Multi-trunked small tree or large shrub with light gray bark

NATIVE RANGE: Southeastern U.S., throughout Florida and the Caribbean; Zones 6–11

HABITAT: Pinelands, swampy areas and other moist sites, often growing behind dunes and in the Everglades, where it is a pioneer plant

PROPAGATION: Seed, division

Wax myrtle is a fast-growing small tree or large shrub, and a fine choice for seaside plantings as it is very salt-tolerant. It also is cold-hardy and will take anything from wet to well-drained soil. It can be pruned into tree form, but doesn't take well to being sheared as a hedge; sections of the plant may die out. In the landscape it is prone to fungal disease. Its dense foliage makes it a good screening plant and a habitat for birds, and its waxy berries can be used in candle-making.

A dwarf variety, *M. cerifera var. pumila*, growing to only 3 feet, has a horizontal form and smaller leaves.

MYRSINE, RAPANEA
Myrsine guianensis

HEIGHT: 15–20 feet

LIGHT: Sun to part shade

BLOOM: Tiny clustering greenish-white flowers, blooming in winter and spring

FRUIT: Small, blue-black berries carried in the leaf axils

LEAVES: Alternate leaves, clustered at the ends of the branches, may be elliptical to oblong, with smooth margins curving downward

TRUNK: Usually shrubby, with light gray bark

NATIVE RANGE: South Florida, the West Indies and tropical America; Zones 10–11

HABITAT: A variety of habitats, from dry woodlands or coastal areas to boggy sites

PROPAGATION: Seed

Myrsine is an attractive native whose versatility is one of its greatest assets. It tolerates dry or moist soil, sun or shade equally well. It has good salt-tolerance but will grow well inland. Use it for natural screening or as a specimen plant; with training, it can be a small columnar tree suitable for narrow spaces. Its fruit will bring jays, woodpeckers, cardinals, thrashers, and other birds to the garden.

PRICKLY PEAR
Opuntia spp.

HEIGHT: 2–8 feet

LIGHT: Sun

BLOOM: Flat to cupped flowers, 1–3 inches across, are predominately yellow, although red, purple, and white forms sometimes are seen.

FRUIT: A fig-like fruit, up to 3 inches long, spatulate, usually red, and either smooth or spiny; edible in some species

LEAVES: The rounded or oval pads, 3–5 inches across, contain chlorophyll and function as leaves. Pads generally are spiny, although some species are spineless.

TRUNK: Rough and brownish on old trunks

NATIVE RANGE: Throughout most of the U.S., with most species occurring in the Plains and western states; Zones 3–11

HABITAT: Open, excessively drained sandy soils near the seashore or in dunes or sandy ridges

PROPAGATION: Seed; cuttings

Depending on the species, prickly pear can range from a ground cover to a small tree. It is an interesting, low-care plant, but difficult to use in the landscape. One possible use would be at a beach house, where its low maintenance and salt- and drought-tolerance would be appreciated. The flowers are showy, and the unusual form the plant often takes is certainly distinctive. To propagate, separate the pads, letting them dry for a few days, then plant to about one-fourth of its length.

PISONIA
Pisonia rotundata

HEIGHT: 10–15 feet

LIGHT: Sun to part shade

BLOOM: Dense clusters of flowers appearing at the bases of the leaves in spring are greenish-white, somewhat fuzzy, and have no petals. Male and female flowers are on separate plants.

FRUIT: Very small cylindrical fruits are dry and angled, with sticky glands along the angles that stick to humans and animals, spreading the seed.

LEAVES: Opposite, stiff, dull green leaves are 1-4 inches long with prominent depressed veins, oval in shape with rounded tips, looking a little like a miniature ficus leaf.

TRUNK: The multistemmed trunk is light gray, with pronounced leaf scars. Unlike some of its relatives, pisonia's trunk and stems do not bear thorns.

NATIVE RANGE: Lower Florida Keys and the West Indies; Zone 11

HABITAT: Hammocks and pinewoods at or near sea level

PROPAGATION: Seed

Pisonia is a coarse-textured shrub that can offer a contrast to finer-leaved, salt-tolerant vegetation for landscaping in the Keys. The denseness of this rather rare shrub makes it a good choice for hedges, screens, and other privacy plantings.

SCRUB PLUM
Prunus geniculata

HEIGHT: 4–5 feet

LIGHT: Sun to part shade

BLOOM: Solitary white flowers, ⅓ inch across, with pink sepals and yellow stamens, blooming in winter

FRUIT: Reddish, 1-inch plums

LEAVES: Deciduous, oval, ½ inch long, with finely serrated edges

TRUNK: Shrubby and densely branched with gray bark often covered with lichens

NATIVE RANGE: Central Florida along the Lake Wales Ridge; Zone 9

HABITAT: Pine scrub and sandhills with well-drained, sandy soil and open vegetation

PROPAGATION: Seed

This little plum can be distinguished from its larger relatives by its low, rounded form and zigzag branches with thorny tips, adaptations to the poor soil of its natural environment. As most of its native habitat has been cleared for development, it has become an endangered species, but some native nurseries are propagating it. The winter blooms are attractive, the small plums are a food source for birds, and the dense branches provide cover for wildlife.

Wild coffee *Psychotria nervosa*   Bahama coffee *Psychotria bahamensis*

WILD COFFEE
Pyschotria nervosa

HEIGHT: 5–10 feet

LIGHT: Sun to shade

BLOOM: Small white flowers in clusters, appearing in spring and summer

FRUIT: Oval red berries about ⅓ inch long

LEAVES: Dark green, glossy, opposite, oval, pointed leaves, to 6 inches long, have prominent veins and a quilted appearance.

TRUNK: Multistemmed, shrub-like, with brown bark

NATIVE RANGE: South Florida and the West Indies; Zones 10–11

HABITAT: A common understory plant in tropical woodlands

PROPAGATION: Seed, cuttings

Wild coffee is an excellent understory native for shady areas, useful for massing or as a screen. Its shiny evergreen foliage is conspicuous even in a shady situation, and even more so when a little sunlight is reflected from the leaves. The plant is sensitive to drought and may need additional irrigation.

This is the most common species of wild coffee in Florida. Another species, *P. sulzneri*, has dull, gray-green foliage and greenish-white flowers, while the least common, Bahama coffee *(P. bahamensis or P. ligustrifolia)*, found in the Keys and Caribbean, has smaller leaves. All three species attract butterflies to their flowers and birds to the fruit.

WHITE INDIGO BERRY
Randia aculeata

HEIGHT: 10 feet

LIGHT: Sun to part shade

BLOOM: The ½-inch, tubular white flowers are fragrant, as befits a gardenia relative. The blooms, appearing year around, are five-petaled and scattered over the plant in the leaf axils or on the stems individually or in small clusters.

FRUIT: Round, ½-inch, white berries enclose seeds set in a dark, almost indigo-blue pulp.

LEAVES: Oval to rounded opposite leaves, glossy light green and ¾ to 2 inches long, with pointed tips

TRUNK: Single or multi-trunked shrub or small tree with gray bark

NATIVE RANGE: South Florida, the Caribbean and the Bahamas; Zones 10–11

HABITAT: Open dry, grassy fields and edges of hardwood hammocks

PROPAGATION: Seed

This is a tough, slow-growing, subtly decorative evergreen plant, suitable for difficult sites with no irrigation. It has strong wood that is used sometimes for fishing poles requiring strength and flexibility. The branches may be spiny at the tips, so care is needed in handling the plant.

MISTLETOE CACTUS, PENCIL CACTUS
Rhipsalis baccifera

HEIGHT: Individual stems 2 feet or more in length

LIGHT: Sun to part shade

BLOOM: Small, white, ½-inch flowers with five petals

FRUIT: Small white berries with black seeds

LEAVES: Drooping, yellowish-green branches are bare of foliage.

NATIVE RANGE: Coastal areas of central and south Florida; Zones 10–11

HABITAT: Mangroves and buttonwood forests, growing on trunks and branches

PROPAGATION: Seed, division of clumps

This endangered cactus (also listed as *R. cassutha*) has probably disappeared from its native habitats. Usually found on a stump or tree branch and appearing to be an epiphyte, it is more like a shrub, attached to earth by long, ropy stems. It starts life when a seed, usually carried by a bird, finds a bit of humus in a fissure on a tree and germinates, later sending roots to the ground. Cultivated plants may be naturalized on tree branches or grown on cork or driftwood.

WILD AZALEA
Rhododendron canescens

HEIGHT: 10 feet

LIGHT: Sun to part shade

BLOOM: Fragrant, tubular, 3-inch blooms, ranging from white to pink or rose, open in early to mid-spring before leaves appear.

FRUIT: Inconspicuous woody capsule

LEAVES: Elliptic, pointed, deciduous green leaves, 1–4 inches long and covered with white hairs, grow in whorls at the branch tips.

TRUNK: Suckering stems with smooth brown bark

NATIVE RANGE: North Carolina and Tennessee to north Florida and west to Texas; Zones 5–9

HABITAT: Open fields, edges of woodlands, and along streams

PROPAGATION: Seed, cuttings, suckers

This common but striking southeastern shrub is highly prized for its colorful, fragrant spring flowers. It is lovely in a woodsy setting in acid soil; in ravines and on steep river banks, its suckering growth helps hold soil, preventing erosion. Wild azalea hybridizes readily with other species of azalea.

CHAPMAN'S RHODODENDRON
Rhododendron chapmanii

HEIGHT: 9 feet

LIGHT: Part shade

BLOOM: Showy pink, ruffled flowers, 1–2 inches across and carried in clusters, appear before new growth in spring.

FRUIT: A brown capsule, ½-inch long

LEAVES: Evergreen, alternate, elliptic, dark green and leathery, to 4 inches long, with small dark spots above and yellowish to rust-colored scales beneath

TRUNK: Shrubby, with dark brown bark

NATIVE RANGE: Northern Florida, including the Panhandle; Zones 8–9

HABITAT: Pine woods, along swamps and bays

PROPAGATION: Seed, cuttings

Dark evergreen leaves and the colorful spring flower display make this endangered Florida shrub highly ornamental in the landscape. Most rhododendrons will not grow this far south, so this species deserves special attention. It makes an excellent companion to the wild azalea in acid woodland soils.

ROUGE PLANT
Rivina humilis

HEIGHT: 3–5 feet

LIGHT: Sun to shade

BLOOM: Tiny white flowers on a spike

FRUIT: Showy red berries on spikes borne throughout the year

LEAVES: Alternate oval, pointed leaves with wavy edges

NATIVE RANGE: Central and south Florida; Zones 9–10

HABITAT: Open woodlands and disturbed sites

PROPAGATION: Seeds, cuttings

Rouge plant, a relative of pokeweed, is a small, carefree, colorful border plant for informal, shady settings. Its brightly colored fruits are striking throughout the year and will attract several species of birds.

BLACKBERRY
Rubus spp.

HEIGHT: To 6 feet

LIGHT: Sun to part shade

BLOOM: Five-petaled white flowers, 1 inch across, blooming in early spring

FRUIT: Edible black fruit, ripening in late summer

LEAVES: Three or more leaflets on thorny stems; leaflets are deeply quilted, toothed at the edges and usually pale and fuzzy on the underside.

TRUNK: Sprawling shrubs with arching, thorny stems

NATIVE RANGE: Southeastern U.S. and through most of Florida, depending on species; Zones 7–10

HABITAT: Roadsides, ditches, fields, edges of woods

PROPAGATION: Division, cuttings

Several species of native blackberry grow and produce fruit in Florida. The sweet, juicy berries, a favorite with our pioneers, are excellent for eating out-of-hand and for pies and preserves, although birds and small mammals are likely to get there first. Dried leaves sometimes are used to make tea. Grow blackberries in rich, well-drained soil near a fence or trellis where the canes can be trained to grow upright, and cut the stems back almost to the ground after the fruiting season.

Elderberry *Sambucus simpsonii*   Elderberry *Sambucus simpsonii*

ELDERBERRY
Sambucus simpsonii

HEIGHT: 10–15 feet

LIGHT: Sun to part shade

BLOOM: Small, fragrant, white flowers borne in flattish heads, blooming most of the year

FRUIT: Edible, 1/4-inch, shiny, round, black berries, usually ripening in summer

LEAVES: Glossy, opposite, pinnate foliage with five to nine pointed leaflets, each to 3 inches long and with jagged edges

TRUNK: Normally multistemmed, with rough bark

NATIVE RANGE: Eastern United States, the Caribbean, and tropical America; Zones 3–11

HABITAT: Pioneer plant found in moist, open fields and along canals and ponds, establishing quickly on disturbed sites

PROPAGATION: Seed, cuttings

Elderberry is a good filler plant in the landscape where it can be used as a shrub or small tree. Its coarse texture and thick growth make a good screen to block objectional views. The fruit may be used for wine, jelly, and pies. Some work has been done on northern elderberries to find larger fruiting forms with improved flavor; similar research could occur in Florida.

SCAEVOLA, INKBERRY
Scaevola plumieri

HEIGHT: 3–5 feet

LIGHT: Sun

BLOOM: White to pinkish flowers, like halves of small daisies in appearance, are carried in small clusters near branch tips in spring and summer.

FRUIT: Glossy black and juicy, ½-inch in diameter, the bitter fruit contains two woody pits.

LEAVES: Succulent, glossy, evergreen foliage is 1–3 inches long and alternately arranged. Short petioles are winged, and leaves are spatulate with smooth margins.

TRUNK: Shrubby and sprawling over the ground

NATIVE RANGE: South Florida and the West Indies; Zones 10–11

HABITAT: Sunny dry beaches and low hammocks

PROPAGATION: Seed, cuttings; branches naturally layer and root as they spread.

Scaevola is a tough survivor, salt- and drought-tolerant and suitable for arid beach-front properties where it can be used as a specimen or a hedge. The layering branches catch wind-blown sand and help to form dunes; they also provide shelter for birds. A nonnative species with white fruit, *S. frutescens*, has become naturalized in Florida and now is more common than the native species because of its invasive habit.

NECKLACE POD
Sophora tomentosa

HEIGHT: 5–10 feet

LIGHT: Sun

BLOOM: One-inch, yellow, pea-like flowers are carried on spikes, 6–15 inches long, at the branch tips, with flowers opening first at the bottom of the spike and blooming most of the year.

FRUIT: Fuzzy brown pods, 4–6 inches long, are beadlike, narrowing between the seeds. Seeds are poisonous if eaten.

LEAVES: Foot-long leaves are pinnately compound, with 1- to 2-inch oval, dark green leaflets. New growth is grayish and velvety with a silvery tint.

TRUNK: A shrubby grower with gray-brown bark

NATIVE RANGE: South Florida, West Indies, and South America; Zones 10–11

HABITAT: Sunny, open, scrubby areas at the edge of hammocks

PROPAGATION: Seed, cuttings

Necklace pod is a showy, loose-growing native shrub whose yellow flowers are highly attractive to butterflies and hummingbirds. Its high salt- and drought-tolerance makes it a candidate for beach plantings, but as it tends to become leggy, it works best as a background plant.

BLUE PORTERWEED
Stachytarpheta jamaicensis

HEIGHT: 3–4 feet

LIGHT: Sun to part shade

BLOOM: A rough, slender spike on which several ¼-inch tubular blue or purple flowers open at a time, blooming year around

LEAVES: Opposite, 1- to 3-inch long, dark green leaves are oval and pointed with sawtooth edges. The woody, brown lower stem may be single or multistemmed; newer stems are green and square.

NATIVE RANGE: Central and south Florida and the tropics; Zones 9–11

HABITAT: Open woodlands, clearings, and disturbed, well-drained sites

PROPAGATION: Seed, cuttings

Porterweed is a low, sprawling shrub with a subtle beauty, usually alive with zebra and other butterflies. It is a fairly long-lived, semi-woody perennial that should live at least four years. It reseeds after it becomes established, but it is not a pest. Flowers generally are open in the morning, closed in the afternoon. Some authorities separate blue porterweed from Keys porterweed, a dwarf form. Another non-native form, larger and sturdier, is commonly used in landscaping and is equally attractive to butterflies.

Photo by Dr. Edward F. Gilman

SNOWBELL
Styrax americana

HEIGHT: 10 feet

LIGHT: Part shade to shade

BLOOM: Fragrant, white, bell-shaped, 1-inch flowers, occurring April to June

FRUIT: A fuzzy, grayish, ½-inch capsule

LEAVES: Oval to rounded, 3-inch leaves are fuzzy and gray below, dark green above, and alternate along the stem.

TRUNK: Shrubby, gray-brown bark may become fissured with age.

NATIVE RANGE: Virginia to central Florida and west to Texas; Zones 7–10

HABITAT: Usually an understory plant along stream banks in moist, acid soil

PROPAGATION: Seed

This rather ordinary shrub has attractive blooms in spring and early summer. It is particularly ornamental when planted as a specimen emerging from a bed of ferns or other ground cover in a shady spot. Be sure to keep it out of full sun. The related big-leaf snowbell, *S. grandiflora*, of northern Florida, reaches 15 feet, has larger flowers in hanging racemes of 8 to 10 blossoms, and larger leaves. It will take drier soil than its smaller relative.

BAY CEDAR
Suriana maritima

HEIGHT: 10 feet

LIGHT: Sun to part shade

BLOOM: The ½-inch, five-petaled yellow flowers are subtle but attractive, contrasting nicely with the grayish foliage.

FRUIT: Hard, round, woody and nutlike, carried in the calyx that remains on the plant after the fruit and seeds are dispersed

LEAVES: Dense clusters of foliage occur at the tips of the branches. Individual leaves, about an inch long, are paddle-shaped with rounded tips, fleshy, gray, and somewhat fuzzy.

TRUNK: Multistemmed and shrubby; the dark brown or gray bark becomes shaggy with age and peels, revealing light yellow inner bark.

NATIVE RANGE: Coastal regions of south Florida, the Bahamas, the Caribbean, and tropical America; Zones 10–11

HABITAT: Dry, sandy beaches and dunes

PROPAGATION: Seed

Bay cedar is a pretty shrub that can tolerate the full blast of salt winds and even short periods of salt water inundation. It is a tough plant that will continue to look neat despite a harsh environment, and is valuable in helping to control beach erosion. In a more sheltered spot, it may grow to the size of a small tree.

FLORIDA TETRAZYGIA, WEST INDIES LILAC
Tetrazygia bicolor

HEIGHT: 15 feet

LIGHT: Sun to part shade

BLOOM: Flat white flowers with four to six petals and curved yellow stamens, carried in long, open clusters. They bloom from late spring through summer.

FRUIT: Half-inch, blue-black berries in open, elongated clusters, ripening in late summer and fall

LEAVES: Lance-shaped, quilted leaves are 3–5 inches long, smooth-edged and have three parallel main veins, the typical foliage pattern of the melastoma family, which includes the ornamental tibouchinas. The species name, "bicolor," refers to the foliage, which is dark green above and silver beneath.

TRUNK: Single or multistemmed and brown

NATIVE RANGE: In Florida, only in Miami-Dade County; similar species found in the West Indies; Zones 10–11

HABITAT: Pine woods and open hammocks, usually in acid, well-drained soil

PROPAGATION: Seed, cuttings

This rare and beautiful plant has a reputation for being difficult to establish, but its distinctive and colorful leaves and decorative flowers make it worth the effort. Incorporating some of the acid soil of its local native habitat probably would help it immensely in becoming established in the landscape. The fruit is eaten by many kinds of birds.

SEA LAVENDER
Tournefortia gnaphalodes

HEIGHT: 5–6 feet

LIGHT: Full sun

BLOOM: Small, clustered, five-petaled white flowers on spikes

FRUIT: Black, ¼-inch, rounded fruit

LEAVES: Fuzzy, silvery and narrow, to ¾ inch long, clustered at the branch ends in whorls

TRUNK: Multistemmed and dark, not usually visible because of the dense, clumping leaf growth

NATIVE RANGE: Coastal south Florida and the Caribbean; Zones 10–11

HABITAT: Beach front

PROPAGATION: Seed, layering

Sea lavender is one of our most elegant native coastal plants. It is extremely rare, hard to transplant, and has a reputation for being difficult and delicate, but every effort should be made to grow it in appropriate environments, which include full sun and no extra irrigation once it is established. Some native nurseries are attempting to grow this beautiful plant commercially, as it is so hard to find in the wild.

BLUEBERRY
Vaccinium darrowii

HEIGHT: 2–3 feet

LIGHT: Sun to partial shade

BLOOM: Clusters of white to pinkish, urn-shaped flowers, blooming in early spring

FRUIT: Edible blue berries

LEAVES: Alternate, oval, evergreen, light blue-green, ½ inch long, changing color to red and yellow in fall

TRUNK: Woody, branched shrub; the plant spreads by underground stolons, forming colonies

NATIVE RANGE: North and central Florida; Zones 8–9

HABITAT: Sandy woodlands

PROPAGATION: Seed, division, cuttings

Almost everyone loves blueberries; their only drawback is that the birds usually find them first. These low evergreen shrubs make nice border plants in moist, well-drained, acid soil. Plants also may be grown in containers. For good fruit production, mulch them well and prune back old growth every year. Highbush blueberry, *V. corymbosum*, is a 9-foot shrub with pinkish flowers and black berries. Shiny blueberry, *V. myrsinites*, is a shrubby little plant to 2 feet tall, with small, glossy leaves, pinkish flowers, and blue-black fruit. Both are native to north and central Florida.

SPANISH BAYONET
Yucca aloifolia

HEIGHT: 10–15 feet

LIGHT: Sun to part shade

BLOOM: Large panicles of 2½-inch white flowers from May to September, on branch tips

FRUIT: Drooping brown capsules, 3 inches long

LEAVES: Rosettes of hard, sharp-pointed, dark green leaves, 2 feet long and 2 inches wide, tapering to a sharp point

TRUNK: Overlapping leaves form a rough, woody trunk as the plant ages.

NATIVE RANGE: Coastal U.S., from the Carolinas through Florida, and the Gulf Coast to Mexico; Zones 8–11

HABITAT: Dry, sandy areas near the coast

PROPAGATION: Seed, division of clumps and root suckers

Spanish bayonet is a tough, hardy plant that needs minimal care. All it demands is well-drained soil. But any plant with stiff, sharp-pointed leaves such as this must be located with care. Its best use is where security screening or a dramatic accent is desired. It is very salt- and wind-tolerant and is excellent for beachfront landscaping or any sandy, arid location if surrounded with a ground cover or low plants to protect the unwary. Give it plenty of space, as the clumps tend to spread. The blossoms are edible and the roots provide a natural soap.

COONTIE
Zamia pumila

HEIGHT: 2–3 feet

LIGHT: Sun to shade

BLOOM: Brown cones; on male plants the cones are slender, to 7 inches long; female plants carry shorter, squatter cones.

FRUIT: Female cones split open, exposing fleshy, orange-red, 1-inch seeds.

LEAVES: Stiff, feathery fronds to 3 feet in length, with a dozen or more narrow, opposite, shiny, dark green leaflets.

NATIVE RANGE: Widespread throughout Florida; Zones 8–11

HABITAT: Open pine woods, coastal woodlands

PROPAGATION: Seed, offsets

Despite its appearance, coontie is neither a fern nor a palm, but a cycad, an ancient cone-bearing plant. While not usually defined as a shrub, it will serve that purpose. Cold-tolerant, it makes a tough, attractive ground cover or low border for a woodsy, somewhat shady site with well-drained soil. The underground stems of coontie were ground into a flour and used for making bread by the Seminole Indians in the early days. It also is a primary larval food source for the endangered atala, a small black and blue butterfly. Listed by the state as commercially exploited in the wild, it now is being produced by a good many native nurseries. The plant is listed also as *Z. floridana*.

WILDFLOWERS

FALSE FOXGLOVE, GERARDIA, AGALINIS
Agalinis spp.

HEIGHT: To 3 feet

LIGHT: Sun

BLOOM: Pink, five-lobed, funnel-shaped, 1-inch flowers, with purplish dots and yellow streaks inside the throat appear on tall, thin, branched stems during the summer and fall.

LEAVES: Narrow, rough, inch-long, opposite except for upper leaves, which are alternate

NATIVE RANGE: Atlantic and Gulf coasts to Texas and central Florida; Zones 6–9

HABITAT: Damp roadsides, woodlands, ditches, and meadows

PROPAGATION: Seed

Several species of agalinis are native to Florida. Although they are common roadside annuals, their delicately colored flowers create a delightful display, and the plants could be used in a casual wildflower garden in moist but not soggy soil. Don't let them dry out. They will attract butterflies, which use them as larval plants.

MILKWEED, BUTTERFLY WEED
Asclepias spp.

HEIGHT: 2 to 3 feet

LIGHT: Sun to part shade

BLOOM: Five-petaled flowers in clusters, white, greenish, yellow, or orange depending on species, with a long blooming season from spring through fall

LEAVES: Usually opposite (varying according to species), oval, lance-shaped, or long and narrow; stems usually have a milky sap.

NATIVE RANGE: Eastern U.S. throughout Florida; Zones 5–11

HABITAT: Pine woods, fields, damp meadows

PROPAGATION: Seed

A dozen or so species of milkweed are native to Florida, some growing throughout the state and others with a more limited range. These common perennials are essential to any butterfly garden, where they serve as larval and nectar plants. To encourage flowering, clip off old, faded clusters. The plants usually are found growing in poor, dry soil but respond to irrigation and better soil by producing larger clumps and more flowers. Butterflyweed, *A. tuberosa*, found throughout the state, is popular in native landscaping for its bright orange flowers. It has alternate leaves and the sap is not milky. *A. perennis*, with white, pink-tinged flowers, is native to central and northern Florida and blooms most of the year. Swamp milkweed, *A. incarnata*, usually found in damp areas, has pink flowers.

Scarlet milkweed, *A. curassavica*, a common perennial with orange and yellow flowers, is not native, but is loved nevertheless by monarch and queen butterflies.

CLIMBING ASTER
Aster carolinianus

HEIGHT: Vine-like, to 10 feet

LIGHT: Sun to part shade

BLOOM: Aster-like, 2 inches across, with narrow, pink to lavender rays and yellow to orange centers, blooming all year

LEAVES: Alternate, oval, gray-green; either rough or smooth, on woody stems

NATIVE RANGE: South Carolina to south Florida and the Gulf Coast; Zones 8–11

HABITAT: Swamps, edges of streams

PROPAGATION: Seed

Because this aster tends to sprawl or climb other shrubs, its best use is in an informal, woodsy setting where a little untidiness can be overlooked. It will add color in damp areas and along stream banks, perhaps planted with elderberry. Cut it back now and then to keep it flowering and growing vigorously.

GREENEYES
Berlandiera subacaulis

HEIGHT: To 18 inches

LIGHT: Sun to part shade

BLOOM: Solitary, daisy-like, eight-petalled flowers, 2 inches in diameter, with yellow rays and a distinctly green center, borne singly on hairy stems

LEAVES: Lobed and somewhat hairy leaves, 4–5 inches long, in a rosette at the base of plant

NATIVE RANGE: Only through Florida; Zones 8–10

HABITAT: Sandy pine woods, roadsides, meadows

PROPAGATION: Seed, division of clumps

Greeneyes are delightful little perennial plants that will add welcome color to a green woodland setting. In an open area they are wonderful combined with tropical sage or ruellia. Once established, they are drought-tolerant, need little care, and will bloom most of the year.

SPANISH NEEDLE, BEGGAR-TICKS
Bidens spp.

HEIGHT: 2–3 feet

LIGHT: Full sun

BLOOM: Aster-like flowers with a few ½-inch yellow or white rays and yellow centers, blooming all year

LEAVES: Stalked, usually divided but sometimes entire, with toothed edges

NATIVE RANGE: Throughout North America; all zones

HABITAT: Roadsides, disturbed areas; a common lawn weed

PROPAGATION: Seed

To most gardeners, Spanish needle is a noxious weed—invasive, ugly, and something to be uprooted immediately. To butterflies, however, it is the most attractive plant in the neighborhood, and a patch of it in bloom will lure multitudes of ruddy dagger wings, julias, and other species. Removing seed heads will help keep the plants from spreading and encourage the production of more flowers. *Bidens mitis*, usually called beggar-ticks, has all-yellow flowers; *B. pilosa* has white rays and yellow-orange centers.

SEA OX-EYE DAISY
Borrichia arborescens

HEIGHT: 3–4 feet

LIGHT: Sun

BLOOM: Daisy-like yellow flowers, 1 inch in diameter

LEAVES: Pale green or grayish, opposite, succulent, 1–3 inches long and spatulate in shape

TRUNK: Woody and shrubby

NATIVE RANGE: South Florida, West Indies, and tropical America; Zones 10–11

HABITAT: Beaches, marshes and low hammocks near the sea

PROPAGATION: Seed, rooted cuttings

The drought- and salt-tolerant sea ox-eye daisy is an excellent small, carefree shrub for oceanside planting. Its flowers make a good display throughout the year, while its suckering roots stabilize beach sand, growing and spreading to form an attractive colony of plants. A similar species, *B. frutescens*, also called ox-eye daisy, is a bit smaller and grows throughout the state. The two species sometimes hybridize naturally.

SEA ROCKET
Cakile lanceolata

HEIGHT: To 18 inches

LIGHT: Sun

BLOOM: Small (¼-inch), four-petaled, white to pale lavender flowers in clusters, blooming from spring to fall, followed by fleshy, angled seed pods, 1 inch long.

LEAVES: Succulent, alternate leaves, 3–5 inches long, varying in shape and either smooth-edged or deeply lobed

NATIVE RANGE: East coast of U.S. from North Carolina to the Keys; Zones 8–11

HABITAT: Sandy beaches and dunes

PROPAGATION: Seed

Few plants are as accepting of sand, hot sun, and salt air as this attractive little succulent, which often forms dense, bright green clumps right on the beach. A member of the mustard family (its leaves have a peppery taste), it is one of the small number of plants well suited to oceanfront landscaping where it also will help prevent erosion.

FLORIDA PAINTBRUSH
Carphephorus corymbosus

HEIGHT: 3 feet

LIGHT: Sun

BLOOM: Flat heads of small pink to purple, rayless, fragrant flowers blooming in late summer and fall

LEAVES: Alternate, light green, oval leaves, 1–3 inches in length, which clasp the hairy stem and become smaller and narrower as they ascend

NATIVE RANGE: Coastal plain from the Carolinas to north and central Florida; Zones 8–9

HABITAT: Dry, sandy sites, pine woods

PROPAGATION: Seed

This tall, colorful perennial in the aster family is not only highly ornamental but is an excellent nectar source in a butterfly garden. In a grassy meadow it is truly spectacular. It does best in an acid soil. Related species also native to Florida are deer tongue, *C. paniculatus*, and vanilla plant, *C. odoratissimus*, which is said to have a vanilla-like scent.

PARTRIDGE PEA
Cassia fasciculata

HEIGHT: 4 feet

LIGHT: Sun to light shade

BLOOM: Bright yellow, five-petaled flowers, touched with red at the base are about 2 inches across and bloom from spring to early winter.

LEAVES: Compound, alternate, feather-like, with about 12 pairs of tiny light green, sensitive leaflets that fold up when they are touched; stems may be reddish.

NATIVE RANGE: Eastern U.S. from Massachusetts to Texas, throughout Florida; Zones 6–10

HABITAT: Well-drained, sandy soils, roadsides

PROPAGATION: Seed

Partridge pea is a colorful, low-maintenance choice for an informal setting. It is an annual but will reseed by itself. The leaves and flowers are larval plants for several kinds of butterflies, and its peas, carried in 2- to 3-inch pods, attract birds. The plant also is listed in the genus *Chamaecrista*.

FLORIDA ASTER, GOLDEN ASTER
Chrysopsis spp.

HEIGHT: To 3 feet

LIGHT: Sun

BLOOM: Daisy-like flowers, usually an inch or less in diameter with bright yellow rays and yellow, sometimes hairy disks, are borne on branching, generally hairy stems. Blooming is usually in late summer and fall, although some species bloom year-round.

LEAVES: Alternate, long, lance-shaped or oval, often aromatic and dotted with glands

NATIVE RANGE: Various species throughout the eastern U.S. and throughout Florida; Zones 3–11

HABITAT: Pine woods, sandy coastal areas

PROPAGATION: Seed, division

Many species share the name golden aster; they also may be listed in the genus *Heterotheca*. The plants are a bit on the weedy side, but they offer colorful flowers, attract butterflies and are accepting of heat, drought and poor soil, even near the beach. Use them to add a woodsy, casual look to the wildflower garden. Taller species may be used as background plants or low shrubs.

DAYFLOWER
Commelina erecta

HEIGHT: 8–10 inches

LIGHT: Sun to shade

BLOOM: One-inch flowers with two large sky-blue petals and one small white petal; flower centers are yellow. They appear in clusters on an erect stem, blooming most of the year.

LEAVES: Alternate leaves are narrowly elliptic or lance-shaped, hugging the stems.

NATIVE RANGE: New York to Texas and throughout Florida; Zones 5–10

HABITAT: Sandy areas, fields

PROPAGATION: Seed, division of tubers

Commelinas are tuberous perennials related to the wandering jew. They owe their common name to their habit of opening in the morning and closing by mid-afternoon. Dayflower may not be a particularly gorgeous plant, but it does provide that clear blue color so rare in flowers. Don't confuse it with *C. diffusa,* a low, creeping species, which is a common lawn weed with little landscaping value.

AGERATUM, MISTFLOWER
Conoclinium coelestinum

HEIGHT: 1–2 feet

LIGHT: Full to part sun

BLOOM: Many dense, puffy heads of small, fuzzy lavender-blue flowers, blooming summer and fall

LEAVES: Triangular, toothed and crinkled, 1½–2 inches long, on branched stems

NATIVE RANGE: Eastern U.S., from Michigan throughout Florida; Zones 5–11

HABITAT: Wetlands, ditches, edges of woods

PROPAGATION: Seed

A small annual in the aster family and a good nectar plant for butterflies, ageratum does best in well-drained soil in a sunny garden. It is listed also as *Eupatorium coelestinum*, and many cultivated forms are popular garden flowers.

Conradina *Conradina etonia*   Apalachicola rosemary *C. glabra*

CONRADINA, SCRUB MINT
Conradina spp.

HEIGHT: To 2 feet

LIGHT: Sun

BLOOM: Clusters of two-lipped flowers up to 1 inch long and ranging from white to pink and lavender-blue, blooming spring to fall

LEAVES: Small, to ½-inch, needlelike, rolled leaves, green to gray in color, on shrubby, woody stems

NATIVE RANGE: North and central Florida, eastern Alabama; Zones 8–9

HABITAT: Scrub pine woods, sand ridges, bluffs, in well-drained soil

PROPAGATION: Seed, cuttings

Several species of these rare aromatic mints, which flower prolifically, occur in various parts of the state and are known by an assortment of common names. Apalachicola rosemary, *C. glabra*, with white flowers, is native to north Florida. Short-leaved rosemary, *C. brevifolia*, has white flowers and tiny grayish leaves and is found in a very limited range in central Florida. Scrub mint, *C. grandiflora*, in southeastern Florida, has inch-long lavender flowers and green leaves that resemble rosemary. *C. canescens* and *C. etonia* have smaller lavender-pink flowers with the larger lower lip spotted in dark purple. Conradinas will do well in a sunny area in dry, sandy soil, but need irrigation until they are established. A few native nurseries, fortunately, are propagating these plants; their natural habitats are shrinking.

COREOPSIS, TICKSEED
Coreopsis spp.

HEIGHT: 3 feet

LIGHT: Sun

BLOOM: Daisy-like flowers, an inch across, with bright yellow rays and deep brown or purplish centers on slender branched stalks, bloom mainly in spring and summer but flowers may appear at any time of the year.

LEAVES: Varying by species; may be alternate or opposite, long and narrow or oval, and smooth to hairy

NATIVE RANGE: East and Gulf coasts, throughout Florida; Zones 4–10

HABITAT: Ditches, roadsides, damp woodlands

PROPAGATION: Seed

Several species of tickseed, perennials in the aster family, grow in various parts of Florida in either damp or dry soils and flowering at different seasons. They need full sun to flower well. One, *C. nudata* or swamp coreopsis, a wetland plant of northern Florida, has pink rays and a bright yellow center and is a particularly attractive flowering plant for a wild garden. Coreopsis reseed readily, are simple to grow, and may be used as cut flowers. They also are nectar plants for butterflies.

STRING LILY, SWAMP LILY
Crinum americanum

HEIGHT: To 2½ feet

LIGHT: Sun to part shade

BLOOM: Snow white and fragrant, with three long, slim, curved petals and three sepals joined at the base, and purple anthers, appearing in clusters at the top of a tall stalk in spring and summer

LEAVES: Long, strap-like, dark green with slightly toothed edges

NATIVE RANGE: Throughout Florida and Gulf Coast to Texas; Zones 8–10

HABITAT: Edges of fresh water swamps and other damp sites

PROPAGATION: Seed, bulb division

The string lily is a real eye-catcher in both the wild and the home garden. Give it rich soil and plenty of water and it will respond with a lush display of dark foliage and spectacular flowers. String lily may be distinguished from its look-alike relative, the spider lily (*Hymenocallis latifolia*), by the lack of a central crown in its blossom.

LAKELA'S MINT
Dicerandra immaculata

HEIGHT: To 2 feet

LIGHT: Sun

BLOOM: Two-lipped flowers, with the upper lip having two lobes and the lower lip three lobes. Flowers, which have long anthers, are clustered in the leaf axils along the top branches and bloom in summer and fall.

LEAVES: Small, narrow, opposite, aromatic, on square stems

NATIVE RANGE: Some species grow from southern Georgia to northern Florida, Zones 8–9; others are limited to a small area of central Florida, Zone 9

HABITAT: Well-drained sandy soil, scrub pinelands

PROPAGATION: Seed

Dicerandras are shrubby, branching mints, with a strong mint-like aroma. Scrub balm, *D. frutescens,* is white-flowered with pink spots. Lakela's mint, *D. immaculata,* has almost vanished from the wild. Limited to a tiny part of central Florida, its habitat has been almost destroyed by development. In addition, its prolific masses of bright rosy-pink flowers probably have made it irresistible to collectors. *D. linearifolia,* of central and north Florida, has pinkish-purple flowers. Garret's mint, *D. christmanii,* is native only to the Lake Wales Ridge. These species will grow somewhat out of their restricted ranges if given well-drained soil, and it is fortunate that a few botanical gardens, such as Bok Tower Gardens, are propagating them.

PURPLE CONEFLOWER
Echinacea purpurea

HEIGHT: 2–3 feet

LIGHT: Sun to part shade

BLOOM: Daisy-like, 3-inch flowers, usually borne singly on hairy stems, have red-purple rays and a reddish-brown, cone-shaped center. They bloom from early summer through fall.

LEAVES: Coarse, prickly, oblong, alternate, to 6 inches in length

NATIVE RANGE: Southeastern U.S. to Texas and through Florida; Zones 7–10

HABITAT: Fields, disturbed areas, dry woods

PROPAGATION: Seed, division of clumps

This hardy perennial, offering very showy flowers, asks for little care, tolerates heat and drought, but needs good drainage. Plants die back in cold weather but leaf out again in spring. The long-lasting flowers, whose nectar attracts butterflies, are fine in cut arrangements. When the flowers die, the petals fall but the seed-bearing cones remain, attracting birds. In addition to the native variety, hybrids and selected forms are available from nurseries and seed companies.

BUTTERFLY ORCHID
Encyclia tampensis

HEIGHT: To 1½ feet

LIGHT: Sun to shade

BLOOM: Several 1½-inch flowers appear alternately on a tall, thin stalk, flowering from spring to fall. Blooms usually are yellow-green or brownish with a whitish lip; petals and lip are touched with a rose-purple spot or stripe. There are many variations in color, including white forms.

LEAVES: One to three long slim leaves, from a few inches to a foot or more in length, grow from a gray-green pseudobulb. Leaves tend to be longer on plants growing in the shade.

NATIVE RANGE: North central Florida to the Keys and the Bahamas; Zones 9–11

HABITAT: An epiphyte, or air plant, the butterfly orchid is found growing on the branches and trunks of mangroves, pond apples, oaks, pines, and even occasionally on rocks.

PROPAGATION: Seed, division

This is Florida's most common orchid. Like other Florida orchids, it is protected by law, but private growers sometimes propagate and share it. Old plants often form large, dense masses on tree limbs. They are not parasites and take nothing from the host tree, but merely use it as a platform. Many lovely orchids—clamshell, vanilla, cowhorn, ghost orchids, and more—once were common in Florida but have almost vanished. More than 60 native orchid species are listed as threatened or endangered.

ERYNGIUM, SNAKEROOT
Eryngium aquaticum

HEIGHT: To 3 feet

LIGHT: Partial sun

BLOOM: Dense, rounded heads of tiny, powder-blue flowers, surrounded by pointed bracts, on branched stalks

LEAVES: Long, alternate, spineless

NATIVE RANGE: Southeastern U.S. to north and central Florida; Zones 8–9

HABITAT: Moist pine woods, ditches, edges of woods

PROPAGATION: Seed

This is the most attractive of the several eryngium species found in Florida. The flowers change color as they age, from greenish-white through unusual shades of blue, rose, and rust. Give this celery relative a damp spot to grow and its flowers will attract butterflies to the garden. The related button snakeroot, *E. yuccifolium*, grows throughout Florida and has spiny leaves.

SEASIDE GENTIAN
Eustoma exaltatum

HEIGHT: 2 feet

LIGHT: Sun or light shade

BLOOM: Five-petaled, bell-shaped flowers, 2 to 3 inches across, lavender to purple with a darker purple center and bright yellow stamens, in bloom most of the year

LEAVES: Two-inch-long oval or oblong gray-green or bluish-green, opposite leaves on a straight stem to 2 feet tall

NATIVE RANGE: The Gulf Coast, central and south Florida and the Caribbean; Zones 9–11

HABITAT: Beaches, sand dunes, wet ditches, and marshland

PROPAGATION: Seed

Despite the silky, delicate appearance of its blooms, the annual seaside gentian will tolerate salty conditions, wind and poor soil. One of Florida's showier native wildflowers, it is a relative of the Texas bluebell and the commercial lisianthus. Its combination of striking flowers and grayish foliage puts it high on the list of desirable ornamentals for beach-front landscaping.

YELLOWTOP
Flaveria linearis

HEIGHT: To 3 feet

LIGHT: Sun

BLOOM: Flat, branched heads composed of many small, bright yellow aster-like flowers, usually with only one ray flower to a cluster, blooming mainly in fall and winter

LEAVES: Narrow, about 4 inches long

NATIVE RANGE: Central and south Florida and West Indies; Zones 9–11

HABITAT: Pine woods, roadsides, damp coastal sites, and salt marshes

PROPAGATION: Seed

This colorful perennial will serve the same function in the wildflower garden or grassy meadow as goldenrod, although its use probably is limited to the southern and perhaps central parts of the state. Its flowers provide nectar for butterflies, and it is an attractive plant even when not in bloom.

BLANKET FLOWER
Gaillardia pulchella

HEIGHT: 1½ feet

LIGHT: Sun

BLOOM: Zinnia-like flowers are usually orange or maroon with yellow tips and a darker center disk, but colors vary. Flowers appear singly on long stems that may sprawl or remain upright.

LEAVES: Narrow, alternate, lance-shaped, with the lower leaves toothed at the edges

NATIVE RANGE: Southeast U.S. throughout Florida; Zones 6–10

HABITAT: Beaches, roadsides, open waste sites

PROPAGATION: Seed, division of clumps

An annual, gaillardia flowers year-round and reseeds prolifically. A tough little plant, it tolerates heat and drought and is fairly tolerant of salt, so it often is used in plantings near the beach. However, it will grow and bloom almost anywhere. The showy blossoms attract butterflies and may be used as cut flowers. Remove the old flower heads to encourage more bloom.

NARROW-LEAF SUNFLOWER, SWAMP SUNFLOWER
Helianthus angustifolius

HEIGHT: 6 feet

LIGHT: Sun

BLOOM: Flowers are 3 inches in diameter, with bright yellow rays and purplish centers, displayed at the top of tall stems; blooming season is late summer and autumn.

LEAVES: Alternate, rough, narrow, almost grasslike, to 6 inches in length, on rough, hairy stems

NATIVE RANGE: New York to eastern U.S. and into north and central Florida; Zones 5–9

HABITAT: Wetlands, disturbed areas

PROPAGATION: Seed, division of clumps

A tall, slim, branching perennial in the aster family, narrow-leaf sunflower is beautiful when planted toward the rear of a wildflower garden or used as a striking and colorful accent against a background of green shrubs. Moist soil suits it best.

BEACH SUNFLOWER, DUNE SUNFLOWER
Helianthus debilis

HEIGHT: 1–2 feet

LIGHT: Sun

BLOOM: A 2-inch yellow sunflower with a brown center, blooming all year

LEAVES: Triangular, hairy foliage, alternating along the trailing stems

NATIVE RANGE: Along the coast from the Carolinas to Texas and throughout Florida; Zones 8–10

HABITAT: Beaches and dunes

PROPAGATION: Seed, cuttings

This bright drought- and salt-resistant plant is an annual, but can be considered permanent because of its profuse seeding. It is an indispensable part of the coastal landscape, forming large colonies and adding color year-round, and is a perfect no-work ground cover if irrigation is used sparingly. It also is a nectar plant for butterflies.

SPIDER LILY
Hymenocallis latifolia

HEIGHT: 2–3 feet

LIGHT: Sun to part shade

BLOOM: Loose clusters of 10–15 fragrant, white, 5-inch blossoms are carried on a tall stalk above the foliage. Each tubular flower has a crown-like center, six slender, curving petals, and six long stamens. They bloom from spring to fall, and are followed by large oval seed pods.

LEAVES: Strap-like, 2 inches wide and 2½ feet long, dark green, rising from a central bulb base and forming dense clumps

NATIVE RANGE: South Florida and the West Indies; Zones 10–11

HABITAT: Beaches, elevated sites in mangrove swamp areas and open rocky areas through the Keys

PROPAGATION: Seed, division of bulbs; it takes about a year to get a good-sized plant from seed, but the underground bulbs multiply rapidly and may be separated and replanted.

The spider lily is one of Florida's most beautiful native flowers and is becoming very popular for low-maintenance landscaping as a ground cover, accent plant, or border planting. It is highly tolerant of beach conditions and most types of soil, but the bright green leaves are a favorite of lubber grasshoppers. Like the related alligator lily and string lily, it belongs to the amaryllis family.

ALLIGATOR LILY
Hymenocallis palmeri

HEIGHT: 1½–2 feet

LIGHT: Sun to part shade

BLOOM: Fragrant, six-petaled white flowers have a six-pointed crown at the center. They resemble the spider lily, but only a single flower appears on each stalk and the central crown has a toothed edge.

LEAVES: Long, narrow, ½-inch wide, and smooth

NATIVE RANGE: Central and south Florida; Zones 9–11

HABITAT: Damp areas, roadsides

PROPAGATION: Seed, bulb division

Less frequently seen in landscaping than *H. latifolia,* the alligator lily is a delicately beautiful native flower that deserves to be propagated and used more widely. It is smaller and more delicate in appearance than the spider lily, and probably a little fussier about soil and water.

STANDING CYPRESS
Ipomopsis rubra

HEIGHT: To 3 feet

LIGHT: Sun to part shade

BLOOM: Brilliantly red, tubular, 1¼-inch flowers, touched with yellow, have flaring lobes. Clustered at the top of leafy stems, they bloom mainly in summer and early fall.

LEAVES: Delicate, finely divided alternate leaves are larger toward the base of the tall stalks, becoming smaller as they ascend.

NATIVE RANGE: The Carolinas to Texas and north and central Florida; Zones 7–9

HABITAT: Dry, sandy fields, edges of woodlands

PROPAGATION: Seed

If you love red flowers, standing cypress is a magnificent choice for the wild garden or meadow. Individual plants are tall and slim; plant them in a mass for a spectacular display. They have been reported to reach 5 feet or more with extra good care. The plant is a perennial and will reseed in the garden. A member of the phlox family, standing cypress is also listed as *Gilia rubra*.

IRIS
Iris spp.

HEIGHT: To 4 feet

LIGHT: Sun to light shade

BLOOM: Striking, unmistakable flower with three upright petals and three drooping outer sepals up to 4 inches long, sometimes touched with yellow, blooming in spring on tall, fleshy stalks rising well above the leaves

FRUIT: Oval, ridged, 3-inch seed pods

LEAVES: 2-foot, sword-like leaves with parallel veins, clasping the flower stalks

NATIVE RANGE: Virginia through Florida; Zones 7–10

HABITAT: Damp pine woods, lake banks, marshy sites

PROPAGATION: Seed, division of rhizomes

Florida is fortunate to have several native iris, prized for their magnificent blue or purple blooms. Prairie iris, *I. hexagona*, found in moist areas throughout the state, can be identified by its zigzag stems. Southern blue flag, *I. virginica*, is similar but straight-stemmed; it grows only into northern Florida. Purple flag, *I. tridenta*, with deep purple flowers streaked in white, also is limited to northern Florida.

LIATRIS, BLAZING STAR, GAYFEATHER
Liatris spp.

HEIGHT: To 3 feet

LIGHT: Sun

BLOOM: Small, fuzzy blossoms, usually rose-purple but occasionally white, are clustered densely on a tall, leafy spike. They are unusual because the flower buds at the top of the stalk open first, succeeded by those lower on the stalk.

LEAVES: Narrow, alternate; either smooth or hairy depending on the species

NATIVE RANGE: Eastern U.S. through Florida and the Gulf Coast; Zones 3–9

HABITAT: Roadsides, open woodlands, damp or dry soils depending on species

PROPAGATION: Seed, root division

A dozen or so species of liatris, which belong to the aster family, are found throughout Florida. The most desirable, such as *L. spicata,* have dramatic and striking flowers. Let them stand by themselves or mix them with an assortment of other native wild-flowers in well-drained soil. They are undemanding and hardy plants in the garden, where they will reseed, and are long-lasting as cut flowers. Butterflies love them. Several named cultivars, with white, purple, or lavender flowers, are on the market.

CARDINAL FLOWER
Lobelia cardinalis

HEIGHT: 3–4 feet, occasionally taller

LIGHT: Sun to part shade

BLOOM: Brilliantly red, two-lipped flowers, with two upper and three lower lobes, to 2 inches long, on tall spikes, blooming summer through fall

LEAVES: Oval to lance-shaped, alternate, with toothed edges, on leafy, usually unbranched stems

NATIVE RANGE: Eastern U.S. into north and central Florida; Zones 2–9

HABITAT: Damp meadows, edges of rivers, and marshes

PROPAGATION: Seed

Few native wildflowers are more boldly red than the cardinal flower, and hummingbirds like it as much as gardeners do. Almost an aquatic plant, it needs plenty of water and does well when naturalized at the edge of a lake or pond in dappled shade. Plant it in a mass for an eye-catching display; it's a short-lived perennial but will reseed in good soil. Several commercial hybrids of this lobelia are on the market.

Swamp lobelia, *L. glandulosa*, also found in wet areas, has similarly shaped but smaller blue or purplish flowers with white centers and slender leaves. It blooms most of the year.

MIMOSA, SENSITIVE PLANT
Mimosa strigillosa

HEIGHT: Low ground cover, 3–4 inches

LIGHT: Sun

BLOOM: Pink puffballs about 1 inch across, on short stems, blooming from spring to early fall and followed by inch-long, rough, jointed pods

LEAVES: Small, fern-like leaflets that fold up when touched

NATIVE RANGE: Georgia to north and central Florida; Zones 8–9

HABITAT: Woodlands, disturbed areas, damp sites

PROPAGATION: Seed, division

Mimosa, with its sensitive leaves, is a time-honored source of entertainment to children. As a perennial ground cover, it provides subtle color. A potential substitute for lawn grass, it can be mowed, preferably when it is not in bloom. Either moist or well-drained soil suits it, and it will grow south of its natural range. The similar sensitive briar, *Schrankia microphylla*, found statewide, has thorny stems.

MONARDA, HORSEMINT
Monarda punctata

HEIGHT: To 3 feet

LIGHT: Sun to part shade

BLOOM: The "flower" is actually an inflorescence composed of lavender bracts surrounding small, spotted yellow flowers tightly clustered around the square, leafy stem. They bloom from late spring to fall.

LEAVES: Aromatic, opposite, oval to lance-shaped with toothed edges

NATIVE RANGE: New York to central Florida and along the Gulf Coast to Texas; Zones 6–9

HABITAT: Sandy fields, disturbed areas

PROPAGATION: Seed, cuttings, division of clumps

While monarda is fairly large and ornamental, it has a soft, almost dusty pastel color. Despite that subtle tone, the flowers of this perennial, a mint relative, will attract hummingbirds and butterflies to the wild garden. While it is hardy, it responds to good care: Give it water and a rich but well-drained soil. Cut older plants back each year after blooming to make them fuller and encourage flowering; you can use the cuttings for new plants.

PALAFOXIA
Palafoxia spp.

HEIGHT: To 5 feet

LIGHT: Sun

BLOOM: Heads of small, white to pinkish-lavender, tubular, rayless flowers on stalked, hairy stems, blooming in late summer and fall

LEAVES: Alternate, oval to lance-shaped, 1–2 inches long and wider near the base of the plant

NATIVE RANGE: Central and south Florida; Zones 9–10

HABITAT: Pine woods, scrub areas

PROPAGATION: Seed

Palafoxias are members of the aster family. Up close, the tiny flowers have a ragged look, but at a distance the dense clusters present an airy light appearance. They need a well-drained, sandy soil in a sunny location. One showy species, sometimes called many-wings, *P. integrifolia,* has pinkish flowers and rather short stems. *P. feayi* is a taller, shrubbier species with whitish flowers.

WHITE PENSTEMON, BEARDTONGUE
Penstemon multiflorus

HEIGHT: 2½ feet

LIGHT: Sun to light shade

BLOOM: Pale lavender-white, tubular, five-lobed flowers up to an inch long, similar in shape to snapdragons and blooming from spring to fall

LEAVES: A rosette of basal leaves, with smaller leaves arranged oppositely on the branched flower stalks

NATIVE RANGE: Virginia to Alabama and throughout Florida; Zones 7–10

HABITAT: Pinelands, disturbed areas

PROPAGATION: Seed

This is one of many species of penstemon, perennial natives found throughout the country. Another species, found in north and central Florida, is *P. australis*, with pink to purple flowers. They'll do well in the wild garden with good irrigation and a well-drained soil, and will reseed. The blooms are popular in flower arrangements.

FALSE DRAGONHEAD, OBEDIENT PLANT
Physostegia purpurea

HEIGHT: To 3 feet

LIGHT: Sun to part shade

BLOOM: Two-lipped lavender flowers,
1 inch long, resembling snapdragons and
borne in spikes on slender, square-edged
stalks in late summer and fall

LEAVES: Opposite, lance-shaped, toothed

NATIVE RANGE: Eastern U.S. to central
Florida; Zones 5–9

HABITAT: Damp woodlands, swamp edges

PROPAGATION: Seed, root division

A perennial in the mint family, false drag-
onhead may be used near the water's edge,
yet it will tolerate dry conditions. It is attractive in a border and as a cut flower. If the
plant is killed back by frost, it will regrow
from the roots in the spring. Move a single
flower on the stalk in any direction and it
will remain in that position—thus the name
"obedient plant." Several species occur in the
southern U.S.

PENNYROYAL
Piloblephis rigida

HEIGHT: 2 feet

LIGHT: Sun

BLOOM: Small, fragrant, two-lipped lavender flowers have two lobes on the upper lip and three on the lower lip, which is spotted with purple. The flowers, carried in dense heads, bloom most of the year.

LEAVES: Dense, opposite, evergreen, ½-inch, needlelike leaves on branching stems have a minty aroma.

NATIVE RANGE: Central and south Florida; Zones 9–10

HABITAT: Dry pine woods, scrub land

PROPAGATION: Seed, cuttings

As it tends to sprawl, this aromatic mint makes a good small-leaved ground cover. It prefers sandy, well-drained, rather acid soil and is tolerant of cold and drought but not salty conditions. Pennyroyal is a good nectar plant for butterflies, and its leaves can be used to make a tea.

SILKGRASS, SILVER-LEAFED ASTER
Pityopsis graminifolia

HEIGHT: To 2½ feet

LIGHT: Sun

BLOOM: Bright yellow aster-like flowers, an inch across, with up to 10 rays, blooming from summer to fall on branching stems held above the grassy foliage

LEAVES: Grasslike, 1 foot in length, with a silvery sheen

NATIVE RANGE: Eastern U.S., throughout Florida, West Indies; Zones 5–11

HABITAT: Dry fields, sandy areas

PROPAGATION: Seed, division of clumps

What separates this aster from most of its relatives is its attractive silvery foliage. Less coarse in appearance than many asters, this perennial is pretty even when out of bloom, especially when the leaves are backlit by the sun. It would work in a border or flower bed with other wildflowers, such as liatris or tropical sage. Full sun and a well-drained acid soil suit it best. Silkgrass also is listed as *Heterotheca graminifolia*.

PLUCHEA
Pluchea rosea

HEIGHT: 3 feet

LIGHT: Sun

BLOOM: Rounded clusters of small, bright purple-pink, rayless flowers, blooming from spring to fall

LEAVES: Oval or oblong, alternate, 2–4 inches long, hairy and aromatic

NATIVE RANGE: Coastal New England to south Florida and the West Indies; Zones 6–10

HABITAT: Pine woods, fence rows, marshes

PROPAGATION: Seed

This coarse but colorful annual isn't common in cultivation, but might deserve a spot in a native plant garden with damp soil. It reseeds readily. A similar species, *P. odorata*, grows in dry soil along the edges of salt marshes. Both species are quite salt-tolerant.

JOINTWEED
Polygonella spp.

HEIGHT: 2 feet

LIGHT: Sun, light shade

BLOOM: Loose spikes of tiny, fragrant, white, cream or pinkish flowers on leafy stems, blooming in summer and fall

LEAVES: Small (less than 1 inch), narrow, alternate, on woody, branching stems

NATIVE RANGE: Coastal region from Virginia throughout Florida; Zones 7–10

HABITAT: Sandy woodland, scrub forests

PROPAGATION: Seed

Several species of polygonella, perennials in the buckwheat family, are found in Florida. Most are erect plants but *P. myriophylla* is a rather sprawling plant that flowers prolifically and has a delicate, almost smoke-like appearance. Native to a small region of central Florida, it would be a lovely addition to a wildflower garden.

MEADOW BEAUTY, RHEXIA
Rhexia spp.

HEIGHT: 1–3 feet

LIGHT: Sun to light shade

BLOOM: Delicate, four-petaled flowers, usually rose pink to white and up to 2 inches across, with yellow stamens, blooming from spring to fall

LEAVES: Narrow, opposite, up to 3 inches long, with three distinct veins; stems may be smooth or hairy, branched or not, depending on species

NATIVE RANGE: Southeastern U.S. to north and central Florida; Zones 7–9

HABITAT: Damp meadows, ditches

PROPAGATION: Seed, division

Meadow beauty is a dainty little perennial with bright but short-lived flowers, requiring a boggy garden setting where it will multiply by way of its tuberous roots. There are a number of species that grow in various parts of the state; one uncommon species found in northwestern Florida has yellow flowers.

BLACK-EYED SUSAN
Rudbeckia hirta

HEIGHT: 2 feet

LIGHT: Full sun to partial shade

BLOOM: Two- to 3-inch flowers with daisy-like yellow rays and brownish-black centers bloom all year.

LEAVES: Alternate, with a rough surface and toothed edges, on hairy stems

NATIVE RANGE: Canada through eastern U.S. to south central Florida; Zones 2–9

HABITAT: Roadsides, meadows

PROPAGATION: Seed

A bright, cheerful addition to the wildflower garden, black-eyed Susan tolerates most conditions but it will look its best in a fairly rich, well-drained soil with good irrigation. A short-lived perennial, it reseeds readily. It is popular as a cut flower, and a number of commercial garden plants have been developed from it. Butterflies are attracted to its nectar and birds to the seeds.

RUELLIA, WILD PETUNIA
Ruellia caroliniensis

HEIGHT: 1–2 feet

LIGHT: Sun to part shade

BLOOM: Showy blue to lavender tubular flowers are open only in the morning or all day on cloudy days. The native species has stalkless blooms. Flowers average 1–2 inches across and appear from spring to fall, followed by a long, thin capsule that splits when ripe, ejecting the seed.

LEAVES: Oval, pointed, fuzzy, 2–2½ inches long

NATIVE RANGE: The Carolinas to all of Florida and west to Texas; Zones 8–11

HABITAT: Open woodlands

PROPAGATION: Seed, cuttings

These perennial plants tend to vary in size and growth habit. Easy to grow, they add a lovely amethyst color to the wildflower garden and are butterfly attractants. Several species of ruellia appear in Florida, and there is a great deal of disagreement as to which are native and which are introduced. In spite of its common name, it is not related to the garden petunia.

SABATIA, MARSH PINK
Sabatia spp.

HEIGHT: From a few inches to 3 feet, depending on species

LIGHT: Sun to part shade

BLOOM: White to deep pink flowers with a yellow eye are usually five-petaled although there may be as many as 12, depending on species. Flowers may be as much as 2 inches across but generally are smaller, appearing from spring to early winter at the tips of the stems, which usually are branched.

LEAVES: Opposite, varying in shape but most often long and narrow

NATIVE RANGE: Virginia to south Florida and Alabama; Zones 7–10

HABITAT: Marshy meadows, low pinewoods

PROPAGATION: Seed

At least a half dozen species of sabatia, which belong to the gentian family, may be found in Florida's damp, grassy meadows. Most will grow anywhere in the state although a few are limited to north and central Florida. They'll do well in a boggy garden with rich soil.

TROPICAL SAGE, SCARLET SAGE
Salvia coccinea

HEIGHT: 2 feet

LIGHT: Sun or light shade

BLOOM: Bright red, inch-long, two-lipped flowers on a tall, squared, leafy stem, blooming all year

LEAVES: Opposite, oval, with toothed edges, to 2 inches in length

NATIVE RANGE: South Carolina to Texas, all of Florida and tropical America; Zones 8–11

HABITAT: Open, disturbed sites and roadsides in well-drained soil

PROPAGATION: Seed

Tropical sage, our only native sage with red blossoms, is one of our most colorful wildflowers. A short-lived perennial, it tends to get woody as it ages, but will reseed and spread. It is drought-tolerant and attracts butterflies and hummingbirds. Larger, showier commercial varieties have been developed from this plant.

LYRELEAF SAGE
Salvia lyrata

HEIGHT: 2 feet

LIGHT: Sun to light shade

BLOOM: Purple-blue, two-lipped flowers clustered in whorls around a square stem, blooming spring to fall

LEAVES: Purple-green leaves, usually lobed, grow in a rosette at the base of the plant; the stem also may have a few leaves.

NATIVE RANGE: Eastern U.S. to south Florida; Zones 6–10

HABITAT: Roadsides, sandy, disturbed areas

PROPAGATION: Seed

An annual, lyreleaf sage will reseed and spread. It tends to become weedy unless contained in a planting bed, but it is attractive enough that it deserves a place in an informal wildflower garden.

PITCHER PLANT, TRUMPETS
Sarracenia flava

HEIGHT: 2 feet

LIGHT: Sun to part shade

BLOOM: Yellow, five-petaled flowers with a musky odor, appearing in spring

LEAVES: Long, upright, hollow leaves are yellow-green, spotted or streaked with red, and flaring at the top.

NATIVE RANGE: Coastal U.S. from North Carolina into north and central Florida; Zones 8–9

HABITAT: Bogs, edges of ponds, usually growing with peat or sphagnum moss

PROPAGATION: Seed, division of underground stolons

This carnivorous plant's hollow leaves trap insects, which are then digested, supplying some nutrients to the plant. The entire group of pitcher plants is fascinating, and consequently they have been collected from the wild to the point where they are rare and endangered. Other species found in Florida, although limited to the northern section, are the hooded pitcher plant (*S. minor*), the white pitcher plant (*S. leucophylla*), and a few red-flowered forms such as *S. rubra*. They are seldom available commercially, but if your property includes a boggy, sandy area, it already may be home to one or more pitcher plants, which should be protected and enjoyed.

LIZARD'S TAIL
Saururus cernuus

HEIGHT: 3 feet

LIGHT: Sun to part shade

BLOOM: A fairly showy spike of tiny whitish flowers that droops at the tip, blooming from spring to fall

LEAVES: Fresh green, pointed, heart-shaped leaves, alternating up thin stems

NATIVE RANGE: Eastern U.S. and throughout Florida; Zones 5–10

HABITAT: Shallow water or along banks of streams and ponds and in swamps and wet woods

PROPAGATION: Division

Lizard's tail is an attractive little native with interesting blooms, useful in wet sites. It's one of those plants that children notice because of its amusing flowers. It sometimes becomes weedy, however, as large colonies may be formed by the underground roots.

SEA PURSLANE
Sesuvium portulacastrum

HEIGHT: 6 inches to 1 foot

LIGHT: Sun

BLOOM: Pink, succulent, star-shaped flowers with many stamens, growing singly on short stems and appearing year-round; sepals are greenish on the underside. The small seed pods contain numerous small black seeds.

LEAVES: Fleshy, narrow, 1½-inch long, on reddish creeping stems

NATIVE RANGE: Southeastern U.S., throughout Florida, West Indies, and Central America; Zones 7–11

HABITAT: Sandy beaches, dunes

PROPAGATION: Seed, rooted cuttings

This is a small, neat, non-invasive ground cover for dry, sandy areas or other poor soils in full sun. Its high salt tolerance makes it an excellent selection for seaside plantings, where its stems form a thick mat, helping to hold sand in place. Although considered an annual, sea purslane grows as a perennial in south Florida.

BLUE-EYED GRASS
Sisyrinchium atlanticum

HEIGHT: To 2 feet

LIGHT: Sun

BLOOM: Six-petaled, bluish-purple flowers with yellow centers, about ½-inch in diameter, appearing singly at the top of slender, flat stalks in spring

LEAVES: Long, slender, and grasslike, growing in a tuft

NATIVE RANGE: Maine to southern Florida; Zones 3–10

HABITAT: Open woods, fields, marshes, roadsides

PROPAGATION: Seed, division of clumps

These dainty and familiar little wildflowers are not a grass but a perennial plant in the iris family, forming dense but tidy clumps. They might be used along the edge of a bed of larger wildflowers. Cold-hardy, they'll do better in the north and central parts of the state. Several similar species grow in Florida in varying habitats.

GOLDENROD
Solidago spp.

HEIGHT: To 6 feet, depending on species

LIGHT: Sun to light shade

BLOOM: Spikes or clusters of small, aster-like flowers atop tall, leafy stems

LEAVES: Oval to linear leaves, either smooth or with toothed edges, appearing alternately on tall, sometimes hairy, stems

NATIVE RANGE: Eastern U.S. throughout Florida; Zones 3–11

HABITAT: Roadsides, pine woods, salt marshes, dry to damp soils

PROPAGATION: Seed, division

Goldenrods, largely acquitted of the old charge that their pollen causes hay fever (blame ragweed instead), are wonderful in a natural, informal garden, especially when mixed with other wildflowers, especially those with pink or purple blossoms. They spread from underground runners so may need to be contained. Many species are found through the state, blooming mainly in summer and fall. All are perennials and somewhat similar in appearance, although some branch and others do not. One of the most attractive is seaside goldenrod, *S. sempervirens*, with dense spikes of vivid flowers blooming all year. It has a finer look than some of the other species. *S. fistulosa* can reach 6 feet in height and has feathery, arching flower heads. *S. canadensis*, with loose panicles of flowers, grows mainly in northern Florida.

STOKES' ASTER, STOKESIA
Stokesia laevis

HEIGHT: 2 feet

LIGHT: Partial sun

BLOOM: Bluish, lavender, or sometimes white aster-like flowers, 3–4 inches across, appearing in summer on tall, leafy stems

LEAVES: A rosette of thick, narrow, grayish leaves, to 8 inches long

NATIVE RANGE: South Carolina to central Florida and Louisiana; Zones 8–10

HABITAT: Pine woodlands

PROPAGATION: Seed, division of clumps

Stokes' aster is easy to grow and quite drought-tolerant, even though it often is found in damp wooded areas. Plant it where it gets a little shade in the afternoon, and trim off dead flower heads to keep the plant blooming. Cutting it back will encourage clump formation. Its long-lasting blossoms are a source of nectar for butterflies. Several cultivated forms of this large, showy perennial are on the market.

WOOD SAGE
Teucrium canadense

HEIGHT: To 3 feet

LIGHT: Sun, part shade

BLOOM: Pale lavender, two-lipped, ½-inch flowers in spikes atop tall, leafy, square stems, blooming most of the year

LEAVES: Opposite, lance-shaped and pointed, 1–4 inches long, with toothed edges; foliage is dull green, paler on the underside.

NATIVE RANGE: Southern U.S. to south Florida and west to Texas; Zones 7–10

HABITAT: Moist woodlands

PROPAGATION: Seed, root division

A perennial in the mint family, wood sage is not particularly showy, but it is undemanding and will tolerate poor soils as long as drainage is good. Cultivated forms may be found in nurseries.

TILLANDSIA *Tillandsia balbisiana*
TILLANDSIA, WILD PINE, AIR PLANTS
Tillandsia spp.

HEIGHT: A few inches to several feet

LIGHT: Sun to shade

BLOOM: Small, tubular, purple, white, or yellow flowers almost concealed by colorful bracts, often scarlet but sometimes yellow or green, on prominent spikes

LEAVES: Stiff leaves gathered into a rosette at the base of the plant, forming a cup that collects water as well as insects and debris that provide nutrients

NATIVE RANGE: Central and southern Florida; Zones 9–11

HABITAT: Hammocks, cypress forests

PROPAGATION: Seed; division of offsets, called "pups"

A dozen or so tillandsias, Florida's most common bromeliads, are native to the state. The name "wild pine" indicates their resemblance to their relative, the pineapple. Most have a rosette of long, spiky leaves and a central flower spike, which may be quite colorful. Several are attractive enough to naturalize on trees (rough-barked trees such as buttonwood make good platforms), or driftwood. Although many tillandsias are listed as threatened or endangered, their feathery seeds are blown about freely and plants may appear on trees in parks and residential landscapes. Giant wild pine, *T. utriculata*, the largest species, has tapering leaves as long as 2 feet, a branched stalk and white flowers. Stiff-leaved wild pine, *T. fasciculata*, is one of the most common species, with stiff, down-curved leaves, large

Tillandsia *Tillandsia setacea*

red and yellow bracts and violet flowers. Needle-leaved air plant, *T. setacea,* forms clumps of thin, dark green to coppery leaves, up to a foot in length. Reflexed wild pine, *T. balbisinia,* has long, twisted leaves, a bulbous base and long stems with red or green bracts and purple petals. Hoary air plant, *T. pruinosa,* is a small, bulbous plant with a silvery white coating.

Tillandsias are "air plants," or epiphytes, not parasites, and use tree boughs and stumps only as platforms. If they fall to the ground they often take root and continue to grow. The common "ball moss" and Spanish moss also are tillandsias; they have no relationship to moss despite their common names. Two other bromeliads, catopsis and guzmania, are native to Florida; both are scarce.

SPIDERWORT
Tradescantia ohiensis

HEIGHT: To 2 feet

LIGHT: Sun to part shade

BLOOM: Three-petaled blue to lavender or occasionally white, 1-inch flowers with yellow stamens, tightly clustered at the tips of smooth, leafy stems and blooming most of the year

LEAVES: Narrow, grasslike, rather succulent, up to 15 inches long, creased along the center rib and clasping the stem

NATIVE RANGE: Eastern U.S., throughout Florida; Zones 5–10

HABITAT: Roadsides, disturbed sites, damp meadows

PROPAGATION: Seed, division of clumps

Spiderwort is a low-care, drought-tolerant little plant, fine as a ground cover or low border. Its attractive flowers add a cool color to the wild garden even though they last only a few hours, like the related dayflower. The plant spreads by underground rhizomes, forming clumps, but it is not likely to grow out of control.

TAMPA VERBENA *Verbena tampensis*
VERBENA *Verbena spp.*

HEIGHT: 1–2 feet

LIGHT: Sun

BLOOM: Five-lobed, rose-pink to purple, 1-inch flowers in flat-topped clusters, blooming most of the year

LEAVES: Opposite, oval, lance-shaped or lobed, usually with toothed edges, on branching stems

NATIVE RANGE: Central and south Florida; Zones 9–10

HABITAT: Beach dunes, dry woodlands

PROPAGATION: Seed, stem cuttings, division of clumps

Although the native verbenas aren't as showy as the hybrid garden varieties, they will serve much of the same purpose in the garden. Their nectar is a food source for butterflies. Beach or seaside verbena, *V. maritima* (also listed as *Glandularia maritima*) has lobed or oval leaves on stems which may reach 2 feet. Tampa verbena, *V. tampensis,* is generally shorter; it also requires richer soil. Moss or sand verbena, *G. pulchella,* an introduced species from South America, is a low, creeping plant common in Florida along roadsides and in disturbed areas; its flowers are pink, purple, or white.

ZEPHYR LILY, ATAMASCO LILY
Zephyranthes atamasco

HEIGHT: 1 foot

LIGHT: Sun to light shade

BLOOM: White, six-petaled, lily-like flowers with yellow stamens, 3 inches long and 4 inches across, borne singly on straight stems above the foliage and blooming from late winter through spring

LEAVES: Long, flat, and grasslike, 4–8 inches long, with sharp margins

NATIVE RANGE: Virginia to north and central Florida and Mississippi; Zones 7–9

HABITAT: Damp roadsides, meadows, pine woods

PROPAGATION: Seed, division of bulbs

These showy amaryllis relatives are wonderful in a mass planting, making a nice substitute for northern spring-blooming bulbs. Bulbs may be divided at the end of the blooming season. The plants prefer a low, damp, but not soggy, area.

VINES

TRUMPET VINE
Campsis radicans

HEIGHT: Vining stems to 30 feet or more

LIGHT: Sun to part shade

BLOOM: Orange to red, 3-inch long, trumpet-shaped blooms, carried in showy terminal clusters from June to September

FRUIT: A 3- to 5-inch capsule containing winged seeds

LEAVES: Dark green, coarse-textured, pinnate leaves, 7–14 inches long, with toothed oval leaflets 1–4 inches long, appearing late in spring and turning yellow in autumn before falling

NATIVE RANGE: Pennsylvania to central Florida and west to Texas; Zones 4–9

HABITAT: Open fields, roadsides, near beaches

PROPAGATION: Seed, cuttings, root suckers

This is a showy native plant suitable for difficult sites, but it is invasive and can take over its surroundings, climbing on and over anything in its path. It clings to rough surfaces with hold-fast rootlets, like ivy. It is best used on a well-built trellis or pergola where its growth can be controlled. Nevertheless, trumpet vine is colorful, cold-hardy, and salt-tolerant, and will bring hummingbirds to the garden. Plant it in a well-drained, sunny site.

BEACH BEAN, BAY BEAN
Canavalia maritima

HEIGHT: Low, creeping plant whose vines may reach 30 feet or more

LIGHT: Sun

BLOOM: Attractive pink, pea-type, 1-inch flowers, blooming all year

FRUIT: Thick, green, 4- to 5-inch pods that turn brown as they ripen

LEAVES: Thick, leathery, oval, alternate, 3–4 inches long, growing in groups of three and tending to fold upward along the mid-vein in hot weather

NATIVE RANGE: Central and south Florida; Zones 9–10

HABITAT: Beaches and dunes

PROPAGATION: Seed, rooted cuttings

Also listed as *C. rosea*, beach bean is a tough, salt-tolerant vine, rooting at the nodes and helping to hold sand in place. The deeply rooted stems may extend several yards, and can clamber up trees, fences, or trellises. The plant also reseeds readily, forming large mats. Although it occurs naturally on the seashore, it will grow inland on richer soil, often even more vigorously.

CAROLINA JESSAMINE, YELLOW JESSAMINE
Gelsemium spp.

HEIGHT: Vining stems, 10–20 feet long

LIGHT: Sun to shade

BLOOM: Fragrant, yellow, trumpet-shaped flowers, 1½ inches long, appear in winter or from fall to spring, depending on species.

LEAVES: Opposite, oval, dark evergreen, 1–3 inches long

TRUNK: Brown, wiry, multistemmed vine, growing thicker in full sun

NATIVE RANGE: Virginia to central Florida, west to Texas; Zones 6–9

HABITAT: Open woodlands, wetlands, disturbed areas, and along the edges of roads where it climbs small trees and fences

PROPAGATION: Seed, air layers, cuttings

Two similar species of these showy vines are found in Florida. Carolina jessamine, *G. sempervirens*, common in woodlands of north and central Florida, blooms in winter and is highly fragrant. Yellow or swamp jessamine, *G. rankinii*, which grows farther south and prefers moister conditions, has a lighter fragrance but a longer blooming period, fall through spring. Both are cold-hardy, twining vines useful in the landscape as they are colorful and will bloom in the shade. The flowers attract hummingbirds, and the dense foliage supplies cover and nesting sites for other birds. They are not overly large or aggressive but use caution if you plant one next to a tree as the vines can choke branches or a small tree. The plant is good as a ground cover or for disguising a wire fence. A double-flowered form, 'Pride of Augusta,' is occasionally seen; its flowers may be a little longer-lived than the single form.

RAILROAD VINE
Ipomoea pes-caprae

HEIGHT: To 6 inches in height, but the ground-hugging vines may reach 100 feet in length

LIGHT: Sun

BLOOM: Pink to lavender, morning-blooming, funnel-like flowers appear all year.

FRUIT: Brown ½-inch pods containing four seeds

LEAVES: Leathery green 4-inch leaves are carried on 6-inch petioles. Leaves are two-lobed like a goat's foot (thus the species name, *pes-caprae*). The flexible half-inch thick stems run across the sand, rooting at nodes.

NATIVE RANGE: Beaches of the Old and New World tropics and from Texas to Georgia on the coast; Zones 9–11

HABITAT: Dunes and beaches above the high tide line, often coexisting with sea oats as the first line of defense against the sea

PROPAGATION: Seed, cuttings

Railroad vine is a pioneer plant on the beaches, and as resilient as sea oats against salt, heat, and wind. All it demands is plenty of sunshine. Cuttings will take root very quickly. The plant sends down roots at nodes along its runners, helping to stabilize sand dunes and serving as a ground cover where little else can survive.

BEACH MORNING GLORY
Ipomoea stolonifera

HEIGHT: 6-inch ground creeper; trailing stems may reach 50 feet or more

LIGHT: Sun

BLOOM: Two-inch, trumpet-shaped white flowers with yellow centers appear in summer and fall.

FRUIT: Small pod

LEAVES: Leathery leaves, 1–1½ inches long, usually oval or occasionally lobed, on long trailing stems

NATIVE RANGE: Southeast U.S., including all of Florida; Zones 8–11

HABITAT: Dunes and beaches above the high-tide line

PROPAGATION: Seed, cuttings, or division

Not as common a coastal plant as railroad vine, beach morning glory can play a similar role in seafront landscaping. Its flowers are more delicate and subtle than those of the morning glory. Stems root at the nodes where they touch the soil, forming dense mats that help prevent sand erosion.

Jacquemontia *Jacquemontia curtissii*

Beach jacquemontia *J. reclinata*

JACQUEMONTIA
Jacquemontia curtissii

HEIGHT: Vine to 6 feet

LIGHT: Sun to part shade

BLOOM: Five-lobed, bell-shaped white flowers, an inch in diameter, similar to morning glory, and usually closing by mid-afternoon

LEAVES: Usually less than an inch long, the leaves vary in shape, from oval to spatulate and with blunt or pointed tips. Leaves are alternate, on slender, vining stems growing from a woody base.

NATIVE RANGE: Southernmost Florida in Dade, Collier, and Monroe counties; Zones 10–11

HABITAT: Pine woods near the coast

PROPAGATION: Seed, cuttings

Jacquemontia is a perennial vine related to the many species of morning glory but lacking their aggressive character. This delicate little low, spreading plant has almost disappeared from the wild because of habitat destruction, and is on the state's endangered list, along with its relative, beach jacquemontia, *J. reclinata*. Fortunately, it is being cultivated by a few native nurseries. Bringing such rare, nursery-grown species into well-planned native landscaping helps assure their survival.

CORAL HONEYSUCKLE
Lonicera sempervirens

HEIGHT: 10–15 feet

LIGHT: Sun to part shade

BLOOM: Tubular, 2-inch, orange-red flowers, growing in clusters, appear throughout the year. A yellow variety is rare.

FRUIT: A red berry about ⅓ inch across, usually appearing in autumn

LEAVES: Blue-green leaves are 1–3 inches long and ovate in shape. On blooming plants, several leaves without a petiole surround each blossoming stem.

TRUNK: A light brown, twining stem

NATIVE RANGE: Eastern U.S. to south Florida; Zones 6–10

HABITAT: Edges of woodlands where it can twine up trees and shrubs, reaching for light

PROPAGATION: Seed, cuttings

Lonicera is a showy evergreen vine that blooms heavily in the spring, attracting butterflies and hummingbirds. Its small fruit also provides a good display and will bring thrushes, orioles, mockingbirds, catbirds, and other birds to the garden. It is slower growing and less invasive than some members of the honeysuckle family, and does nicely when trained up a trellis or fence. Moist, fertile soils suit it best. Foliage sometimes is thinned out by leaf spotting, a fungal problem; aphids also may distort new growth.

VIRGINIA CREEPER, WOODBINE
Parthenocissus quinquefolia

HEIGHT: Vine to 50 feet or more

LIGHT: Sun to shade

BLOOM: Panicles of yellow-green flowers appear in spring, carried under the leaves so that they are barely noticeable.

FRUIT: Panicles of purplish-black, round, ¼-inch fruit in fall

LEAVES: Palmately compound leaves usually have five oval, pointed, toothed leaflets 2–4 inches long, dull medium-green above and paler green beneath. Fall color can be brilliant purple to red, but the vine is almost evergreen in south Florida.

TRUNK: A brown, vining trunk, attaching by branched tendrils that will cling to almost any surface

NATIVE RANGE: New England to south Florida; Mexico; Zones 3–11

HABITAT: Virginia creeper will grow anywhere, in city or country, tolerating wind, poor soil, pollution and any light condition.

PROPAGATION: Seed, cuttings

While Virginia creeper usually is looked upon as a weed (and it is aggressive enough that it can become a pest), it has its uses. It's fine for difficult sites such as ugly retaining walls along highways, urban areas that will benefit from any greenery, and beach situations where most plants won't survive. And, at least in northern Florida, it adds a colorful accent in the fall. Birds are attracted to its fruit, which is most noticeable after the leaves have fallen from the vine. It clings by tendrils, as grapes do, so keep it away from wood or brick walls.

PASSIONFLOWER, MAYPOP
Passiflora incarnata

HEIGHT: Creeping stems may reach several feet, lying prostrate on the ground or climbing over fences and shrubs

LIGHT: Sun

BLOOM: Showy, fringed, bluish-purple flowers, 2–3 inches across, with five petals and five sepals, blooming most of the year

FRUIT: Oval, green to yellow edible berry, 2 inches long, with dark brown seeds

LEAVES: Three-lobed, 3–6 inches long

NATIVE RANGE: Texas to Virginia and south throughout Florida; Zones 7–11

HABITAT: Dry roadsides, fields

PROPAGATION: Seed, root shoots

This perennial vine may be considered a weed and can be invasive, but it is a superb host plant for butterflies. The larvae of zebra longwing, julia and gulf fritillary butterflies feed on its leaves. Plant it where it can climb and cover an unattractive landscape element such as a chain-link fence; pruning will be required to keep it within bounds.

FLORIDA PEPEROMIA
Peperomia spp.

HEIGHT: 1 foot; if vining, to several feet

LIGHT: Part shade

BLOOM: Small greenish flowers on a spike 2–4 inches long

LEAVES: Oval, leathery, dark-green leaves, 2–4 inches long, on thick stems

NATIVE RANGE: South Florida, mainly Dade and Collier counties; Zones 10–11

HABITAT: Moist soil or growing as an epiphyte on trunks and branches of trees, sometimes with orchids, bromeliads, and other air plants

PROPAGATION: Cuttings

Several species of peperomia, either spreading, clumping, or vining in habit, once spread throughout Everglades hammocks and cypress swamps but few plants now survive in the wild. Peperomias are on the state's list of endangered species. Now and then you'll come across a nursery that is propagating them. Most native peperomias have pale to dark green leaves, but one, *P. humilis*, has colorful pinkish-red foliage.

CATBRIAR, BAMBOO VINE
Smilax laurifolia

HEIGHT: Vine, variable in height but often reaching 20 feet

LIGHT: Sun to part shade

BLOOM: Inconspicuous clustered green flowers in spring

FRUIT: Small blue-black berries

LEAVES: Oval, pointed foliage with prominent veins on thorny, green, vining stems that use tendrils to climb

NATIVE RANGE: Southeastern states from the Carolinas south through Florida; Zones 8–10

HABITAT: Damp woodlands, swamp edges, dunes, and pine woods

PROPAGATION: Seed, cuttings

Catbriar usually is not considered a landscape plant but could be useful for covering chain-link fencing. It has potential security value, as its spines would discourage intruders. It serves as a good nesting site and food source for birds, especially mockingbirds and catbirds. The young shoots are edible.

WILD ALLAMANDA
Urechites lutea

HEIGHT: Vining stems, to 6–8 feet

LIGHT: Sun to part shade

BLOOM: Golden yellow, five-lobed, flaring, trumpet-shaped blossoms, 2 inches across, blooming most of the year

LEAVES: Bright green, opposite, oval to round, 2-inch long leaves

NATIVE RANGE: South Florida and the West Indies; Zones 10–11

HABITAT: Pine woods, coastal hammocks

PROPAGATION: Seed, cuttings

This woody, vining plant is in the same family as the cultivated allamanda widely used as a shrub in South Florida. Salt- and drought-tolerant, it is useful in seaside plantings, and while it is fast growing, it is not an invasive vine. It could serve as a ground cover in an open sunny area or be grown on a trellis. Flowers and foliage are reported to be poisonous if eaten.

GRAPE
Vitis spp.

HEIGHT: Vines reaching 40 feet or more

LIGHT: Sun to part shade

BLOOM: Panicles of small, greenish, five-petaled flowers in leaf axils

FRUIT: Clusters of purple to black edible fruits appearing from late summer to fall and varying in size and flavor by species

LEAVES: Alternate and variable in form, generally heart-shaped; three-lobed or unlobed, with or without serrations at the edges.

TRUNK: A woody, vining stem that climbs by tendrils into and over the tops of nearby trees and other vegetation; mature trunks have shredding, dark brown bark.

NATIVE RANGE: Many species of native grape are found throughout the country, having an extensive range and found in almost every habitat; All zones

HABITAT: Swamps, woods, sandy and rocky areas, edges of rivers and lakes

PROPAGATION: Seed, cuttings, grafting for cultivated varieties

Several species of native grape grow in the state; the best known is the muscadine or southern fox grape *(V. rotundifolia)*, which grows from Delaware, through Florida, and into the midwest. A number of cultivated forms have been developed; their fruit is used for wine-making and in jams and juices. In the landscape, a shady grape arbor sheltering a table and a few chairs is a wonderful addition to the garden. The fast-growing vines will cover an unsightly chain-link fence and provide food and shelter for birds and animals.

GRASSES

SHORTSPIKE BLUESTEM
Andropogon brachystachys

HEIGHT: 5–6 feet

LIGHT: Sun

BLOOM: Small bluish to reddish-purple flowers on tall, arching stalks, blooming in the fall; flowers turn light brown as they age.

LEAVES: Bright green, stiff, foot-long leaf blades

NATIVE RANGE: North and central Florida; Zones 8–9

HABITAT: Moist sandy woods, edges of swamps

PROPAGATION: Seed

Shortspike bluestem is a dense, clumping grass useful in wildflower areas where its fibrous root system will help keep weeds from invading. Although it prefers damp soil, it will adapt to drier conditions. Many other species of andropogen, known as bluestem or broomsedge, are native to the U.S. and made up a large part of our original prairies. Some cultivars have been selected for size and fall color.

WHITE-BRACTED SEDGE, STAR RUSH
Dichromena spp.

HEIGHT: 6 inches to 2 feet

LIGHT: Sun to part shade

BLOOM: Tiny yellowish flowers are
  surrounded by prominent narrow, pointed,
  white bracts about an inch long. The
  heads appear singly on stems rising above
  the leaves, usually blooming from spring
  through fall.

LEAVES: Narrow, smooth, and grasslike

NATIVE RANGE: Southeastern U.S. to Texas,
  throughout Florida; Zones 7–10

HABITAT: Moist woodlands, open fields

PROPAGATION: Seed, division of rhizomes

These sedges are appreciated for their
handsome, striking terminal spikes, which
have the appearance of spidery flowers. The
number of bracts depends on the species.
D. latifolia, probably the showiest, has seven
or more; *D. colorata* and *D. floridensis* have
fewer. *D. floridensis,* found in South Florida
pinelands, will grow in drier sites than the
other species. The genus sometimes is listed
as *Rhynchospora.*

ELLIOTT LOVE GRASS
Eragrostis elliottii

HEIGHT: 1 foot

LIGHT: Sun

BLOOM: Misty panicles of lavender-beige flowers, blooming in autumn and carried on stems above the foliage

LEAVES: Graceful, rather sprawling clumps of fine, blue-green, grassy leaves, ¼-inch wide

NATIVE RANGE: The Carolinas to Texas, Gulf Coast and southern Florida; Zones 7–10

HABITAT: Tolerates a range of conditions: roadsides, dunes, dry prairies to wet woodlands

PROPAGATION: Seed, division of clumps

This is a compact little bunchgrass that makes a striking border and mixes well with wildflowers, contributing its own ethereal blooms. It will tolerate dry conditions and sandy soils, and reseeds easily on its own. Love grasses may be used fresh or dried in flower arrangements.

PURPLE LOVE GRASS
Eragrostis spectabilis

HEIGHT: 1-1½ feet

LIGHT: Sun

BLOOM: Delicate panicles of tiny, reddish-purple flowers hover above the foliage, turning pale beige as they age.

LEAVES: Rounded clumps of soft, light green leaves, ½ inch wide, are up to a foot in length. In cool climates leaves turn reddish in the fall.

NATIVE RANGE: Most of U.S. through central Florida; Zones 5–9

HABITAT: Roadsides, damp to dry sites

PROPAGATION: Seed

Purple love grass is useful as a fine-textured accent plant or in a massed planting; it also is small enough to use as a border or in a bed of wildflowers. It will take hot, dry conditions, but a wet, shady site won't suit it at all.

MUHLY GRASS, MIST GRASS
Muhlenbergia capillaris

HEIGHT: 1–3 feet

LIGHT: Sun to light shade

BLOOM: Delicate, silky violet plumes appear in late summer on stalks rising well above the foliage, creating an iridescent, pinkish-gray haze.

LEAVES: Fine-textured, rolled leaves, forming small but dense clumps

NATIVE RANGE: Massachusetts to central U.S., to southern Florida, the Gulf Coast and West Indies; Zones 7–10

HABITAT: Sandy alkaline soils, dunes to Everglades

PROPAGATION: Seed, division

When muhly grass is in bloom, its shimmering beauty is outstanding. Salt- and cold-tolerant, it makes an adaptable ground cover even in poor, sandy soils. In dry sites it stays at about a foot but reaches twice that height when it has sufficient irrigation. This is one of several species of muhlenbergia used as ornamentals across the South.

LOPSIDED INDIANGRASS
Sorghastrum secundum

HEIGHT: 4–5 feet

LIGHT: Sun

BLOOM: Small, narrow, drooping spikes of tiny golden-tan seed heads in late summer and early fall, with the spikes arranged along one side of the tall stalk

LEAVES: Rounded clumps of narrow, flat, hairy blades about 12 inches long

NATIVE RANGE: The Carolinas south to central Florida and west to Texas; Zones 7–9

HABITAT: Damp to dry woods, meadows

PROPAGATION: Seed

Not a spectacular grass, but pretty and graceful, this plant is well-suited to acid soils. Use it in a wild garden with Florida paintbrush, liatris, or cardinal flower, or with pines and palmetto. A related and somewhat larger species, Indiangrass *(S. nutans),* is a common prairie grass throughout the midwest.

SAND CORDGRASS
Spartina bakeri

HEIGHT: 3–5 feet

LIGHT: Sun

BLOOM: Insignificant

LEAVES: Soft, fine, arching blades growing in a dense, rounded clump

NATIVE RANGE: Georgia and throughout much of Florida; Zones 8–10

HABITAT: Wetlands, woods, prairies

PROPAGATION: Seed

Sand cordgrass has a delicate look, but its clumps are large enough to make a definite design statement. Give it plenty of room when you plant it; individual plants should be spaced 6–7 feet apart. In nature, cordgrass usually is found growing in moist locations, but it adapts well to dry and even salty areas, and will not dry out and turn brown in the manner of pampas grass. It is popular for large projects such as golf courses and commercial landscapes, either massed or as an accent plant, and is useful for controlling erosion along lakes and streams. Other native species used in landscaping include saltmeadow cordgrass, *S. patens*, and smooth cordgrass, *S. alternifolia*.

FAKAHATCHEE GRASS
Tripsacum dactyloides

HEIGHT: 4–6 feet

LIGHT: Sun to part shade

BLOOM: Red-brown spikes at the top of tall, nodding stems

LEAVES: Dark green, arching, 1-inch wide leaves, growing in tall, dense clumps

NATIVE RANGE: Eastern U.S. throughout Florida; Zones 5–10

HABITAT: Wetland, river banks

PROPAGATION: Seed, division of clumps

A rich, damp, well-drained soil suits Fakahatchee grass best, although it tolerates most soil conditions and will survive drought. With good care, it grows taller. It makes an excellent substitute for pampas grass, which has a tendency to become messy. Evergreen in south Florida, it turns brown in winter in colder areas and during a freeze may die back to the ground.

FLORIDA GAMAGRASS
Tripsacum floridanum

HEIGHT: 2 feet

LIGHT: Sun to part shade

BLOOM: Insignificant clusters of tiny flowers on long, slim stalks

LEAVES: Glossy, long, and narrower (½- to ¼-inch wide) than Fakahatchee grass

NATIVE RANGE: South Florida, although now it is being cultivated much farther north; Zones 7–10

HABITAT: Ditches, bogs, and other damp areas

PROPAGATION: Seed, division of clumps

This is a dense, compact grass, suitable as a ground cover. Although it likes damp, rich soil, it tolerates most conditions. While it will survive drought, it needs sufficient irrigation to look its best. In the southern part of the state the plant is evergreen if it gets enough water; farther north it turns brownish-yellow in cold weather. Smaller and finer than *T. dactyloides,* it is called dwarf Fakahatchee grass by the nursery trade, even though it is a different species.

SEA OATS
Uniola paniculata

HEIGHT: 3–6 feet

LIGHT: Sun

BLOOM: Tiny, insignificant flowers in panicles

FRUIT: Decorative tan, wheat-like, nodding seedheads

LEAVES: Grassy, tough, pale green leaves, rolled inward at the edges

NATIVE RANGE: Coastal Texas to Virginia to south Florida; Zones 8–11

HABITAT: Beach, dunes

PROPAGATION: Seed, division of rhizomes

Sea oats, whose clumps collect sand blown about by the wind, are our foremost plants for erosion control and establishing dunes. Stabilized dunes provide significant protection against hurricanes, and many seaside communities construct boardwalks to cross the sea oat dunes to avoid damaging the plants' root systems. These grasses will accept salt, wind, and poor, dry soil. A protected plant in Florida, it is available through a limited number of commercial nurseries.

FERNS

LEATHER FERN
Acrostichum danaeifolium

HEIGHT: 7–8 feet

LIGHT: Sun to part shade

LEAVES: Large, stiff, lance-shaped pinnate leaves are dark green above, paler green below, vertical or arching and arising from a central clump. The reproductive spores are carried on the spore-bearing leaves, which are reddish-brown on the underside.

NATIVE RANGE: Central and south Florida and tropical America; Zones 9–11

HABITAT: Brackish or freshwater wetlands or partly moist areas

PROPAGATION: Spores, division of clumps

This adaptable species, Florida's largest native fern, will grow in almost any damp area, forming thick clumps. It tolerates more sun than most ferns. Use it as a vertical accent near a pool or pond, or as a complement to some of the native grasses for a change of texture. It is a tough, problem-free plant that should be used more. Coastal or golden leather fern, *A. aureum*, has smaller fronds and is found nearer the seacoast, usually in brackish water and often in mangrove swamps.

SWAMP FERN
Blechnum serrulatum

HEIGHT: 2 feet

LIGHT: Sun or shade

LEAVES: Fronds are stiff and crinkled with toothed edges; new growth is pinkish in color.

NATIVE RANGE: North central to south Florida; Zones 8–11

HABITAT: Swamplands and upland hammocks

PROPAGATION: Spores, division of rhizomes

A common fern of damp areas, blechnum is fast-growing and a good choice for damp, acid soil. It is at its best in a moist, shady site with plenty of compost added to the soil. Nevertheless, it will grow so readily in either sun or shade that some horticulturists call it "weedy."

FLORIDA TREE FERN
Ctenitis sloanei

HEIGHT: 3 feet

LIGHT: Shade

LEAVES: Large, arching, bright green, triangular fronds, divided three times, on fuzzy, reddish stems growing from a reddish base that may form a small trunk

NATIVE RANGE: South Florida; Zones 10–11

HABITAT: Shady hammocks in rich, moist soil

PROPAGATION: Spores, division of clumps

This lacy Florida fern makes a pretty, tropical ground cover in open shade. It is fairly easy to grow if it has rich, damp soil. It may be grown in a container outdoors if you never let the soil dry out. This fern is listed also in the genus *Dryopteris*.

FISHTAIL FERN
Nephrolepsis biserrata 'Furcans'

HEIGHT: 3¼–4½ feet

LIGHT: Part to full shade

LEAVES: Pinnately compound, arching, dark green foliage, with distinctive fishtail tips

NATIVE RANGE: South Florida and the tropics; Zones 10–11

HABITAT: Moist tropical woodlands

PROPAGATION: Spores, division

Fishtail fern is a wonderful tall ground cover, perfect under trees such as oak. The ferns will absorb fallen leaves and acorns, eliminating much raking. The plants also can serve as a foundation planting on the north side of a building, substituting for a clipped hedge, which would need pruning. Avoid planting them in bright sunlight that will cause fronds to bleach out. Sword fern, *N. biserrata*, has unnotched leaf tips.

BOSTON FERN
Nephrolepsis exaltata 'Bostoniensis'

HEIGHT: 2–4 feet

LIGHT: Sun to shade

LEAVES: Long, pinnate, tapering fronds, speckled with round or kidney-shaped spore cases on the underside

NATIVE RANGE: All Florida; Zones 8–11

HABITAT: Moist woodlands

PROPAGATION: Spores and division of clumps; Boston fern puts out runners or stolons that produce new plants where they take root.

This is the most common fern found in Florida. Dozens of different forms have appeared naturally, some with ruffled or divided fronds, and many have become popular house plants. Related to fishtail and sword ferns, the Boston fern can get out of bounds and become weedy, but nothing excels as a fast, inexpensive ground cover in poor soil or under trees where little else will grow. Planted on a slope, it will help control erosion. It also may be used in a pot or hanging basket. While it will do well in either shade or sunlight, it will be a richer, darker green in a shady site.

ROYAL FERN
Osmunda regalis

HEIGHT: To 6 feet

LIGHT: Light to heavy shade

LEAVES: Light green, twice-divided fronds with an open, airy appearance, usually dying back in winter; leaflets, reddish when young, have rounded tips.

NATIVE RANGE: Eastern U.S. to all of Florida; Zones 5–10

HABITAT: Swamps and similar moist to wet sites

PROPAGATION: Spores, division of rhizomes

In damp acid soil, grow royal fern in a clump for a dramatic effect, in a border, or as an accent plant where it adds a lush, tropical touch. Don't let it dry out. The related cinnamon fern, *Osmunda cinnamomea*, has a less tidy appearance but still is attractive in a massed bed or as an accent plant. Plant it in a marshy area with acid soil, in a ravine, or along a shady pond edge where it will get plenty of water. In chilly winters, it will die back. Most ferns carry their reproductive spores on the underside of the leaves; osmunda carries them in clusters on separate, specialized fronds.

GOLDEN POLYPODY, SERPENT FERN
Polypodium aureum

HEIGHT: To 3 feet or more

LIGHT: Sun to shade

LEAVES: Light green, lobed, wavy fronds, not entirely divided, with long petioles and fleshy, furry, golden-brown rhizomes

NATIVE RANGE: Central and south Florida and tropical America; Zones 9–11

HABITAT: Sabal palm trunks, where they grow from the "boots" or bases of old palm fronds, on stumps and in crotches and bark crevices of live oaks and other trees. Rarely, this fern is found growing in the earth in damp, rich, rather acid soil.

PROPAGATION: Spores, division of rhizomes

Golden polypody sometimes is called cabbage palm fern for its habit of taking up residence on these native trees. Its spores are carried by the wind, and it is rare to see a wild cabbage palm in the southern part of the state that is not draped with these graceful plants. They often inhabit landscape palms as well, moving in without human help. To start a colony, tuck a piece of the fern, with rhizome and a few roots attached, into a suitable niche or hanging basket. It also works well in a shady rock garden. The species is listed also as *Phlebodium aureum*.

STRAP FERN
Polypodium phyllitidis

HEIGHT: 2 feet

LIGHT: Partial shade

LEAVES: Long, ribbon-like, undivided fronds; the upper surface bears small bulges that duplicate the spore-bearing sacs on the underside.

NATIVE RANGE: Central and south Florida, tropical America; Zones 9–10

HABITAT: Tree stumps and trunks in swamps and other moist sites

PROPAGATION: Spores, division of clumps

This is a lovely fern for a moist, rather shady spot with well-drained organic soil, or even in a container if you pay close attention to watering. Also listed as *Campyloneurum phyllitidis*, it sometimes is mistaken for the much rarer bird's nest fern, *Asplenium serratum*.

RESURRECTION FERN
Polypodium polypodioides

HEIGHT: 6–8 inches

LIGHT: Light to medium shade

LEAVES: Small, deeply divided fronds that are open and dark green when they have plenty of moisture, curling up and appearing brown and dead in dry periods

NATIVE RANGE: Southeastern U.S. and throughout Florida; Zones 8–11

HABITAT: Rough bark of tree limbs and trunks, rocks, occasionally taking root in damp, acid soil

PROPAGATION: Spores, division of rhizomes

This is a common but interesting and attractive fern, which gets its name from its apparent ability to return from the dead after a rain shower. The plant is unlikely to be found in a nursery, but often appears on favorable branches because the spores are carried by the wind. It is not a parasite and will do no harm to the tree, so leave it alone and enjoy its delicate beauty.

BRACKEN
Pteridium aquilinum

HEIGHT: 1–3 feet

LIGHT: Sun

LEAVES: Coarse, open, twice-divided fronds on arching stems arising from a hairy, creeping rhizome

NATIVE RANGE: Varying forms are found throughout the U.S.; Zones 3–10

HABITAT: Open woods, fields

PROPAGATION: Spores, division of rhizomes

Bracken is a tough, hardy fern that will grow almost anywhere, but it does tend to spread and has a reputation for being weedy. Nevertheless, it will make a pleasant ground cover in poor soils where few other ferns will survive. It is at its best in a sunny to partly shaded spot with damp to partly dry soil.

AQUATICS

YELLOW CANNA
Canna flaccida

HEIGHT: 2½ feet

LIGHT: Sun to part shade

BLOOM: Rich, golden yellow flowers about 3 inches long grow in clusters on a tall, stout, leafy stem, appearing mainly in spring and early summer. The three petals and three sepals make the flower somewhat similar to an iris, but with a rather droopy appearance.

LEAVES: Oval to lance-shaped, alternate, a foot or more in length and 3 to 6 inches wide

NATIVE RANGE: North Carolina to south Florida and the Gulf Coast; Zones 8–10

HABITAT: Bogs, marshes, wet ditches

PROPAGATION: Seed, division of rhizomes

This showy perennial is a colorful addition to the native water garden, especially when it is combined with the purple-flowered pickerel weed. Although not often seen in the wild, it is grown commercially and used successfully in marshland restoration projects.

HORSETAIL
Equisetum spp.

HEIGHT: 4 feet

LIGHT: Sun to part shade

LEAVES: Tall, stiff, jointed, leafless, hollow
stems, evergreen in mild climates

NATIVE RANGE: Throughout the U.S.;
all Zones

HABITAT: Pond banks, shallow water

PROPAGATION: Division of rhizomes

These ancient, rush-like plants, which reproduce from spores, not seed, are useful for controlling erosion on river banks, but the creeping rhizomes can make it extremely invasive. You might plant it at the edge of a pond in a few inches of water and remove unwanted shoots as they appear, or better yet, plant a clump in a large, sturdy pot placed in shallow water where growth can be controlled. A dwarf form only a few inches in height is available.

SOFT RUSH
Juncus effusus

HEIGHT: 1½–2½ feet

LIGHT: Partial shade

BLOOM: Small brownish flowers at the top of the stem, blooming in summer

LEAVES: Soft, round, medium green, grasslike stems, turning brown in cold weather

NATIVE RANGE: Throughout the U.S.; Zones 3–10

HABITAT: Marshes, ponds, stream edges

PROPAGATION: Seed, division of clumps

Soft rush will grow in wet soil or shallow water and it makes a fine accent plant at the edge of a water garden or even in a large tub if the potting soil is kept moist. As they grow in height, the dense, grassy clumps acquire a graceful, arching appearance. They help stabilize stream banks and provide shelter and nesting sites for birds.

SPATTERDOCK, COW LILY
Nuphar luteum

HEIGHT: Foliage and flowers may reach a foot above the water surface.

LIGHT: Sun to part shade

BLOOM: The 2- to 3-inch, yellow, cup-like bloom does not open like a water lily. The flower, which is not very showy, is held above the water and appears in the spring and summer.

FRUIT: A pod that drops beneath the water and eventually splits, releasing its seeds

LEAVES: The green pads, growing from a thick stalk, are variable, ranging from round to heart- or arrow-shaped, and up to a foot or more across.

NATIVE RANGE: Eastern Canada and New England south through Florida; Zones 3–10

HABITAT: Slow-moving fresh water rivers, ponds, and lakes everywhere in the state except the Keys

PROPAGATION: Seed, division of rhizomes

Spatterdock is a common water plant in Florida. Many localized forms can be seen. The large leaves are attractive, but the flowers are small and uninteresting compared to the showy native water lily. Nevertheless, it is an excellent breeding ground for many fish, and its seeds are eaten by water birds.

WHITE WATER LILY
Nymphaea odorata

HEIGHT: Underwater stem may reach several feet

LIGHT: Sun to part shade

BLOOM: Highly fragrant white flowers with bright yellow stamens, 5 inches across, with numerous pointed petals, float on or sometimes are elevated above the water surface. Flowers, blossoming from spring to fall, close at night and reopen in the morning for up to four days.

LEAVES: Circular to oval, thick, up to 10 inches across and split where they are attached to the stem, floating on the water surface

NATIVE RANGE: Eastern U.S., throughout Florida, to Louisiana and Texas; Zones 3–10

HABITAT: Quiet ponds, lakes, ditches

PROPAGATION: Seed, division of rhizomes

Beautiful and fragrant, the white water lily is highly prized for water gardens and has been used in hybridizing many commercial varieties. Rhizomes may be planted in shallow water (up to 18 inches) and held in place by a rock until they are well established. Plants multiply readily and rapidly. They may be grown in water-filled tubs, too, but the flowers will be smaller.

PICKERELWEED
Pontederia lanceolata

HEIGHT: 3–4 feet

LIGHT: Sun to part shade

BLOOM: Spikes of small, tubular, blue-violet flowers bloom on top of tall stems in spring and summer. The flower's upper lip may be spotted in yellow.

LEAVES: Variably lance-shaped or heart-shaped, dark green, on thick stems

NATIVE RANGE: New England to Texas and south Florida; Zones 3–10

HABITAT: Shallow fresh water sites

PROPAGATION: Seed, division

This perennial plant (also listed as *P. cordata*) is excellent for lake shores, shallow ponds, and bog gardens, where it may form large, colorful clumps. Plant it in water about 6 inches deep. Pickerelweed is easy to grow and may even become a bit weedy, but it does provide a good habitat for fish and water birds, which eat the seeds.

DUCK POTATO, ARROWHEAD
Sagittaria spp.

HEIGHT: 3 feet

LIGHT: Sun, part shade

BLOOM: Three-petaled white flowers with yellow centers are about 1 inch across. Depending on the species, they may appear in spring and summer or year-round, on leafless stalks rising well above the leaves.

LEAVES: Variable by species; *S. lancifolia* has lance-shaped leaves, *S. graminea* is grass-like, and *S. latifolia* has leaves shaped like an arrowhead. The smooth, glossy leaves grow from a starchy tuber.

NATIVE RANGE: Canada to Texas and throughout Florida; Zones 3–10

HABITAT: Ponds, ditches, edges of stream and canals

PROPAGATION: Seed, division of rhizomes

Not only are these perennial water plants decorative, but they help prevent erosion when planted along a lake front. They also may help improve water quality by absorbing excess nutrients. At one time, the tubers were a source of starch for native Americans. The tubers also are eaten by ducks and muskrats and the seeds are a food source for water birds.

GIANT BULRUSH
Scirpus spp.

HEIGHT: 9 feet

LIGHT: Sun to light shade

BLOOM: Clusters of small brownish flowers at the top of slender stalks

LEAVES: Cylindrical, erect, grass-like stems are round or triangular, about an inch across at the base and thinner at the top. Leaves are reduced to sheaths on the stem.

NATIVE RANGE: Numerous and similar species of these perennials are found throughout the U.S.; all Zones.

HABITAT: Marshes, shallow ponds

PROPAGATION: Seed, division of rhizomes

Giant bulrush, a member of the sedge family, is useful in a water garden or along a lake edge where a tall screening or specimen plant is desired. The Florida Game and Fresh Water Fish Commission lists giant bulrush as one of the most desirable aquatic plants. Its large, dense clumps make a good habitat for small fish. To get it started, plant clump divisions about 6 inches under water.

THALIA, ARROWROOT, ALLIGATOR FLAG
Thalia geniculata

HEIGHT: 6 feet

LIGHT: Sun, part shade

BLOOM: Small, purplish, drooping flowers, somewhat orchid-like in shape, appear in panicles on stems that reach 8 feet or more.

LEAVES: Thick, lance-shaped leaves are a foot wide and up to 2 feet in length, on reddish, 3-foot stems. Upper surfaces may have a powdery white appearance.

NATIVE RANGE: South Carolina through Florida; Zones 8–10

HABITAT: Stream and pond banks, marshes

PROPAGATION: Seed, division

Thalia is rank-growing but attractive when grown at the edge of a large pond or lake. It likes plenty of space, but lacking that, you can grow it in large pots sunk into the water. Another species, *T. dealbata*, is found from North Carolina to Texas and Florida.

FLORIDA NATIVE NURSERIES

The Association of Florida Native Nurseries (AFNN) is the largest native nursery association in the United States. It is a not-for-profit corporation whose members include nurseries, landscape architects and designers, and other companies and individuals in related fields who support the preservation, conservation, and propagation of Florida's native plants.

The following AFNN member growers and nurseries are listed for 1997–98. They are specified as wholesale (W) or retail (R), although many wholesalers offer retail service by appointment. Contract growers grow and supply plants on order.

Alexander Landscaping & Plant Farm,
910 S. Flamingo Road, Davie 33325;
954-472-5039 (W, R)

Apalachee Native Nursery, Route 3, Box 156;
Monticello 32344; 850-997-8976 (W, R)

Aquatic Plant Management, 5722 S.
Flamingo Road, Suite 265, Cooper City
33330; 800-641-6892 (W)

Aquatic Plants of Florida, Inc., 1491 Second
St., Suite C-1, Sarasota 34236;
1-800-952-9886 (W)

Bartow Ornamental Nursery, 3890 Highway
60E, Bartow 33830; 941-534-1350 (W)

Bent Tree Farm, Inc., 4273 NW CR 225-A,
Ocala 34482; 352-732-9564 (W, R)

Biosphere Consulting, 14908 Tilden Road,
Winter Garden 34787; 407-656-8277 (W)

Breezy Oaks Nursery, 23602 SE Hawthorne
Road, Hawthorne 32640; 352-481-3795
(W, R)

Bullbay Creek Farm, 1033 Old Bumpy Road,
Tallahassee 32311; 904-878-3989 (W)

Central Florida Native Flora, Inc., P.O. Box
1045, San Antonio 33576; 352-588-3687
(W)

Chiappini Farm Native Nursery, Chiappini
Farm Road, Melrose 32666;
1-800-293-5413 (W, R)

Coastal Aquatic Services, Inc., 1790 Celestine
Pass Road, Sarasota 34240; 941-378-5320
(W)

D.R. Bates Seeds, P.O. Box 68, Loxahatchee
33470; 561-790-3246 (W)

Ecological Consultants, Inc., 5121 Ehrlich
Road, Suite 103A, Tampa 33624;
813-264-5859 (W)

Ecoshores, Inc., 3869 S. Nova Road, Port
Orange 32127; 904-767-6232 (W)

EnviroGlades, 248 C Road, Loxahatchee
33470; 561-798-4995 (W)

Environmental Equities, Inc., 12547 Denton
Ave., Hudson 34667; 813-861-1194
(W, R)

Erhardt Nursery, 5099 Second Road, Lake
Worth 33467; 561-967-7181 (W)

Florida Environmental, Inc., 18505 Paulson
Drive, Bldg. B, Port Charlotte 33954;
941-624-2911 (W)

Florida Keys Native Nursery, Inc.,
102 Mohawk St., Tavernier 33070;
305-852-2636 (W, R)

Florida Native Flora, Inc., 3401 N. Galloway
Road, Lakeland 33810; 941-853-8695
(W, R)

Florida Native Plants, Inc., 730 Myakka
Road, Sarasota 34240; 941-322-1915
(W, R)

Gann's Native Tropical Greenery, 22140 SW
152nd Ave., Miami 33170; 305-248-5529
(W, R)

Gourd Garden and Curiosity Shop, 4808 E.
County Road 30-A, Santa Rosa Beach
32459; 850-231-2007 (R)

Gone Native Nursery, 2704 SW Horseshoe
Trail, Palm City 34990; 561-283-8420 (W)

Green Images/ Native Landscape Plants,
1333 Taylor Creek Road, Christmas
32709; 407-568-1333 (W, R)

Green Seasons Nursery, P.O. Box 539,
Parrish 34219; 941-776-1605 (W)

Hard Scrabble Farms, 1881 Bayshore Drive,
Terra Ceia 34250; 941-722-0414 (W, R)

Hickory Hill Native Nursery, Inc., 27212
Hickory Hill Road, Brooksville 34602;
352-754-9701 (W, R)

Horizon Nursery, 1300 SW Ninth St., Vero
Beach 32962; 1-800-753-7151 (W, R)

Horticultural Systems, Inc., 13620 Golf
Course Road, Parrish 34219;
1-800-771-4114 (W, R)

Indian Trails Native Nursery, 6315 Park Lane
W., Lake Worth 33467; 561-641-9488 (W)

LCEI (Central Florida Lands & Timber),
Route 1, Box 899, Mayo 32066;
904-294-1211 (W)

Liner Farm, Inc., 4020 Packard Ave., St.
Cloud 34772; 1-800-330-1484 (W)

Maple Street Natives, 2395 Maple St., West
Melbourne 32904; 407-729-6857 (W, R)

Marshall Tree Farm, 17350 SE 65th St., Morriston 32668; 1-800-786-1422 (W)

Meadow Beauty Nursery, 5782 Ranches Road, Lake Worth 33463; 561-966-6848 (W, R)

Mesozoic Landscapes, Inc., 7667 Park Lane W., Lake Worth 33467; 561-967-2630 (W, R)

Native Creations, 35540 N. Treasure Island Road, Leesburg 34788; 352-343-3854 (W)

Native Green Cay, 12750 Hagen Ranch Road, Boynton Beach 33437; 561-496-1415 (W)

Native Nursery, Inc., 13686 55th St. S., Lake Worth 33467; 561-793-2680 (W)

Native Tree Nursery, Inc., 17250 SW 232nd St., Goulds 33170; 305-247-4499 (W)

Natural Habitats, Inc., 3001 SW 121st Ave., Davie 33330; 954-370-9887 (Contract grower)

Norman's Native Plants Plus, 2150 US 27 N., Avon Park 33825; 941-453-6303 (W, R)

Northeast Florida Native Nursery, Inc., 2615 Dawin Road N., Jacksonville 32207; 904-443-0084 (W, R)

Okefenokee Growers, P.O. Box 4488, Jacksonville 32201; 1-800-356-4881 (W)

Ornamental Plants & Trees, 1171 SR 20-A, Hawthorne 32640; 352-481-4067 (W)

Peltons Landscaping Service, Inc., P.O. Box 560912, Miami 33256; 305-447-7667

Possum Hollow Orchards & Nursery, 10106 NW 156th Ave., Alachua 32615; 352-462-5455 (W, R)

Rigsby Nursery, Inc., 18671 Palm Creek Drive, North Fort Myers 33917; 941-543-3379 (W)

RSS Field Services, Inc., P.O. Box 549, Plant City 33564; 813-757-1990 (W, R)

Runway Growers, Inc., 2891 SW 36th St., Fort Lauderdale 33312; 954-584-0269 (W, R)

Sabay Trees, P.O. Box 2232, Bradenton 34208; 941-322-2367 (W)

San Felasco Nurseries, Inc., 7315 NW 126th St., Gainesville 32653; 1-800-933-9638 (W)

SCCF Native Plant Nursery, 3333 Sanibel Captiva Road, Sanibel 33957; 941-472-1932 (R)

Simonton Farms Nursery, Route 2, Box 551-A, Micanopy 32667; 352-591-2271

Sinclair Landscape Nursery, Inc., 11011 Hagen Ranch Road, Boynton Beach 33437; 561-737-6904 (W)

Southern Landscape & Nursery, Inc., 16351 Van Gogh Road, Loxahatchee 33470; 561-798-1172 (W, R)

Southern Roots Tree Nursery, 1810 Bold Springs Road, Ochlocknee, GA 31773; 912-377-6237 (W, R)

Spurling Nursery, P.O. Box 216, Homestead 33090; 305-247-3307 (Contract grower)

SUNCO, 2269 Second Ave. N., Lake Worth 33461; 561-586-7402 (W)

Sundance Ornamentals, 10689 Heritage Blvd., Lake Worth 33467; 561-965-1344 (W)

Superior Trees, Inc., P.O Box 9325, Lee 32059; 850-971-5159 (W)

Sweet Bay Nursery, 10824 Erie Road, Parrish 34219; 941-776-0501 (W)

The Natives, 2929 JB Carter Road, Davenport 33837; 941-422-6664 (W, R)

The Tree Gallery, 11230 Gallery Lane, Boynton Beach 33437; 561-734-4416 (W, R)

Tindall Growers, Inc., 5801 SW 76th Ave., Davie 33328; 954-434-1161 (W)

Tree of Life Nursery, Inc., 3805 E. County Line Road, Lutz 33549; 813-949-0448 (W, R)

TreeMart, 12505 N. Nebraska, Tampa 33612; 1-800-664-4006 (W)

Urban Forestry Services, Route 2, Box 940, Micanopy 32667; 352-466-3919 (W)

BIBLIOGRAPHY

Ajilvsgi, Geyata. *Butterfly Gardening for the South*. Dallas, TX: Taylor Publishing Co., 1990.

Association of Florida Native Nurseries. *Xeric Landscaping with Florida Native Plants*. San Antonio, FL: AFNN, 1991.

Austin, Dr. Daniel. *Coastal Dune Plants*. Boca Raton, FL: Gumbo-Limbo Nature Center of South Palm Beach County, 1991.

Bell, C.R. and Taylor, B.J. *Florida Wild Flowers and Roadside Plants*. Chapel Hill, NC: Laurel Hill Press, 1982.

Broschat, T.K. and Meerow, A.W. *Betrock's Reference Guide to Florida Landscape Plants*. Hollywood, FL: Betrock Information Systems, Inc., 1991.

Craighead, Frank C. *Orchids and Other Air Plants of the Everglades National Park*. Coral Gables, FL: University of Miami Press, 1963.

Dirr, Michael A. *Manual of Woody Landscape Plants*. Champaign, IL: Stipes Publishing Co., 1990.

Dressler, R.L., Hall, D.W., Perkins, K.D., and Williams, N.H. *Identification Manual for Wetland Plant Species of Florida*. Gainesville, FL: University of Florida, 1987.

Elias, Thomas S. *The Complete Trees of North America*. New York, NY: Van Nostrand Reinhold Co., 1980.

Fleming, G., Genelle, P., and Long, R.W. *Wild Flowers of Florida*. Miami, FL: Banyan Books, Inc., 1976.

Florida Cooperative Extension Service, Daniel B. Ward, editor. *Rare and Endangered Plants of Florida*. Gainesville, FL: University Presses of Florida, 1979.

Florida Division of Forestry. *Coastal Plants of Florida: A Key to Good Land Management*. Tallahassee, FL: Florida Department of Agriculture and Consumer Services, 1979.

Florida Division of Forestry. *Forest Trees of Florida*. Tallahassee, FL: Florida Department of Agriculture and Consumer Services, 1972.

Florida Game and Fresh Water Fish Commission. *Florida's Endangered Species, Threatened Species and Species of Special Concern*. Tallahassee, 1996.

Greene, Wilhelmina F. and Blomquist, Hugo L. *Flowers of the South*. Chapel Hill, NC: University of North Carolina Press. 1953.

Greenlee, John. *The Encyclopedia of Ornamental Grasses*. Emmaus, PA: Rodale Press, 1992.

Halfacre, R. Gordon and Shawcroft, Anne R. *Landscape Plants of the Southeast*. Raleigh, NC: Sparks Press, Inc., 1971.

Little, Elbert L. Jr. *Forest Trees of the United States and Canada*. New York, NY: Dover Publications, 1979.

Meerow, A.W. *Betrock's Guide to Landscape Palms*. Hollywood, FL: Betrock Information Systems, Inc., 1992.

Nellis, David W. *Seashore Plants of South Florida and the Caribbean*. Sarasota, FL: Pineapple Press, Inc., 1994.

Nelson, Gil. *The Shrubs and Woody Vines of Florida*. Sarasota, FL: Pineapple Press, Inc., 1996.

Scurlock, J. Paul. *Native Trees and Shrubs of the Florida Keys*. Pittsburgh, PA: Laurel Press, 1987.

Stevenson, George B. *Trees of the Everglades National Park and the Florida Keys*. Miami, FL: Banyan Books, 1969.

Suncoast Native Plant Society. *The Right Plants for Dry Places*. St. Petersburg, FL: Great Outdoors Publishing Co., 1997.

Sunset Books and Sunset Magazine. *Sunset National Garden Book*. Menlo Park, CA: Sunset Books Inc., 1997.

Tasker, Georgia. Wild Things: *The Return of Native Plants*. Winter Park, FL: Florida Native Plant Society, 1984.

Taylor, W.K. *The Guide to Florida Wildflowers*. Dallas, TX: Taylor Publishing Co., 1992.

Wasowski, Sally and Andy. *Native Texas Plants, 2nd Edition*. Houston, TX: Gulf Publishing Co., 1997.

Wasowski, Sally and Andy. *Gardening With Native Plants of the South*. Dallas, TX: Taylor Publishing Co., 1994.

Workman, Richard W. *Growing Native*. Sanibel, FL: The Sanibel-Captiva Conservation Foundation Inc., 1980.

Wyman, Donald. *Wyman's Gardening Encyclopedia*. New York, NY: Macmillan Publishing Co., 1977.

INDEX

Page numbers in italics refer to photographs and illustrations.

Please Note: The photo on page 147 is *Ilex cornuta*, not *I. opaca.*